EDUCATION AND CULTURE IN THE POLITICAL THOUGHT OF ARISTOTLE

EDUCATION AND CULTURE
IN THE POLITICAL THOUGHT OF
Aristotle

By CARNES LORD

CORNELL UNIVERSITY PRESS
Ithaca and London

CORNELL UNIVERSITY PRESS GRATEFULLY ACKNOWLEDGES
A GRANT FROM THE ANDREW W. MELLON FOUNDATION THAT
AIDED IN BRINGING THIS BOOK TO PUBLICATION.

First published 1982 by Cornell University Press.
Published in the United Kingdom by Cornell University Press Ltd.,
Ely House, 37 Dover Street, London W1X 4HQ.

International Standard Book Number 0-8014-1412-1
Library of Congress Catalog Card Number 81-15272
Printed in the United States of America

Librarians: Library of Congress cataloging information
appears on the last page of the book.

The paper in this book is acid-free, and meets
the guidelines for permanence and durability of
the Committee on Production Guidelines for Book Longevity
of the Council on Library Resources.

To my mother

Contents

Preface   11

Abbreviations   13

Introduction   17

1 EDUCATION   36

  1. Education and Ruling *36*
  2. The Parts of the Soul *38*
  3. Education and Leisure *40*
  4. The Stages of Education (I) *41*
  5. The Stages of Education (II) *44*
  6. Education and the City *48*
  7. The Nature of Education *51*
  8. The Purposes of Education *53*
  9. Useful Education and Liberal Education *57*
  10. The Stages of Education (III) *59*
  11. Liberal Education *62*

2 MUSIC AND EDUCATION   68

  1. Music and Music Education *68*
  2. Music and Virtue (I) *73*
  3. Aristotle, Homer, and the Ancients *75*
  4. The Power of Music (I) *78*
  5. Pastime and Play *79*
  6. The Power of Music (II) *82*
  7. The Meaning of *Mousikē* *85*
  8. Music and Poetry in the *Poetics* *89*

Contents

9. Music and Virtue (II) *92*
10. The Music Education of the Young *96*
11. Music and Liberal Education *98*

3 MUSIC AND CATHARSIS   105

1. Music and the Best Regime *105*
2. The Uses of Tunes or Harmonies *110*
3. Tunes or Harmonies in the *Politics* and the *Problems* *113*
4. The Catharsis Question *119*
5. Catharsis in Greek Culture *122*
6. Enthusiasm, Pity, and Fear *126*
7. The Character of Tragic Catharsis *135*
8. Theatrical Music and the Citizen Class *138*
9. The New Music and the Old *141*
10. Citizen and Vulgar Harmonies *143*
11. The End of the *Politics* *146*

4 POETRY AND EDUCATION   151

1. Poetry and Education *151*
2. Education and Law in the *Nicomachean Ethics* *153*
3. Moral Weakness *156*
4. Catharsis and Spiritedness *159*
5. Tragic Error *165*
6. Comedy *174*
7. Poetry and Prudence *177*

5 POLITICS AND CULTURE   180

1. Education and Culture *180*
2. The Best Way of Life (I) *181*
3. The Best Way of Life (II) *183*
4. The Problem of Political Rule *189*
5. Spiritedness and the Best Regime *192*
6. Politics and Philosophy *196*
7. Culture and Gentlemanship *200*

Contents

APPENDIX   Aristotle, Damon, and Music Education   203

Selected Bibliography   220
Index   223

Preface

This book was undertaken in the conviction that the encounter between Greek philosophy and the world in which it arose—a world at once richly articulated and essentially prescientific— remains an event of immense importance for the self-understanding of modern man. I was attracted to the specific question of the relation between politics and culture in Greek philosophy by a sense that clarification of this question could illuminate an issue whose fundamental contours had somehow been lost from sight in the contemporary world. This sense and that conviction I owe above all to my teacher Allan Bloom; and it is to him also that I owe my long-standing preoccupation with Aristotle. These are debts that can be only very inadequately acknowledged here.

Parts of this book have appeared previously in different form. The final chapter is a revised and abbreviated version of my "Politics and Philosophy in Aristotle's *Politics*," *Hermes* 106 (1978), 336–57, and the Appendix is a slightly expanded version of "On Damon and Music Education," *Hermes* 106 (1978), 32–43. For permission to use this material I thank Franz Steiner Verlag. I also express my appreciation to Thomas L. Pangle, who gave the manuscript several sympathetic and helpful readings; to Barbara Jones for her help in typing the final version; and to Craig Waggaman for preparing the index.

CARNES LORD

Washington, D.C.

11

Abbreviations

C & M	*Classica et Medievalia*
CP	*Classical Philology*
CQ	*Classical Quarterly*
CR	*Classical Review*
HSCP	*Harvard Studies in Classical Philology*
LSJ	H. G. Liddell, R. Scott, and H. S. Jones, *A Greek-English Lexicon*, 9th ed. (Oxford, 1940; reprinted 1961)
MH	*Museum Helveticum*
Mnem.	*Mnemosyne*
RE	A. Pauly, G. Wissowa, and W. Kroll, *Realenzyklopädie der klassischen Altertumswissenschaft* (Stuttgart, 1894–)
REG	*Revue des Etudes Grecques*
RhM	*Rheinisches Museum für Philologie*
TAPA	*Transactions of the American Philological Association*

The works of Aristotle are abbreviated as follows:

Ath. Pol.	*Constitution of Athens*
De An.	*De Anima (On the Soul)*
Eth. Eud.	*Eudemian Ethics*
Eth. Nic.	*Nicomachean Ethics*
Gen. An.	*Generation of Animals*
Hist. An.	*History of Animals*
Met.	*Metaphysics*
Poet.	*Poetics*
Pol.	*Politics*
Rhet.	*Rhetoric*
Top.	*Topics*

Abbreviations

Note: Except for the *Constitution of Athens,* references to the works of Aristotle follow the conventional system based on the pages, columns, and lines of the edition of Immanuel Bekker (Berlin, 1831). References to Plato follow the pagination established by Stephanus. All translations of Aristotle as well as of other classical and modern writers are by the author. References throughout the text that are not otherwise identified are to the *Politics.*

EDUCATION AND CULTURE IN THE POLITICAL THOUGHT OF ARISTOTLE

Introduction

To speak of a political role for literature and the arts is to speak a language that is no longer congenial or even completely intelligible to modern man, at least in the West. If those in the Marxist tradition persist in regarding culture as an instrument of political and social revolution, what may be broadly labeled liberal thought has championed the autonomy of culture regardless of costs and consequences, viewing with hostility all attempts to press culture into the service not only of party or regime but of moral or political imperatives of any sort. Liberal thought allies itself in this respect (though the alliance is not always fully reciprocated) with the dominant tendency of modern literary and aesthetic criticism. The repudiation of realism (and by anticipation of "socialist realism") and the rejection of meaning and representation urged by the aesthetic of modernism in its most uncompromising form are perhaps the clearest evidence of the revolt of modern culture against the conditions of life in the contemporary West.[1] But the aesthetic of modernism only radicalizes the fundamental assumption of modern literary and aesthetic criticism generally—the assumption of a sharp disjunction between aesthetic experience and ordinary experience, culture and society, "art" and "life." According to this understanding, literature or art necessarily

1. A recent development of this argument may be found in Daniel Bell, *The Cultural Contradictions of Capitalism* (New York, 1976).

17

represents a creative transformation—effected and appreciated by a faculty of "imagination"—of reality as it is ordinarily experienced. The aesthetic experience is said to be one that transcends essentially the concerns and the imaginative capabilities of ordinary persons. If culture serves a purpose at all, that purpose is essentially private—the amusement of an imaginatively privileged few or of a public in search of entertainment. It should not—if it is genuine culture, it cannot—consciously undertake or indirectly serve to improve the tastes, educate the opinions, or shape the behavior of the public or its leaders.

The alternative view—the alternative to what an eminent Marxist thinker has called the "false extremes" of revolutionary agitprop and an apolitical aestheticism[2]—is the classical view. The place that is held in modern literary and aesthetic criticism by the creative imagination was occupied in classical thought by the notion of "imitation." In the classical understanding, literature and art reflect, represent, or imitate reality as it is ordinarily experienced. Above all, they imitate human reality, the world of moral and political action. In the well-known formulations of Aristotle's *Poetics*, poetry imitates "men acting," or "action" (*praxis*) in the full sense that the term holds for Aristotle—human action as it expresses man's humanity and fundamental sociality. At first glance, one might suppose the effect of a theory of this sort is to reduce literature or culture to the role of mere recorder of the society to which it belongs. Yet Aristotle makes quite clear that imitation

---

2. "In all artistic questions, classical aesthetics . . . saw public issues, questions of social pedagogy. By contrast, modern aesthetics represents, with few exceptions, a step backward. Partly this is because this aspect of art's effect was entirely or largely disregarded and art was essentially reduced to a specialized connoisseurship, but partly too because it was indeed recognized that art exercises such a societal effect, but this effect was understood to operate in a much too direct and too concrete and substantive a fashion—as if art existed simply in order to achieve the implementation of particular concrete societal tasks. In opposition to both false extremes, classical aesthetics . . . adopts a position that is quite true to art's actual societal role" (Georg Lukacs, *Ästhetik* [Berlin, 1963], I, 810).

is not mere replication, or that it is possible to imitate men not only as they are but as they should be.[3] Culture is then not only essentially commensurate with the world of moral and political experience; it is a potential source of models of moral and political behavior. By that fact, it is well equipped to serve as the core of a civic education. For Aristotle and for the classics generally, literature and the arts constitute the core of an education designed to form the tastes, character, and judgment of good citizens and free men.[4]

Theoretical reflection on education and culture as a problem of political life is for all practical purposes inseparable from the study of the political philosophy of classical antiquity. With the notable exception of Rousseau, no modern political thinker of any stature gives thematic attention to the question of the social or political role of literature and the arts. By contrast, very extensive discussions of this theme occupy a conspicuous place in the central works of the tradition of classical political philosophy—Plato's *Republic* and *Laws* and Aristotle's *Politics*. It may seem surprising at first sight that this should be the case. The political writings of Plato are today widely regarded as monuments of illiberality, spiritually akin to the totalitarianisms of modern times in their apparent subordination of individual needs and interests to the requirements of the community. In particular, Plato's *Republic* culminates in the wholesale expulsion of poets and poetry from the best city constructed by Socrates and his companions in the course of that work. Plato's hostility toward literature and the arts stands in apparent contrast to the tolerant attitude typically exhibited within the modern liberal tradition. The paradox disappears,

3. Aristotle distinguishes (*Poet.* 1460b9–11) between imitation of things as they are, as they should be, and as they are said or thought to be. The last category is intended to cover representations of the gods; "imagination" was here particularly conceded a role (consider Plato *Republic* 596c and 598e, Philostratus *Life of Apollonius* VI.19). Cf. Fritz Wehrli, "Die antike Kunsttheorie und das Schöpferische," *MH* 14 (1957), 39–49 = *Theoria und Humanitas* (Zürich, 1972), pp. 120–32.

4. For a fine exposition of this view see Allan Bloom, *Shakespeare's Politics* (New York, 1964), pp. 1–12.

however, when it is realized that the decisive question concerns not so much the posture that should be adopted by those in positions of political authority toward literature and the arts, but rather the inherent capacity of literature and the arts to affect political life for both good and ill. If culture is impotent to move men in politically relevant ways, it can be safely ignored by political men, and therefore ceases to be of interest to political theorists. If and to the extent that it is politically powerful, on the other hand, it acquires of necessity both practical and theoretical importance. Plato's expulsion of the poets testifies in the first instance, then, to a healthy regard for the political importance of culture—an attitude very far from being shared by the leading political thinkers of liberal modernity.

This is not to suggest that the liberal view of education and culture has always been a simple or uniform one. When Rousseau launched his bold attack on the liberalism of the day in his *Discourse on the Sciences and the Arts* (1750), his criticism centered on an idea—the idea that political and moral progress is fundamentally compatible with, if it does not actually presuppose, the free development of the sciences and of culture—which remains a recognizable feature of the liberal landscape even today. A century or so earlier, however, the situation was rather different. Those thinkers who laid the foundations of modern thought in the seventeenth century were more ambivalent in their views of the political role of education and culture, in large part because of their experience of the strength of the traditional education and culture against which their own enterprise was directed. Thomas Hobbes's account of poetry is characteristic and instructive. Hobbes locates the source of poetry in the human faculty of "fancy," which consists primarily in the ability to make comparisons or to construct metaphors. Yet, according to him, metaphors "openly profess deceit; to admit them into counsel, or reasoning, were manifest folly."[5] The poet's metaphors do not reveal or il-

5. Thomas Hobbes, *Leviathan* I.8. As appears from I.2, "fancy" and "imagination" are essentially synonymous.

luminate the world; they disguise or obscure it, constructing in its place a world that belongs wholly to the imagination. The matter would be simple if all men could be persuaded to lead their lives on the basis of a reasoned appreciation of the world as it is in truth. Yet precisely Hobbes's assumptions about the nature of the world as it is in truth make this proposition highly doubtful. "True (that is, accurate) Philosophy professedly rejects not only the paint and false colors of language, but even the very ornaments and graces of the same. The primary bases of all science are not only not alluring, but actually unattractive, dry, and almost repulsive."[6] To the extent that poetry imagines a world that is more attractive than the world as understood by reason and science, it is likely to retain an important hold over men. For this very reason, however, poetry is potentially dangerous. Descartes, in his account of the deficiencies of the education that was traditional in his time, makes the point clearly: "the poetry [of the ancients] makes one imagine many events to be possible which are not so at all, and even their most faithful histories, if they do not change or increase the value of things to make them more worthy of being read, at least almost always omit the lowest and least illustrious circumstances surrounding them; thus it happens that the rest does not appear as what it is, and that those who regulate their morals by the examples they take from it are apt to fall into the extravagances of the knights of our romances, and to conceive designs that surpass their capabilities."[7] Like Hobbes, however, Descartes anticipated that the weight of traditional education and the literary and historical works that formed the core of it would be diminished in due time by the dissemination of scientific knowledge about the world and man. In particular, they expected that men could be brought to abandon their at-

6. Hobbes, *De Corpore* I.1.

7. René Descartes, *Discours de la méthode* 1. Descartes' understanding of the psychological appeal of poetry is visible in his remarks on the passion of "admiration," *Passions de l'âme* 71, 76, and 78. Cf. Richard Kennington, "Descartes," in *History of Political Philosophy*, ed. Leo Strauss and Joseph Cropsey, 2d ed. (Chicago, 1972), pp. 395–413.

tachment to traditional models of piety or political glory by concentrating their attention precisely on the "lowest and least illustrious circumstances" of human life. The requirements of self-preservation or of comfortable self-preservation would make men oblivious of the requirements of virtue or excellence, and thereby supply the foundations for a type of political order more just, prosperous, and enduring than any previously known.

It was Rousseau's rediscovery of the necessity of virtue in the classical sense for decent republican government that led him to reopen the question of the political role of education and culture. Rousseau's treatment of this question appears in the first instance as a return to classical political philosophy. Indeed, Rousseau composed a paraphrase of the tenth book of Plato's *Republic* in preparation for his most extensive treatment of the theme of politics and culture, the *Letter to M. D'Alembert on the Theatre,* an attack on the projected establishment of a theater in republican and Calvinist Geneva.[8] Yet there is reason to wonder whether Rousseau's intransigent rejection in this work of any political role for comic or tragic poetry—not to speak of his elaboration in *Emile* of a model of education that is radically untraditional in avoiding any fundamental reliance on literature and the arts[9]—is not better understood finally as prefiguring a more advanced modernity than as a true revival of classical thought.

In any event, it is certainly arguable that Plato's spectacular eviction of the poets from the regime of his *Republic* has given rise to fundamental misconceptions concerning his larger view and, consequently, the general character of the classical position with regard to the political role of education and culture. It is insufficiently noticed in standard accounts of the subject that

8. See Jean-Jacques Rousseau, *Politics and the Arts: Letter to M. D'Alembert on the Theatre,* trans. Allan Bloom (Ithaca, N.Y., 1968). Contrast Montesquieu's treatment of the role of "music" in republican education, *De l'esprit des lois* V.5.

9. Consider particularly Rousseau, *Emile ou de l'éducation* II, *Oeuvres complètes* (Paris, 1969), IV, 350–59.

Plato's attack on the imitative aspects of poetry in the tenth book of the *Republic* rests on extremely dubious metaphysical assumptions that do not recur elsewhere in his writings; that the attack on poetry is undertaken in the context of an argument concerning philosophic rulership which is highly problematic, and which there are many indications that Plato knew to be highly problematic; that the expulsion of the poets is in any event treated as merely tentative, pending an adequate defense of poetry to be supplied by poetry's "friends"; and that poetry—including under certain conditions even the most troublesome variety of poetry, tragedy—is massively present in the model (but nonphilosophic) regime elaborated by the Athenian Stranger of Plato's *Laws*.[10]

At the same time, the view of Aristotle has been frequently misrepresented by being forced into false opposition to that of Plato. It is widely held at the present time that Aristotle's general view of literature or culture is sufficiently apparent in the argument of his *Poetics,* and indeed in the very existence of that work. The *Poetics* is usually held to be the first systematic work of literary criticism, and Aristotle the founder of literary criticism as a distinct and autonomous field of study. Aristotle is held to have insisted on understanding poetry, in opposition to the procedure of Plato, without reference to moral or political considerations, as a phenomenon possessed of a dignity of its own and governed by its own laws. In thus emancipating poetry from moral and political tutelage, it is often suggested, Aristotle founded or anticipated the characteristic liberal view of the relation between politics and culture.

The chief obstacle to such a view is Aristotle's extensive account of civic education in the last two books of his *Politics,* for it is here that Aristotle comes as close as he comes anywhere to providing a comprehensive statement concerning his

10. On the discussion of poetry in the *Republic,* see particularly Allan Bloom, *The Republic of Plato* (New York, 1968), pp. 426–34. Other recent accounts are J. Dalfen, *Polis und Poiesis* (Munich, 1974), and Iris Murdoch, *The Fire and the Sun* (Oxford, 1977).

understanding of education and culture and their role in social and political life.

Books VII and VIII of Aristotle's *Politics* are devoted to a discussion of the best form of government or the best regime. This discussion, which concludes the *Politics* in the form and condition in which we now have it, is devoted in very large part to an account of education and its role in the best regime. Book VIII contains Aristotle's properly thematic treatment of the subject of education; a considerable part of that book is devoted to an account of "music"—a term that retains for Aristotle much of its original connection with poetry or literary culture generally—and its role in education. The discussion of music and education in the final books of the *Politics* is virtually the only account of those subjects in the extant writings of Aristotle or the Peripatetic school, and it is perhaps the most comprehensive and systematic account surviving from antiquity. And yet this discussion—of critical importance for the study both of classical political thought and of classical poetics—has not, I believe, been adequately served by historical and philological analysis or by interpretation.

There are several reasons for this. The first has to do with a general failure to make the fullest use of the ancient literature on music. Because it is scattered, fragmentary, beset with formidable difficulties, and still poorly understood, this literature has never been properly exploited in its bearing on Aristotle's discussion of music education.[11] I believe considerable light can be shed on Aristotle's argument by the writings or the surviving fragments of Aristoxenus, Aristides Quintilianus, the Peripatetic author of Book XIX of the *Problems,* and the schools

11. The monograph of Ernst Koller, *Musse und musische Paideia: Die Musikaporetik in der aristotelischen Politik* (Basel, 1956), makes a valuable contribution, but fails to exhaust the subject, particularly by omitting any discussion of VIII.7. The chapter on Aristotle in Warren Anderson, *Ethos and Education in Greek Music* (Cambridge, Mass., 1966), is perfunctory and superficial, and the same can be said for the less extensive treatments in the older musicological literature, of which the standard work remains Hermann Abert, *Die Lehre vom Ethos in der griechischen Musik* (Leipzig, 1899).

of Pythagoras and Damon. I have made use of these and similar sources throughout my analysis.[12]

A second and more fundamental reason is the approach that has come to dominate the study of Aristotle in recent years. In 1952 a distinguished scholar could write: "What seems most lacking in Aristotelian scholarship today are interpretations—investigations, that is, which seek to trace the argument of a particular text and to understand the meaning of each sentence in itself and in relation to its context."[13] This remark is nearly as true today as it was then. In Germany, the influence of Heidegger and of the philosophy of hermeneutics has begun to make plausible the notion that the traditional understanding of the texts that form the basis of the tradition of philosophy is radically defective; yet the effect of these currents of thought on Aristotelian scholarship remains limited.[14] Aristotelian scholarship as such continues to take its bearings from the genetic-analytic view of Aristotle's writings associated with the name of Werner Jaeger. By placing a sort of premium on detecting inconsistency and incoherence in the Aristotelian corpus, this approach has tended to discredit and discourage the kind of analysis and explication of the substance of Aristotle's thought with which any authentic interpretation must both begin and end.

Jaeger has claimed that his method is capable in principle of resolving by objective criteria problems of interpretation that older commentators could resolve only by an essentially subjective process of harmonization. Yet one has to ask whether arguments based on the dependence of an Aristotelian text on what are alleged to be Platonic doctrines is a procedure designed to eliminate the possibility of subjective error. Jaeger holds

12. A detailed discussion of these sources and their relationship may be found in the Appendix. See also C. Lord, "A Peripatetic Account of Tragic Music," *Hermes* 105 (1977), 175-79.

13. Olof Gigon, "Aristoteles-Studien I," *MH* 9 (1952), 13.

14. See, for example, Wolfgang Wieland, *Die aristotelische Physik* (Göttingen, 1970), Manfred Riedel, *Metaphysik und Metapolitik: Studien zu Aristoteles und zur politischen Sprache der neuzeitlichen Philosophie* (Frankfurt am Main, 1975).

that the key to understanding both the movement and the substance of Aristotle's thought lies in Aristotle's relationship to Plato, and in particular to Platonic metaphysics. This approach is exposed to the fundamental objection that it attempts to explain the obscure and uncertain by the more obscure and uncertain. At all events, the mass of strata, recensions, and ad hoc hypotheses that the use or abuse of his method has generated seems not infrequently to rival the worst excesses of the scholasticism that Jaeger opposes.

A second objection to Jaeger's approach is that it fails to take sufficient account of the specific character of Aristotle's political writings and of the place of political philosophy or political science in his thought as a whole. Jaeger argues that the *Politics*, like the *Metaphysics*, is an adventitious collection of lecture materials written at various periods of Aristotle's career and embodying very different substantive and methodological views. According to him, the original core of the *Politics*, inspired and guided by a Platonic concern for (if not by the Platonic solution to) the question of the best form of government, consists of Books II–III and VII–VIII, while Books IV–VI, reflecting a supposed disenchantment with such a concern in favor of a more empirical or practical approach to politics, were inserted in their present position by Aristotle or a Peripatetic editor at a later date.[15] Jaeger's understanding of the *Politics* has not gone unchallenged, even among those who accept his basic assumptions. While few would go so far as to speak, with one scholar, of "the utter discrediting of Jaeger's method as applied to the *Politics*," there has been a trend in recent years toward acknowledging the essential unity or coherence of the *Politics* as a whole.[16] No one will deny that the

15. Werner Jaeger, *Aristotle: Fundamentals of the History of His Development*, trans. R. Robinson, 2d ed. (Oxford, 1948), pp. 228–92.

16. Max Hamburger, *Morals and Law: The Growth of Aristotle's Legal Theory* (London and New Haven, 1951), p. 3. Jaeger's view has been most recently elaborated in Willy Theiler, "Bau und Zeit der aristotelischen Politik," *MH* 9 (1952), 65–78. The inner unity of the *Politics* is emphasized in the analysis of Rudolf Stark, "Der Gesamtaufbau der aristotelischen Politik," in *La*

structure of the *Politics* presents real difficulties, or that there are differences in tone, emphasis, or manner of argumentation in its various parts. Yet Jaeger never succeeded in showing that these differences could not be accounted for simply by the differences in subject matter of the various parts. In particular, he never showed that there is a necessary incompatibility between Aristotle's concern with the best form of government or regime in Books VII–VIII and his concern in Books IV–VI with regimes that more closely approach actual regimes. That Aristotle himself was not aware of any such incompatibility seems quite clear from the introductory remarks to Book IV (1288b10–89a7), where the study of the regime that is simply best and the study of the regime that is best (or of regimes that are generally acceptable) for most societies are treated as equally necessary parts of political science. Jaeger's assumed dichotomy between "idealistic" and "practical" elements of the *Politics* rests finally on a failure to appreciate the extent to which the *Politics* is from beginning to end a "practical" book, or the implications of Aristotle's assertion that political science is a practical science directed to practice rather than a theoretical science pursued for the sake of knowledge.

Whether Books VII and VIII were composed at the same time as the other books of the *Politics* is not a question that can be resolved here, if it can be resolved at all. The relatively finished style of Aristotle's account of the best regime has led some scholars to suggest that these books may have been intended for separate publication.[17] Jaeger has assigned to the seventh and eighth books an early date (before Aristotle's first departure from Athens), and this view has for the most part prevailed; but arguments for a later date have continued to find

---

"Politique" d'Aristote, Entretiens Fondation Hardt XI (Geneva, 1965), pp. 3–51; cf. R. G. Mulgan, *Aristotle's Political Theory* (Oxford, 1977), pp. 1–2. A useful review of modern scholarship on this question may be found in Renato Laurenti, *Genesi e formazione della Politica di Aristotele* (Padua, 1965), pp. 25–43.

17. Thus, for example, U. von Wilamowitz-Moellendorf, *Aristoteles und Athen* (Berlin, 1893), I, 356.

support.[18] One may agree with Jaeger that *Politics* VII–VIII are heavily dependent on Plato, particularly the Plato of the *Laws*. But Jaeger and his followers have hardly proved that a reliance on the political writings of Plato—and particularly the eminently practical or empirical *Laws*—is unthinkable in the mature Aristotle. My own view is that while the *Politics* may well incorporate materials written at a relatively early date, the work as a whole is governed by a single conception of its subject matter and may be considered for all practical purposes the work of Aristotle in his maturity.

Beyond a limited reliance on the musical literature as well as on related works by Aristotle himself, my interpretation attempts as much as possible to stand alone. Above all, I have avoided relying on Plato. Interpreting Platonic dialogues is no less hazardous than interpreting Aristotelian treatises, and is arguably much more so if one takes into account their literary character and purpose. Any interpretation of an Aristotelian text that presupposes a specific interpretation of Plato—or pre judges Aristotle's relationship to Plato—must therefore remain radically hypothetical. Accordingly, while I think it legitimate to seek support in Platonic texts for arguable points of interpretation and to indicate suggestive areas of apparent agreement, I have made no attempt at a systematic comparison of the two thinkers.

The difficulties involved in interpreting the final books of the *Politics* can hardly be overestimated. Books VII and VIII stand in particular need of fresh interpretation because the argument of those books is in several senses incomplete, and because this incompleteness and its implications have not been sufficiently appreciated. In the first place and most obviously, the argu-

18. Jaeger, pp. 275–87. The argument for a late date goes back to Hans von Arnim, "Zur Entstehungsgeschichte der aristotelischen Politik," *Sitzungsberichte der Österreichischen Akademie der Wissenschaft in Wien*, Philosophische-historische Klasse, 200/1 (1924); see also Ernest Barker, *The Politics of Aristotle* (Oxford, 1948), pp. xli–xlvi, and David Ross, "The Development of Aristotle's Thought," in *Aristotle and Plato in the Mid-Fourth Century*, ed. I. Düring and G. E. L. Owen (Gothenburg, 1960), pp. 9–10.

ment is physically incomplete: some portion of Book VIII has not survived in the manuscripts of the *Politics* as they have come down to us. There is no way of estimating the loss, unless one is willing to assume that Book VIII would originally have filled an entire book roll and thus been comparable in length to the other books of the *Politics* (it is less than half as long as most of them). But a number of forward references in the existing text permit conjectures as to its content, and there is reason to believe that the missing part was both important in itself and crucial for the understanding of Aristotle's argument.

Perhaps the most serious misconception encouraged by the incompleteness of the text concerns the meaning of the two words that constitute the focus of Aristotle's discussion. "Education" (*paideia*) in its original and narrow sense denotes the education of children or of the young generally; in an extended sense, it may also encompass the education—the "culture"—that can be pursued by mature persons. "Music" (*mousikē*) in its original and extended sense is the study or practice of all that belongs to the domain of the Muses, and hence in particular of poetry. It is usually assumed that the discussion of "music education" in *Politics* VIII is limited wholly to the education of the young in song or music in the narrow sense. I believe a careful reading of the text will indicate that Aristotle also speaks of both music and education in their popular or extended senses—and that this fact would be obvious if the missing segment of Book VIII had been preserved. A greater sensitivity to what may be only implicit in Aristotle's argument as it now stands can also help to make sense of manuscript readings that have been questioned or altered by modern editors.[19]

19. The new text of Alois Dreizehnter, *Aristoteles' Politik* (Munich, 1970), is for the most part properly conservative in retaining the reading of the manuscripts in difficult passages, and will be followed unless otherwise noted. As a rule, I shall take notice only of emendations accepted in the widely used edition of David Ross, *Aristotelis Politica* (Oxford, 1957). In the Appendix, I argue the case against the authenticity of the final paragraph of the *Politics*.

The argument of *Politics* VII-VIII is incomplete in the second place, and most importantly, for the reason that the argument of the *Politics* as a whole is incomplete—because the *Politics* is not intended to give a comprehensive or theoretically precise account of political life. For Aristotle, politics or political science is a practical rather than a theoretical discipline. The inquiry undertaken in the *Politics* and in Aristotle's ethical writings is a "political inquiry of a certain kind." It is not strictly or simply a political inquiry, for it is not directed to practice in an immediate way: concrete political action can be determined only by the statesman who possesses a knowledge of particular circumstances. On the other hand, neither is it simply a philosophical inquiry. Aristotle's inquiry concerns itself primarily with facts or phenomena as distinct from causes, and thus proceeds dialectically rather than by demonstration. His inquiry may on occasion involve or require recourse to philosophy and in particular to "political philosophy"; it is not identical with political philosophy. Rather, it is "political science" in its original form—the knowledge or art proper to the statesman or legislator. Aristotle's science of politics is a practical science above all because it is essentially for the sake or in the service of action rather than thought.[20]

It is frequently argued or assumed that what decisively distinguishes practical from theoretical philosophy for Aristotle

20. Consider *Eth. Nic.* 1094a18-28, 1099b29-32, 1103b26-31, 1179a35-b4, 1180b23-31 ff., *Eth. Eud.* 1216a38-17a18. The *Politics* virtually begins (1252a22-23) with a promise to investigate the various kinds of rule with a view to determining "whether it is possible to acquire a technical expertise [*ti technikon*] in each case." The precise meaning of the term "political philosophy" in its one occurrence in the *Politics* (1281b23) is unclear, but the context suggests it is alien to the general mode of inquiry of the work; cf. 1279b12-15, where it is indicated that this mode of inquiry is at best "not merely directed to action." That the mode of inquiry in question is "dialectic" rather than strict demonstrative science has been recently argued, for example, by Wilhelm Hennis, *Politik und praktische Philosophie: Eine Studie zur Rekonstruktion der politischen Wissenschaft,* Politica XIV (Neuwied, 1963).

is its subject matter.[21] Practical or political science appears to be concerned with "the human things" while theoretical science is concerned primarily with nature and the natural things. Man is in large part a creature of society and convention, and societies and conventions are subject to infinite flux and variation; accordingly, the degree of exactness demanded of political science is less than that required of natural or theoretical science, which is concerned primarily with what is stable and permanent: political science is compelled to be a practical science because the contingent facts of human life do not lend themselves to properly theoretical or philosophic treatment.

This view is not entirely wrong, but it is clearly not sufficient. While it is true that Aristotle distinguishes the human things from the natural things, he does not pretend that this distinction is itself theoretically precise. Aristotle cannot wholly separate the study of man from the study of nature because he regards man as a part of nature. If man is not a being whose characteristics are wholly determined by his instincts or physical nature, neither is he a simply conventional being. Man himself possesses a "nature" that forms the permanent ground and sets limits to the fluctuating uncertainties of human affairs. In fact, then, the teaching elaborated in the *Politics* and in Aristotle's ethical writings must presuppose a certain kind of theoretical knowledge. Aristotelian political science appears to renounce the search for the "causes" of moral and political phenomena and to avoid depending directly on a theoretical psychology or anthropology. Yet the possibility of a theoretical account of these causes is never denied, and occasionally appears to be taken for granted. In the last analysis,

21. The complex of questions connected with the status of practical philosophy in Aristotle's thought can hardly be treated adequately here. Of recent studies see particularly Otfried Höffe, *Praktische Philosophie: Das Modell des Aristoteles* (Munich/Salzburg, 1971), and Günther Bien, *Die Grundlegung der politischen Philosophie bei Aristoteles* (Munich/Freiburg, 1973), pp. 59–69, 103–37.

Aristotelian political science is a practical science, as it seems, not from necessity but from choice.

To repeat: Aristotle's political science is distinguished from theoretical science above all by the fact that it is for the sake or in the service of action. More specifically, the *Politics* together with Aristotle's ethical writings are intended to foster practical or political virtue, and in particular the virtue of prudence. They are addressed not to the young, or not primarily to the young, but to mature men with some experience of moral and political things; and they are addressed only to men who have been raised in decent habits. For all practical purposes, they are addressed to a class of aristocrats or "gentlemen" possessed of the leisure necessary for education and for political activity. In the highest case, they are addressed to men of this sort who are potential or actual statesmen or legislators. It is precisely because Aristotle means to be intelligible to an audience of this kind that he departs as little as possible from the phenomena of political life as they present themselves to the nonphilosophic observer. Aristotle's horizon is common sense or, more precisely, the common sense of the educated gentleman; his principal task is to articulate or clarify what is within that horizon. It is for this reason that Aristotle does not, or does not as a rule, provide the theoretical reasoning that would be required in an exact or comprehensive account of causes or principles.

Moreover, the fact that Aristotle is interested in speaking in a manner that is intelligible and persuasive to practical men means that his manner of argumentation is not without its rhetorical elements. Aristotle's argument proceeds dialectically or rhetorically rather than by strict demonstration in order to engage and transform the opinions of his audience. This approach makes it all the more necessary to pay careful attention to Aristotle's mode of presentation. Not every stage of every argument can be expected to reflect Aristotle's real views: it cannot be assumed that Aristotle shares fully every opinion that he repeats or appeals to, particularly when that opinion reflects a powerful prejudice on the part of his audience. In short, when one reads the *Politics* it is necessary to be alert to the context and the implications of a particular statement if one is to assign it proper weight in Aristotle's argument as a whole. Only through a careful attempt to distinguish what is partial or provisional from what is simply true can one begin to remedy in some measure the incompleteness—the essential limitation—of Aristotelian political science.

It may be asked in what sense the account in *Politics* VII–VIII of the simply best regime—a regime that Aristotle himself admits is very unlikely to be realized in practice—may be regarded as necessary to a practical science of politics. While this question cannot be fully discussed here, the general character of Aristotle's account indicates the direction in which an answer is to be sought. With its emphasis on the education of a ruling class and the leisured activities for which this education is supposed to prepare, and its corresponding neglect of political institutions and processes in the narrow sense, the account of Books VII–VIII can hardly be said to duplicate the account of actual regimes and in particular of the best actual or practicable regime in Books IV–VI. So far from being merely utopian, the account of Books VII–VIII seems intended in very large measure to provide practical guidance for educated and leisured gentlemen even and precisely in regimes where they do not constitute a ruling class in the political sense.

Any interpretation of *Politics* VIII must attempt to deal in some fashion with the problem of tragic catharsis. Aristotle's enigmatic assertion, in Chapter 6 of the *Poetics,* that tragedy effects "through pity and fear a catharsis of such passions" has exercised the speculative gifts of generations of scholars; yet no single interpretation of Aristotle's language and intention has achieved general recognition as the definitive one. But if the precise function of catharsis in the argument of the *Poetics* is obscure, its importance cannot be doubted. When one takes into account the special place accorded tragedy in the analysis of the *Poetics,* it is clear that Aristotle's view of the human purpose of poetry and its role in social and political life must depend to a considerable extent on his conception of tragic catharsis. There appear to be two broad alternatives: either catharsis is a kind of moral improvement, or it is a form of aesthetic or psychological enjoyment. The second alternative—that catharsis affords a pleasant release of emotions generated by tragedy—is the view most widely held today, and it has inevitably affected current interpretations of Aristotle's understanding of the human or political significance of poetry or music generally. This very common view and the structures erected on it rest, however, on a remarkably tenuous foundation—Book VIII of the *Politics*. In the absence of an explanation or elaboration of the notion of catharsis within the *Poetics* itself, the brief discussion of catharsis near the end of the *Politics* remains the only recourse for interpreters who wish to be guided by Aristotle's own words; and prevailing interpretations of catharsis as a rule draw heavily on the evidence supplied by the *Politics*. The difficulty is that the evidence of the *Politics* is itself highly problematic. The argument of the relevant passage and of the final chapter as a whole is very compressed, abounds in difficulties, and in several places seems to contradict earlier statements. If the enigma of catharsis has resisted satisfactory solution, much of the reason lies in a failure to confront these difficulties in a serious and systematic way, and to read Aristotle's remarks in their context and in the light of the argument of *Politics* VII–VIII as a whole rather than in the light of preconceived notions drawn from the *Poetics* and elsewhere.

It is the thesis of this book that the prevailing understanding of catharsis, and with it the prevailing understanding of Aristotle's view of the political role of literature or culture generally, is fundamentally in error. I shall attempt to show that Aristotle regarded music and poetry as essentially educative in a moral sense; that he did not confine their educative role to the music education of the young but extended it to the musical culture of mature men; and that the central place in the musical culture of mature men was assigned by him to a cathartic tragedy

34

designed to reinforce moral virtue and prudence. I shall try to show that the argument of the final books of the *Politics*—so far from prefiguring either liberal or totalitarian ideas—constitutes the classic exposition of the classical view of literature or culture as at once the vehicle of civic education and the central component of a kind of leisure that is essential in any decent political order precisely because it serves to moderate the claims of politics.

The notion that grown men—particularly educated and leisured gentlemen—stand in need of a continuing education in virtue or prudence may be thought to bear the stamp of Plato rather than of the mature Aristotle. That music or poetry rather than science or philosophy forms the core of a moral or political education will strike some as an idea that is more at home in archaic or tragic Greece than in the thought of a follower of Socrates.[22] It is true indeed, I think, that Aristotle fully shares the position of Plato regarding "the ancient quarrel between poetry and philosophy" spoken of by Socrates in the *Republic*. But contemporary interpreters have not generally appreciated what is really at issue in that quarrel. Because they conceive of the relation between theory and practice in the modern manner, such interpreters tend to assume that theory must aspire to transform practice—that the victory of philosophy over poetry in the element of theory must dictate the supercession of poetry by philosophy in the element of practice. They do not see that Plato and Aristotle were unable to dispense with poetry precisely because they recognized that, given the limits imposed on man by nature, philosophy or reason could never be fully effective in political life.

22. Eugen Fink, *Metaphysik der Erziehung im Weltverständnis von Plato und Aristoteles* (Frankfurt am Main, 1970), pp. 18-20, 294-96, and passim, may be taken as a statement of the Heideggerian view.

1

Education

The best introduction to Aristotle's thematic treatment of education in Book VIII of the *Politics* is the unthematic discussion of that subject which concludes Book VII. The question of education is raised for the first time toward the end of Chapter 13 of that book (1332a28 ff.).

1. Education and Ruling

Although Aristotle had earlier devoted considerable space to the question of the conditions or the "equipment" of the best regime, he now declares that possession of the necessary equipment depends decisively on chance for fortune. Whether a city possesses the virtue necessary for a right use of that equipment is, however, no longer a matter of chance but of knowledge and deliberate choice. It is left to the legislator to see that a city becomes "serious" (*spoudaios*)—that is, decent, respectable, or morally good. But a city can become morally good only if its citizens are serious or decent persons (*spoudaioi*). What must be investigated, then, is the question how people become morally good. According to Aristotle, three things contribute to the development of moral goodness or virtue: nature (*physis*), habit or habituation (*ethos*), and speech or reason (*logos*). In the best case, all three will collaborate in forming the morally good person. Now the question of "nature"—of the natural endowment that is necessary or desirable in future citizens of the best regime—has already been treated (1327b19-28a16). What remains, then, is just the question of "education" (*paideia*). "For men learn in part by habituation, and in part by listening" (1332a28-b11).

Aristotle begins Chapter 14 by taking up the question of whether the rulers and the ruled in the best regime ought to be the same or different. At first sight, Aristotle's discussion appears to be little more than a restatement of some earlier remarks in Chapter 9 (1329a2-34). This is not quite correct. In the earlier discussion, Aristotle was concerned primarily with the relation of the ruling citizen body to its subject population. Here he is concerned solely with the relation of rulers and ruled within the citizen body itself. Aristotle's earlier discussion was guided by economic and political considerations; the present discussion is guided by the question of education (cf. 1332b15-16). As Aristotle had indicated earlier, the problem of differentiating rulers and ruled within the citizen body is solved in principle by nature itself: the older citizens are naturally fitted to rule, the younger citizens to be ruled. Rulers and ruled are then in a sense the same, and in a sense different. Accordingly, "education too must be in a sense the same, and in a sense different; for they say that the one who is to rule well must first be ruled" (1332b41-33a3). With this somewhat enigmatic remark, Aristotle allows the matter to drop. In what way, then, will education be affected by the differentiation of rulers and ruled? At first glance, it could seem that there will be in fact only one education, or that the education in being ruled will be at the same time an education in ruling. Or should one say that the young will begin by learning to be ruled, and will then learn through being ruled how to rule?[1]

It seems necessary to assume that Aristotle is thinking of an education with two distinct phases. But I do not think he can be understood to refer to a special education in the art of rul-

1. This is the explanation of W. L. Newman, *The Politics of Aristotle* (Oxford, 1887-1901), III, on 1332b42.

ing—an education which in its later stage is indistinguishable from the experience of being ruled. Aristotle speaks of "education" simply; and he will have nothing to say later on concerning a special education of this sort. Education in ruling and being ruled must be assumed to be a part or an incidental effect of education generally—that is to say, of an education to "moral goodness" or virtue. As regards the twofold character of the education to which Aristotle here alludes, it makes sense to connect it with the two instruments of education mentioned at the end of Chapter 13. The education in being ruled is, it would seem, an education in "habituation" which precedes the experience of rule—of active citizenship and participation in political life—and prepares for it; the education in ruling is an education in "speech" or "reason." And since "the virtue of the citizen and ruler and that of the best man is one and the same" (1333a11-12), it would seem that the citizens are not expected to be fully virtuous, or that their education will not be completed, before they become rulers strictly speaking. These suggestions will be amply confirmed in the sequel.

2. The Parts of the Soul

Aristotle concludes that it will be the legislator's task to see that the citizens become good, and to see what practices will make them so, and "what is the end of the best life" (1333a14-16). In the immediate sequel, Aristotle develops his view of the two kinds or phases of education in their relation to virtue and to the end of the best life. It appears that the human soul may be divided into two parts, one that "possesses reason in itself" and another that does not, though it is capable of obeying reason. To both of these parts belong the virtues "with reference to which a person is called in any way good." But there is one part of the soul in which the "end" is more particularly to be sought, and that is the reasoning part: "the worse is always for the sake of the better," and the better part of the soul is its reasonable part. It appears, however, that the reasonable part of the soul is itself divisible, since there are in fact two kinds of reason—"theoretical" or "speculative" reason (*logos theōrētikos*) and "practical" reason (*logos praktikos*). Actions that proceed from the various parts of the soul are related to each other in an analogous way; and, Aristotle concludes, the actions "belonging to a part that is by nature better are more choiceworthy for those who are capable of a share in all of them or in the two, for the highest that an individual can attain is what is most choiceworthy for him" (1333a16-30).

That part of the soul which is capable of obeying reason without itself being reasonable is elsewhere called by Aristotle the "desiring" (*epithymētikon*) or the "passionate" (*pathētikon, orektikon*) part of the soul. It is the part of the soul that is, in Aristotle's view, the locus of moral or ethical virtue properly so called—of the virtues of "character" (*ēthos*) as distinguished from the virtues of "thought" (*dianoia*).[2] And since moral virtue is engendered above all by habituation, it is with this part of the soul that an education in habituation is primarily concerned. Aristotle's education in habituation is, then, the education of the passionate part of the soul with a view to the inculcation of moral virtue.[3] But "the worse is always for the sake of the better." Moral virtue cannot be understood to be the end of the best life. Moral virtue must be understood as the foundation of a higher form of virtue, and the education in moral virtue as the preparation for a higher kind of education. The higher education in question will be, as it seems, an education in and through reason.

To which division of the reasonable part of the soul will such an education be directed? Is it to be an education in "theoretical reason"—in science or philosophy? Or is it to be rather an education in "practical reason"—in "practical wisdom" or "prudence" (*phronēsis*)?[4] Or, for that matter, will it be an education in both? For the present it must suffice to

2. *Pol.* 1254b4-9, 1334b18-20, *Eth. Nic.* 1102a26-3a10.
3. *Eth. Nic.* 1103a14-b25.
4. *Phronēsis* is the virtue of the lower division (*to doxastikon*) of the reasonable part of the soul (*Eth. Nic.* 1140b25-28).

note that while Aristotle clearly implies that the practical division of the reasonable part of the soul is "for the sake of" its
theoretical division—thus suggesting that the pursuit of science
or philosophy is in fact the end of the best life—he says only
that the actions of a better part of the soul will be choiceworthy
for those capable of sharing in "all of them or in the two." He
suggests, in other words, that a capacity for theoretical reason
or for the pursuit of science or philosophy is not to be expected
in every citizen of the best regime.

3. Education and Leisure

Immediately following his discussion of the parts of the soul,
and in close connection with that discussion, Aristotle introduces the subject of "leisure" (scholē). "All of life, too," he
continues,

> is divided between occupation [ascholia] and leisure and be-
> tween war and peace, and of our activities some are necessary
> and useful and others noble. The same preference must be exer-
> cised here as in regard to the parts of the soul and their ac-
> tivities—war being chosen for the sake of peace, occupation for
> the sake of leisure, and necessary and useful things for the sake
> of noble things. The statesman must legislate with a view to all
> these things—the parts of the soul and their activities, and par-
> ticularly those that are better and have more the character of an
> end, and similarly with regard to the ways of life and the choice
> of preferred actions. For they must be able to be occupied
> [ascholein] and to go to war, but much more to remain at peace
> and at leisure, and they must be able to do necessary and useful
> things, but ought rather to do the noble things. Accordingly, it
> is with these aims in view that they should be educated both
> when they are still children and during the other ages in life that
> require education. [1333a30–b5]

In an earlier chapter, Aristotle had remarked that the
citizens of the best regime will require "leisure" with a view to
"political activities" as well as the acquisition of virtue
(1329a2). At first sight, Aristotle could seem to connect
"leisure" with "political activity" or with the activity of ruling
while connecting "occupation" with military activity: he ap-

pears to suggest that the older citizens will devote their leisure to the "nobler" activity of ruling, while the younger citizens they rule will be "occupied" with the "necessary" activity of defending the city. This impression is misleading. Elsewhere, Aristotle's position is more fully stated:

> Happiness seems to belong to leisure, for we are occupied that we may have leisure, and we wage war in order to live in peace. But the activity of the practical virtues belongs to politics and war, and the actions connected with them seem to be lacking in leisure [ascholoi] and warlike actions completely so . . . ; but the activity of the statesman is also lacking in leisure, since apart from political action it procures the advantages of power, honor, or happiness for him and for the citizens—happiness being different from political activity and something we clearly seek apart from it.[5]

Political activity—the activity of "ruling"—is also a form of "occupation," albeit one that is less "necessary" or more noble than the occupation of war. Political activity is not choiceworthy in itself; compared with the activities of leisure properly speaking, it is necessary rather than noble; it is a means to happiness rather than a source of happiness. Aristotle has indicated that the education of the best regime will indeed be in some sense an education in ruling. But it will also be something more. Education must prepare not only for war but also, and more importantly, for peace; it must prepare not only for the "occupation" of war and politics but also, and more importantly, for leisure. The education of the best regime will surely be an education in things necessary and useful; it will be an education also, and above all, in things noble or beautiful (ta kala). Or, as Aristotle also suggests, it will be an education for "happiness" (cf. 1332a7–27).

4. The Stages of Education (I)

In Chapters 14 and 15 of Book VII, Aristotle raises and answers the question of "the end of the best life." In the latter

---

5. *Eth. Nic.* 1177b4–15.

part of Chapter 15 he turns to the question that remains to be discussed—the question of the "practices" by which the best life as a whole is to be realized (cf. 1333a14–16). At the conclusion of his discussion of the end of the best life, then, Aristotle returns as it were to the beginning. It had previously been determined (1332a38–b11) that "nature," "habit," and "reason" must alike contribute to the formation of the citizens of the best regime. Assuming the appropriate natural endowment as given, what remains to be considered, then, is the question whether their earliest education is to be an education in "reason" or in "habits" (1334b6–9). For, as it seems, the two educations must agree or harmonize in the most perfect manner (*symphonein symphonian tēn aristēn*), and they will not do so if their natural order or sequence is disregarded.

Aristotle's argument is as follows: It is evident that birth is our beginning, and reason and mind our natural end; "so that it is with a view to these [latter] that birth and the training of habits are to be managed." Further, just as body and soul are two, so there are two parts of the soul; and just as the body is prior to soul in birth, so the unreasonable or desiring part of the soul is prior to the part possessing reason. "Accordingly, the training of the body must first of all precede that of the soul; then comes the training of desire; but the training of desire is for the sake of mind, as that of the body is for the sake of the soul" (1334b12–28). Aristotle confirms what had been implied in the earlier discussion of the parts of the soul (1333a16–30). Just as the lower is "for the sake of" the higher, so the education of the lower must precede and prepare for the education of the higher. The education of the body and of the lower part of the soul must be understood as preparing a later education of the "mind" (*nous*) through speech or reason.

In accordance with this scheme, Aristotle proposes in Chapter 16 a number of regulations concerning marriage, sexual intercourse, and the production of children, regulations that are intended to safeguard the physical health and the well-being of future offspring. In Chapter 17 he pursues the

42

development of future citizens from the stage of infancy, with particular emphasis on the importance of "habituation" in the education of the young. It would be more accurate to say that the principal theme of Chapter 17 is the necessary preconditions of education rather than education properly speaking. The education in "habit" itself presupposes both a prior training or habituation designed to "prepare the road" (cf. 1336a32–34) for its reception and public institutions that will support and protect it.

For present purposes, the discussion of Chapter 17 is important primarily for what it reveals about education itself and the precise manner of its organization in the best regime. Aristotle begins with a brief account of infancy and early childhood. It apears that children up to the age of five are not to be exposed to "learning" (*mathēsis*) of any sort; their activity will be limited to "play"—if to a kind of play that affords imitations of the serious concerns of adults (1336a23–34). In the sixth and seventh years, however, children are to become "spectators" of the activities they will soon have to learn themselves (1336b35–37); and in the eighth year their education begins. As regards the character of the training they receive during the first seven years, Aristotle indicates that it will be supervised to a very considerable extent by public officials. He does not make it quite clear whether the responsibilities of those he calls the "superintendents of children" (*paidonomoi*) will extend even to children's play, though he strongly suggests they will;[6] and he insists on public control both of the stories and tales told to young children and of the extent of their association with slaves.

The problem of the corrupting influence of slaves leads Aristotle to an emphatic assertion of the need to banish from

6. Plato requires supervised play from the age of three (*Laws* 793e–94a). Aristotle's argument is misunderstood by Ingemar Düring (*Aristoteles* [Heidelberg, 1966], p. 484), who detects a polemic against Plato: Aristotle does not recommend, he grudgingly concedes that children below the age of seven should be raised primarily at home (1336a41–b2); as appears from the sentence following, he is worried about the influence of domestic slaves.

the city not only vulgar language (*aischrologia*) but every kind of indecency in paintings, statues, and speeches (1336b3-16). To this rule he recognizes, however, two exceptions: those who have attained the proper age may attend festivals of the gods where a certain scurrility is traditionally permitted, and they may attend performances of iambic verses and of comedy. As to what Aristotle means by the proper age, it is indicated rather precisely in his remark concerning comic and iambic performances. Younger persons (*tous neōterous*), he says, are not to become spectators of performances of this kind "until they reach the age when they will be able to take part in reclining at table and in drinking—when education will have made them all immune to the harm that comes from this sort of thing" (1336b20-23).[7] If a measure that reminds of Spartan austerity is to be judged by Spartan practice, the age in question is most probably twenty-one.[8]

5. *The Stages of Education* (II)

Aristotle's most explicit statement concerning the relation between education and the ages or periods of life (*hēlikiai*) occurs toward the end of the chapter. After remarking that children must spend their sixth and seventh years as spectators of the activities they will later have to learn, he adds:

> There are two ages with a view to [*pros*] which education must be distinguished—that following [*meta*] the age from seven to puberty and that following [*meta*] the age from puberty to twenty-one. For those who distinguish the ages by periods of

7. I read *pantas* at b23 with the manuscripts as against Susemihl's *pantōs,* accepted by Ross. It is true that not all mature men appear to be immune to the attractions of *aischrologia* (1336b9-12); on the other hand, an early education in virtue cannot by itself be expected to make men "altogether" good (consider *Eth. Nic.* 1179b29-31 ff.).

8. Cf. Newman on 1336b9. In Athens, adolescent and even younger boys seem to have been regularly present at performances of tragedy and comedy (cf. Plato *Laws* 658d). According to Aristotle (*Ath. Pol.* 42), Athenians became citizens at eighteen, and were granted the right of *syssitia* at that time (though until the age of twenty-one these meals were separate and specially supervised).

seven years are for the most part correct, but one ought to follow the distinctions of nature itself. [1336b37-37a1]

At first glance, there seems to be something wrong with the text of this passage. Does Aristotle not mean to say that it is necessary to distinguish an education that corresponds or is related to the age from seven to puberty and an education that corresponds or is related to the age from puberty to twenty-one?[9] But there is no evidence of textual disturbance, nor is Aristotle's remark unintelligible as it stands. It is not impossible that Aristotle means to distinguish an education that corresponds to the period from puberty to twenty-one (that is, to the period "following" [meta] the age from seven to puberty) and an education that corresponds to the age after twenty-one (that is, to the period "following" the age from puberty to twenty-one). Aristotle had earlier remarked that the citizens of the best regime will be educated "both when they are children and during the other ages in life that require education" (1333b3-5); if an "age" is indeed a period of seven years, this remark implies that education in the best regime will extend beyond the single age following childhood, or in other words that there will be an education beyond twenty-one.[10] But if this is Aristotle's meaning, his remark is an extraordinary circumlocution; and the context as a whole indicates that he is thinking above all of the education of the young (cf. 1336b33-34, 37a3-4). It is preferable, I think, to understand him to refer to two forms of education that indeed correspond to the ages from seven to puberty and from puberty to twenty-one, but which are "distinguished" primarily "with a view to" the ages that follow. Aristotle takes it for granted that there will be different forms of education that succeed one another in

9. This appears to be the view of Ross, who alters meta in a38 and 39 to pros. It is the view taken, though evidently without benefit of emendation, by Barker and by P. Girard, L'éducation athénienne (Paris, 1894), p. 127.

10. Although Newman's interpretation of 1336b37 ff. is not entirely clear, he evidently takes this passage (with 1333b3-5) as suggesting the existence of an education beyond the age of twenty-one. See the remarks in his introductory essay, I, 358 and 370.

time, and of which the earlier or lower forms are "for the sake of" the later or higher; and he argues that it is "with a view to" reason or an education in reason that "birth and the training of habits are to be managed" (1334b15-17; cf. b9).[11] More precisely, Aristotle distinguishes three forms of education or training: education or training of the body, of the desires (the unreasonable part of the soul), and of the mind (the reasonable part of the soul); and he understands the first two as educations by way of habituation, and the third as an education by way of speech or reason. In the present passage, then, his argument seems to be this: Education properly speaking—as distinguished from the practices connected with birth or with the "rearing" (*trophē*) of the first seven years—begins at age seven. The education proper to the period from seven to puberty is primarily an education of the body, and it must be undertaken "with a view to" or in preparation for the period that follows. The education proper to the period from puberty to twenty-one is primarily an education of the desires or of the irrational part of the soul. The education of both periods is an education by way of habituation. At the same time, however, it appears that the education of the irrational part of the soul must itself be undertaken "with a view to" or in preparation for an education that will follow the age of twenty-one.

Some indication as to the character of the education that precedes the age of twenty-one is provided by Aristotle's remark concerning performances of comic and iambic poetry. When Aristotle specifies the age at which the young are to be permitted to attend such performances, he says that their education will by then have made them "immune [*apatheis*] to the harm that comes from this sort of thing" (1336b20-23). What he suggests is that by the age of twenty-one a certain kind of education will have been completed. The education in question would seem to be the education of the lower or irrational

11. Had Aristotle wished to connect the two educations directly with the two ages, he could have written: *helikiai kath' has* (cf. 1331a37-38). Compare in addition the expression *paideuesthai pros tas politeias* (1310a14; cf. 1337a14).

part of the soul in moral virtue, for it is precisely by habituation to the practice of virtue that the soul's desires or "passions" are tamed, trained, or educated. Elsewhere, Aristotle makes clear that twenty-one is an age of crucial importance in the physiological development of the individual. And there is some evidence that he also regarded it as crucially important for the development of "mind." At any rate, a passage in the *Problems* indicates that "learning" as such does not presuppose the full development of mind, and suggests that an education of the mind or of the reasoning part of the soul is appropriate only for mature persons.[12] Finally, it may be observed that it is by no means clear that the education following the age of twenty-one is limited, like the educations of the periods preceding it, to a period of roughly seven years. Aristotle is at the very least reserved in his approval of those who divide human life into seven-year periods, and the ages of fourteen and twenty-one evidently have for him a natural or physiological significance for which there is no real counterpart in the years that begin later cycles.[13]

Book VII ends with a brief statement of the questions to be taken up in Book VIII: "First, then, we must investigate whether some order is to be instituted with regard to children,

12. The author of *Problems* XXX.5 asks why it is that "we possess mind [*nous*] to a greater extent as we grow older but learn more quickly when we are younger" (955b22 ff.; cf. *Pol.* 1340b35–39). The physiological significance of the ages of puberty and twenty-one is discussed in *Hist. An.* 544b25–26, 582a16–33. According to Plato (*Symposium* 181d), the beginnings of *nous* in a young man coincide with the first growth of beard; according to Aristotle (*Hist. An.* 582a32–33; cf. Solon fr 19,3–6 Diehl), the first growth of beard generally occurs around twenty-one.

13. It should be noted, however, that according to the reading of the manuscripts Aristotle in fact says that the division by periods of seven years is for the most part *not* correct (*legousin ou kalōs,* 1336b41–37a1). It is true that the corruption of *kakōs* to *kalōs* occurs elsewhere in the *Politics* (1336b28, 1294a7), but in both cases the true reading occurs in some manuscripts. It is perhaps of some importance that the division in question is of poetic origin (cf. 1335b32–34; it seems to derive from Solon fr. 19 Diehl). Aristotle cannot be said to observe it strictly in his regulations concerning marriage and procreation (1335a28–29, b35–37); and consider *Rhet.* 1390b9–11.

then whether it is more advantageous for this to be a common concern or one managed privately—which is the way it is now in most cities—and third, of what sort this should be" (1337a3–7). Aristotle's immediate concern continues to be education in its emphatic sense—the education (*paideia*) of children (*paides*) or, more generally, of the young. But we have found reason to believe that the question of education is not identical with the question of the education of the young; and if Book VIII appears at first sight to be devoted wholly to the latter question—if, indeed, it appears to identify education altogether with the education of the young—it is necessary to bear in mind both the range and flexibility of the term *paideia* itself and the fact that *Politics* VIII as we have it by no means represents Aristotle's last word on the subject of education. And yet even the extant portions of Book VIII will, as I hope to show, bear witness to the view of education that emerges from the argument of Book VII.

6. Education and the City

The first two questions—whether "some order is to be instituted" regarding the young, and whether it is to be public or private in nature—are disposed of in the first chapter of Book VIII. "That the education of the young is a matter of paramount importance for the legislator," Aristotle begins,

> would be disputed by no one; for its absence in cities damages the regimes. It is necessary to educate with a view to the regime, for the character proper to each regime both preserves it and brings it into being at the first—the democratic character a democratic regime and the oligarchic character an oligarchic one, and the better character is always the cause of a better regime. [1337a11–18]

The city's "regime" is above all its "way of life" (cf. 1295a40–b1). But the way of life of a city is sustained by nothing so much as by the character of its leading and ruling citizens; and character, Aristotle suggests, is formed primarily by education (cf. 1310a12 ff.). Again, every faculty or art requires a preparatory education in connection with the work it is intended to effect, and this applies as well to "the actions of virtue" (1337a18-21). Aristotle probably intends his readers to think in the first instance of those actions of virtue that are manifestly necessary to the city irrespective of its regime—the actions, that is, which relate to war.[14] Aristotle's argument for education appears to be gounded in the most solid and "necessary" requirements of the city.

"Since there is one end for the whole city," Aristotle continues, "it is evident that education, too, must necessarily be one and the same for all, and that it must be a public rather than a private concern" (1337a21-24). Aristotle answers the second question before restating it, but his answer is largely implied in what has preceded. Given the close connection between education and the regime, it is clear that the coexistence of fundamentally different kinds of education, whether public or private, must endanger the cohesiveness of the regime; and it is the regime that lends to the city its unity and singleness of purpose. On another occasion Aristotle goes so far as to suggest that it is education that makes a "multitude" of diverse individuals "one and common" or a city properly speaking (1263b36-37). Education must be one for the sake of the unity of the city; and education must be public for the sake of the unity of education. Aristotle gives precisely no weight to the claims of privacy or of the individual: the concern for each "part," whether of the body or the city, is, it seems, naturally subordinate to the concern for the whole. "And one could praise the Lacedaemonians in this respect; for they pay the most serious attention to the young, and they do so in common" (1337a29-32).

Aristotle's near-praise of Sparta and his apparent surrender to the spirit of Sparta raise an important question. In his discussion of the parts of the soul in Book VII, Aristotle had appeared to indicate that the activities of the "theoretical" part of

14. Cf. Plato *Laws* 641b-c.

the rational division of the soul—the activities, that is, of science or philosophy—are choiceworthy not for everyone or for every citizen of the best regime but only for those who are capable of them (1333a24-30). If the education of the best regime is to be one and the same for everyone, however, it would seem to follow that the education of the best regime cannot include an education in science or philosophy. But is Aristotle really willing to concede so much to Sparta or the demands of political stability? Is it so clear that the claims of the individual are in the highest case naturally subordinate to the claims of the city? Aristotle indicates elsewhere that the pursuit of philosophy provides a kind of happiness to those who are capable of it which is superior to the happiness available to other people;[15] can a regime that is dedicated to securing the highest happiness to its citizens justly neglect such a pursuit?

It is one thing to say that Aristotle must have made provision of some kind for science or philosophy in the education of the best regime. It is another thing to say that he must be assumed to have introduced in that education "a later training in the higher sciences for state purposes."[16] The relation between theoretical science and the political order was not in antiquity what it is today, and Aristotle certainly shared the general view as to the practical uselessness of theoretical science or philosophy.[17] For Aristotle and for antiquity generally, the end of philosophy and the end of the city are not one and the same: it is more than doubtful whether an education in philosophy could be expected to "harmonize in the most perfect manner" with the essentially practical education required by the city and in particular by the best city. One is tempted to suggest that scientific or philosophic education in the best regime will be fundamentally a private affair—or will enjoy, at best, a semi-institutional status along the lines of the "nocturnal council" of

15. *Eth. Nic.* 1177a12 ff.
16. Franz Susemihl and R. D. Hicks, *The Politics of Aristotle* (London, 1894), pp. 50-51 (cf. p. 619). Cf. Newman I, 370, and John Burnet, *Aristotle on Education* (Cambridge, 1903), pp. 134-36.
17. Consider *Met.* 981a12-82b28.

Plato's *Laws*.[18] However that may be, Aristotle elsewhere shows himself to be rather more favorably disposed toward the claims of a private education which, precisely because it is private, is more capable of adapting itself to the needs or talents of individuals.[19]

7. The Nature of Education

In Chapter 2 Aristotle proceeds to consider "what education is"[20] and how it is to be managed in the best regime. For there is disagreement, it appears, regarding the very nature of education. Not everyone agrees as to what it is that the young must learn either with a view to virtue or with a view to the best life; nor is it clear whether education is more properly directed to "thought" (*dianoia*) or to "the character of the soul." When one looks at the current and customary subjects of education, there is only confusion. It is in no way clear whether the young should be trained in "the things useful for life" (*ta chrēsima pros ton bion*), in "the things that contribute to virtue" (*ta teinonta pros aretēn*), or in "unusual and superfluous accomplishments" (*ta peritta*)—for all have their supporters. As regards education for virtue, there is a similar disagreement—which is hardly surprising, considering that virtue is very differently understood by different kinds of men (1337a35–b3).

In attempting to sort out the confusion that is evident in contemporary opinions, Aristotle begins with the one thing that is "not unclear." Everyone would agree, it seems, that it is necessary to teach "those of the useful things that are necessary." That not all useful things will be subjects of education is evident as soon as one distinguishes between liberal and illiberal employments: only those useful things should be taught which do not render the student base, ignoble, or "mechanical" (*banausos*). Any employment, art, or learning is

18. *Laws* 964b ff.

19. *Eth. Nic.* 1180b7–12 ff.

20. I read *esti* with the manuscripts instead of Richards' *estai*, accepted by Ross. The specific question of education in the best regime is not taken up until 1338a30 ff.

"banausic" which renders the body, the soul, or the mind useless with a view to "the uses and actions of virtue."

> For we call banausic those arts that adversely affect the condition of the body, as well as wage-earning employments; for these occupy and debase the mind [*ascholon gar poiousi tēn dianoian kai tapeinēn*]. And though there are certain liberal sciences [*eleutheriai epistēmai*] which it is not illiberal to pursue to a certain point, to attend to them overly much with a view to proficiency [*pros akribeian*] is liable to be harmful in the ways we have indicated. [1337b4–17]

It is necessary to distinguish between what Aristotle calls banausic and what "we"—that is, "we Greeks"—call banausic.[21] In the accepted view, only the manual or wage-earning arts are banausic. In Aristotle's view, the pursuit of proficiency in "certain liberal sciences" may also be banausic. The manual or wage-earning arts necessarily affect in an adverse manner both body and mind. The pursuit of proficiency in certain liberal sciences is "liable [*enochos*] to be harmful"—it is not necessarily or in all circumstances harmful[22]—"in the ways we have indicated"; it may be harmful, that is, with regard to body, soul, and mind. Aristocle indicates, it seems, that the excessive pursuit of proficiency in certain liberal sciences is liable to be harmful above all for the soul. As he goes on to say:

> But the reason for which one undertakes or learns a thing also makes a great difference: to do it for its own sake or for the sake of friends or because of virtue is not illiberal, but the one who does it because of others would often seem to act in a vulgar and slavish manner. [1337b17–21]

To judge from the subsequent argument, the "liberal

---

21. In Barker's translation, *dio . . . banausous kaloumen* emerges as "we may accordingly apply the word 'mechanical'." Susemihl's bracketing of *ē tēn psychēn* in 1337b11 is evidence of the same mistake.

22. Newman's rendering of *enochon* (1337b17) as "bound up with" (for which he appeals to *LSJ* s.v. *enochos* I) is surely incorrect if it is meant to imply a necessary relation. Barker's "liable" gives the normal meaning of the word.

sciences'' of which Aristotle is thinking are those arts that may be pursued or that are primarily pursued ''with a view to the professional contests'' (*pros tous agōnas tous technikous*, 1341a10-11; cf. b8-10) or for the sake of public performance or display. He is thinking in particular of music, and of the corrupting effect of a professional or ''technical'' education in music. An education of this sort is harmful above all to the soul because it encourages the desire to please and hence to adapt oneself to a ''vulgar'' audience of illiberal tastes (1341b8-18). But Aristotle is certainly thinking also of the conventional education in ''gymnastic.'' As appears from the discussion of physical education in Chapter 4, cities that enjoy the greatest repute among the Greeks encourage either a gymnastic training appropriate to professional athletes—a training that ''damages the form and growth of the body''—or (as in the case of Sparta) a severe and martial gymnastic that adversely affects the character of the soul (1338b9ff.). The difference between Aristotle's view of ''liberal education'' and the conventional view is, if anything, more evident in the case of gymnastic than in the case of music.

Aristotle had begun by distinguishing three kinds or uses of education: education is a training either in what is useful for life, in what contributes to virtue, or in ''unusual and superfluous accomplishments'' (1337a41-42). The argument of Chapter 2 has narrowed these possibilities somewhat. Education must exclude in the first place those useful subjects that are both illiberal and unnecessary. In the second place, it will exclude proficiency in subjects that are not useful—in ''superfluous accomplishments''—and which at the same time may be illiberal (cf. 1341a5-13).

8. The Purposes of Education

In Chapter 3 Aristotle approaches the question of the nature of education from the point of view of the subjects taught in current practice. The usual subjects of education are for practical purposes four: ''letters'' (*grammata*), physical training or gymnastic (*gymnastikē*), drawing or painting (*graphikē*), and "music" (*mousikē*). Aristotle reminds us that these subjects are ambiguous (*epamphoterizousin*) as regards the end they serve. Letters and drawing are thought to be "useful for life" in a variety of ways. Gymnastic, on the other hand, is thought to contribute to courage or manliness—that is, it is thought to "contribute to virtue." As for music, one might well be at a loss to identify its purpose (1337b22-28).

In fact, however, a large measure of agreement appears to exist among Aristotle's contemporaries regarding the purpose of music: "most people today study it as being for the sake of pleasure" (*nyn men gar hōs hēdonēs charin hoi pleistoi metechousin autēs*). Accordingly, Aristotle is forced to appeal to the authority of ancient times. "In the beginning," he argues,

> they established it in education for the reason that nature itself seeks, as we have repeatedly said, not only the correct use of occupation but the ability to enjoy noble leisure [*mē monon ascholein orthōs alla kai scholazein dynasthai kalōs*]. For this is the fundamental principle, as we shall say once again. For if, though both are necessary, leisure is more desirable than occupation and is an end, we must find out what ought to constitute the activity of leisure. [1337b28-35][23]

Noble leisure is the fundamental principle of Aristotle's inquiry because, as we have learned from Book VII, it is the end of the best life. In what follows, Aristotle approaches the question that had been nowhere explicitly raised in Book VII, the question of the precise character of the activity that properly belongs to leisure.

Aristotle's first concern is to clarify the difference between the activity that is proper to leisure and what he calls "play" (*paidia*). It is inconceivable that play could be the end of human life. "Play is rather to be used in occupation, for one who labors is in need of relaxation, and play is for the sake of relaxation, while occupation involves pain and tension." Relaxation

23. Ross's *mia* for *hina* in b32 and Susemihl's *d'* for *gar* in b33 (cf. Newman) seem alike unnecessary.

in and through play is indeed pleasant; leisure, on the other hand, is thought to provide not only pleasure but "happiness and a life of bliss," for while occupation is for the sake of an end not yet attained, happiness is itself the end, and is intrinsically pleasant. And yet not everyone thinks that the same pleasure constitutes happiness. Each judges in accordance with himself and his own condition; the best man judges that it is the best pleasure and that deriving from the noblest things (1337b35–38a9).

Aristotle's insistence on a radical distinction between play or amusement and what one may call "serious leisure" underlines once more the central importance of leisure for his analysis as a whole. Play is not the source of happiness because play is inseparable from occupation. Play belongs with occupation because occupation is not in itself satisfying, or because it is always concerned with future happiness or with providing the conditions of happiness and never with the enjoyment of present happiness. Occupation is the "serious" business of life; play is a necessary and at the same time a necessarily unserious refuge from its burdens. Human life would be condemned to an eternal alternation between pain or labor and unmeaning diversion were it not for the fact that nature itself points to the possibility of a way of life or an activity that combines the seriousness of occupation with the pleasures of play.[24]

Aristotle's argument continues as follows:

> It is evident, then, that one must also learn certain things and be educated with a view to the leisure associated with pastime[25] and that these subjects of education and learning must be for

24. R. K. Bury, "Theory of Education in Plato's *Laws,*" *REG* 50 (1937), 312, n. 1 (cf. Newman on 1337b35), has argued that Aristotle's depreciation of play must be understood as a criticism of the importance assumed by it in the *Laws.* But it is easy to see that the Platonic notion of *paidia*—according to Plato it is practically synonymous with *paideia* and is "the most serious thing" for men (*Laws* 803d5–7)—has nothing to do with Aristotle's notion of play, while it has been very much to do with his notion of serious leisure. Cf. Koller, *Musse,* p. 29.

25. Compare the use of *pros* ("with a view to") in 1336b38; cf. note 11 above.

their own sake, while those with a view to occupation will be necessary and for the sake of other things. And it was for this reason that the men of former times established music as a subject of education—not on the grounds that it is necessary (for it is nothing of the sort) or useful (as letters are useful with a view to making money and the management of the household and learning and many political actions, and as drawing is thought to be useful with a view to judging more accurately the works of craftsmen), or again that, like gymnastic, it contributes to health and strength (for we see neither resulting from music). They evidently brought it in for the reason remaining, that is, with a view to the pastime associated with leisure. For they established it in what they regard as the pastime of free men. Hence the verses of Homer: "But call them alone to the rich feast"—and after naming several others, "they call in the singer," he says, "that all may take delight." And elsewhere Odysseus says that this is the best pastime—when men are cheered and "the feasters in the hall listen to a singer, sitting in due order." [1338a9–30]

In the first place, Aristotle makes clear what noble leisure is not. He confirms what had only been suggested in Book VII; noble leisure is not the leisure that is devoted to political actions. Although political activities require leisure, in themselves they are a form of occupation. Like economic or military activities, they partake of the character of the necessary; they cannot be understood to exist for their own sake. When Aristotle speaks of "the leisure associated with pastime" (*hē en tēi diagōgēi scholē*), he does so, it would seem, precisely in order to distinguish the leisure that is associated with political activities from leisure in the proper sense of the term—from the leisured "pastime" that constitutes the end of the best life or the true source of happiness for the citizens of the best regime.[26]

In Aristotle's usage, *diagōgē* (for which "pastime" is a purposely bland if inadequate translation) is a word with a wide range of connotation. In the last chapter of Book VII

26. This explanation does not seem to have occurred to the commentators (see Newman on 1338a9). Cf. 1334a16–17.

(1336a40), it is applied to the activities of young children, and does not seem readily distinguishable from "play" (cf. 1336a27–28, 32–34). In the *Nicomachean Ethics* it is almost exclusively associated with play, relaxation, and the enjoyment of bodily pleasures.[27] Elsewhere, it is used with reference to the contemplative life.[28] In the present passage, Aristotle seems to narrow its meaning; he suggests, at the very least, that pastime can have nothing to do with play. When Aristotle speaks of "the pastime associated with leisure" (*hē en tēi scholēi diagōgē*), he does so in order to distinguish the noble pastime of serious leisure from that pastime which is inseparable from play and relaxation. However understood, *diagōgē* is an essentially pleasant activity; but the *diagōgē* associated with leisure affords a pleasure that is noble rather than necessary.[29] As regards the precise character of *diagōgē* so understood, Aristotle leaves the impression that the Homeric banquet can serve as a model for it. Whether or to what extent Aristotle's view in fact coincides with the view of "the ancients" is a question that must be reserved for later discussion. What can be said is that the central activity of leisure as Aristotle here describes it—or at any rate its most "serious" activity—is the enjoyment of music.

9. Useful Education and Liberal Education

In the sequel, Aristotle returns from his discussion of leisure to the question of education:

> That there exists, then, a certain education that is to be taught to our sons not because it is useful or necessary but because it is liberal and noble is evident. Whether it is one or more than one in number, and what they are and how they are to be taught, these things will be considered later. At present, we have advanced this far: we have some testimony of the ancients drawn from the established subjects of education; for music makes this clear. It has also become clear that certain of the useful things

27. *Eth. Nic.* 1127b33–28a1 (cf. 1171b12–14, 1176b12–14, 1177a9).
28. *Met.* 1072b14; cf. *Eth. Nic.* 1177a27.
29. For this sense consider particularly *Met.* 981b17–23, with the remarks of W. D. Ross, *Aristotle's Metaphysics* (Oxford, 1924), I, 118. Cf. Koller, *Musse*, pp. 35–36.

are to be taught not only on account of their usefulness, such as the learning of letters, but also because they make further kinds of learning possible; and drawing must similarly be taught not in order that they may not make mistakes in their private purchases or that they may be able to guard against deception in the buying or selling of articles, but rather because it makes them observant [*theōrētikon*] of physical beauty. To seek usefulness everywhere is least of all suited to men who are magnanimous and free. [1338a30-b4][30]

There are, it seems, two kinds of education that will be taught to the young. In the first place, there must be an education in "the useful things." But while an education of this kind is indeed indispensable, the requirements of utility must not be allowed to dominate education as a whole. The useful things are to be taught not only on account of their usefulness but because "they make further kinds of learning possible"; they are to be taught "with a view to" a more advanced kind of education, an education wholly unconcerned with the merely useful. In the second place, then, there will be an advanced education that is liberal rather than useful, noble rather than necessary. Compared with useful education—with education "with a view to occupation"—liberal education may be said to exist for its own sake. In the last analysis, however, liberal education too is for the sake of something beyond itself: it is education "with a view to the leisure associated with pastime" (1338a9-13).

Aristotle concludes Chapter 3 with the following remark:

> But as it is evidently necessary to educate in habits before educating in reason, and to educate the body before the mind [*dianoian*], it is clear that the young are to be exposed to gymnastic exercise and training. For the one produces a proper condition of the body, and the other teaches skills. [1338b4-8]

That the training of the body must precede that of the soul had been made clear in Book VII (1334b17-26): the earliest education will be physical education.

30. I read *eleutherois* with the manuscripts rather than *eleutheriois* with Susemihl. Cf. Newman and *Met.* 982b25-27.

It is not necessary to dwell at length on the argument of Chapter 4. Most of the chapter is taken up by Aristotle's criticism of gymnastic as it was taught in the most respected of the Greek cities. Although he rejects the "athletic" or professional gymnastic practiced in many cities, Aristotle's harshest words are reserved for the gymnastic practiced at Sparta with a view to the inculcation of courage; according to him, the severe Spartan discipline serves only to produce "savages" (1338b12–38). What is more important to note, however, is that Aristotle disagrees not only with the methods of Spartan gymnastic but with its aim as well. It is the view of the Spartans—and perhaps not only of the Spartans (cf. 1337b23–27)—that the primary purpose of gymnastic training is to teach the virtue of courage. Aristotle's view, on the other hand, appears to be that the primary purpose of gymnastic training is to develop the health and strength of the body (cf. 1338a19–20 with b6–8 and 42 as well as 1339a21–24). It is true that Aristotle seems to approve a severe gymnastic of the Spartan type—not, indeed, for the earliest years, but for the later years of adolescence (1339a4–7); and it makes sense to understand this later training as an education primarily of the soul rather than the body—that is to say, as an education for virtue. But one is forced to wonder whether the virtue that training is designed to teach is not the virtue of endurance (*karteria*) rather than the virtue of courage (cf. 1334a19–23). Genuine courage will be taught, it could seem, not by gymnastic of any kind but rather by music—or by a certain kind of music (cf. 1338b17–19 with 1340b3–4 and 42b12–14).

10. *The Stages of Education* (III)

Aristotle concludes his treatment of gymnastic with the following statement:

> That gymnastic is to be used, and how it is to be used, is agreed. Up to the age of puberty only lighter exercises are to be employed, and a forced diet and severe labors forbidden, in order not to interfere with growth. . . . But after the three years

following puberty have been devoted to other subjects of learning, it will be suitable for those of the next age to undergo labors [*tois ponois*] and a regime of abstinence. For it is not right to exert [*diaponein*] mind [*tēi dianoiai*] and body at the same time, since these kinds of labor have by nature an opposite effect—the labor of the body interfering with the mind, and that of the mind with the body. [1338b38–39a10]

This passage is of crucial importance for understanding Aristotle's view of the kinds of education and their chronological relationship. In the first place, it both confirms and explains Aristotle's evident insistence that the earliest period of education should be devoted primarily or wholly to gymnastic training. "It is not right," Aristotle asserts, "to exert mind and body at the same time."

This principle, however, is itself in need of clarification. If it is strictly applied, it will be necessary to postpone to the period following puberty—or rather to the three years following puberty—every form of "dianoetic" education: not only will the young not be exposed to music, they will not learn to read and write until the age of fourteen—and their education in all these subjects will be confined to the brief period of three years.[31] Or is the principle not meant to be strictly applied? It is true that Plato had favored the early study of gymnastic, and had restricted the study of letters to a period of three years.[32] But the time allowed—particularly if music and perhaps other subjects are to be included—seems impossibly short, and Aristotle's statement admits of more than one interpretation. What Aristotle objects to, I suggest, is not the simultaneous pursuit of dianoetic and physical education as such but rather the simultaneous "labor" or "exertion" of body and mind. Aristotle's principle is introduced in order to justify the separation of dianoetic and physical education during the years of adolescence—during what had earlier been identified as the second period of education, the period from puberty to twenty-

31. Thus Newman (on 1338b6).
32. *Laws* 794c, 809e. Plato begins instruction in reading and writing, however, at age ten, and before the education in music.

one. But an argument that applies to the severe gymnastic of the period immediately preceding twenty-one may not be intended to apply to the less demanding gymnastic that belongs to the first period of education. The gymnastic training appropriate to younger children might well allow a simultaneous study of letters and of certain other useful or necessary subjects—or at least such study of them as does not require undue labor or exertion. Indeed, Plato himself had shown that the rudiments of arithmetic, geometry, and astronomy may be learned without effort when they are incorporated in children's play.[33]

What, then, of music? Could one not argue that the education in music must also begin prior to the age of puberty (consider 1340b25–31)—as it did, for example, in Athens? Or does Aristotle follow the lead of Plato, who had restricted the study of music (or at any rate of the lyre) to the years from thirteen to sixteen?[34] It may be pointed out in the first place that the learning of music would seem to be distinguished from the learning of letters or arithmetic by at least a degree of labor or exertion (cf. 1339a39, 41a9–14, b21–22). But the decisive consideration, I think, is Aristotle's principle—as stated toward the end of Book VII (1336a37–40) and echoed in the third chapter of Book VIII—that the two periods in the education of the young are to be distinguished above all by their relation to the ages or to the education of the ages immediately following them. Aristotle has indicated that the education in music must be understood as a direct preparation for the leisured activity—the "pastime"—of mature citizens. In a similar way, it seems, the severe gymnastic of the period immediately preceding twenty-one directly prepares the young for the military responsibilities they will have to assume during the early years of manhood. On the other hand, the gymnastic training of the first period of education is clearly intended to prepare for that of the second; and, in a similar way, an early training in the "useful" subject

33. *Laws* 819b–c.
34. *Laws* 809e–10a.

of letters could be understood to contribute to "other forms of learning" (1338a38–40) in the later period, and particularly to the learning of "music"—which traditionally included poetry as well as music in the modern sense of the term.

I suggest, then, the following interpretation: The education of the young is divided into two periods, the period from seven to puberty and the period from puberty to twenty-one. These periods are most fundamentally distinguished by the fact that the first is concerned primarily with the education of the body, while the second is concerned primarily with the education of the soul or the mind. The first period is largely given over to a gymnastic training designed to foster the health and strength of the body; it also includes an education in letters and in the rudiments of certain other necessary or useful dianoetic subjects. The education of the first period may be said to be an education in necessary things that are "useful for life." It is useful in two ways: by preparing directly for the occupations of life, and by preparing for more advanced kinds of learning. If the education of the first period is given over to things necessary and useful, the education of the second period—or at any rate of its first three years—is given over to things liberal and noble. The three years immediately following puberty will be occupied primarily with music; it is the education of this period that most directly prepares the young for a correct use of the leisure they will enjoy as adults. The four years following will be wholly devoted to a severe gymnastic that is designed to prepare them for the military duties required of the younger citizens—for an activity that, while surely noble in a sense, is fundamentally "necessary" or lacking in leisure. The education of the last seven years taken together will constitute an education in moral and political virtue at the same time that it prepares for the exercise of that virtue in later life.

11. Liberal Education

When Aristotle alludes in Chapter 4 to the education of the three years following puberty, he speaks of "subjects of learning" (*mathēmata*). In Chapter 3 he had raised the possibility that the education in things liberal and noble may take more forms than one, or that music is not the only education of this sort; and when Aristotle says that he will consider at a later point what these other subjects are "and how they are to be taught" (1338a32–34), he appears to suggest that music will after all not be the only "liberal" subject to find a place in the education of the second period. Unfortunately, Aristotle's promised discussion of "liberal education" has not come down to us. It is all the more necessary, then, to attempt to identify the subjects in question, and to consider possible implications for Aristotle's argument as a whole.

Of the subjects actually mentioned by Aristotle in the course of Chapter 3, drawing or painting (*graphikē*) is the most likely candidate. Although conventionally regarded as something to be studied for its usefulness, drawing is, as Aristotle makes clear, eminently suited to serve as part of a liberal education: drawing, or drawing correctly taught, encourages a liberal appreciation of physical beauty; it makes one observant—literally, "contemplative" (*theōrētikon*)—regarding the beauty of bodies (1338a40–b2; cf. 1337b25–26, 38a17–19). On the other hand, it must be said that Aristotle does not make it perfectly clear that drawing is to be taught only because it is liberal or noble and not at all for reasons of utility.

However that may be, the conventional subjects of music and drawing are not the only conceivable subjects of a liberal education for the young. In Chapter 2, it will be recalled, Aristotle had spoken of "certain liberal sciences" that are capable of having an illiberal effect on those who pursue them "overly much with a view to proficiency" (1337b15–17); he appeared to be thinking primarily of music (and he may have been thinking of drawing or painting as well). He implies that the "liberal science" of music and similar pursuits must be distinguished from other liberal sciences—from other forms of learning that are not capable of having an illiberal effect. Plato had stressed the necessity of an early education in the rudiments of arithmetic, geometry, and astronomy,[35] and I have suggested that it is likely that Aristotle intended some instruction in these subjects to be included in the education preceding the age of puberty. Might Aristotle not also have recommended an advanced study—prepared by that early instruction—of the unnecessary or less useful parts of these sciences? And would such a study not prepare the later study, by mature men, of the science to which these sciences are ancillary—the study of philosophy? Indeed, are not philosophy and the sciences that lead to philosophy the liberal sciences par excellence?[36] If drawing is to be recommended as a liberal study because it encourages a contemplative attitude toward physical beauty, it seems all the more probable that Aristotle would recommend the study of the properly theoretical sciences.

That some instruction in the theoretical sciences was included by Aristotle in the education of the years immediately following puberty is an eminently plausible assumption. But it would be a mistake to suppose that Aristotle envisioned a rigorous course of scientific or philosophical training. We have seen that Aristotle does not presuppose a capacity for theoretical studies in every citizen of the best regime, and that it is unlikely that the public or official education of the best regime is meant to include an education in philosophy properly speaking. The best regime of the *Politics* is not the best regime of Plato's *Republic*. Aristotle is not concerned to establish the rule of philosophers, and he is not concerned—or not primarily concerned—with the education of philosophers. The

35. *Laws* 817e–18b.
36. Cf. *Met.* 981b17–25 and 982b19–28. It should be pointed out, however, that the expression *hai eleutheriai epistēmai* appears to occur only in the one passage in the *Politics* (1337b15). The classic statement of the liberal character of the theoretical sciences appears in Plato's *Republic* (consider particularly 525b–c, 526c–e, 527c–d). In the *Laws* (817e–18b, 966c–67e), Plato appears to restrict the study of the "useless" parts of the theoretical sciences as well as of philosophy proper to the select few. Xenophon (*Memorabilia* IV.7) presents Socrates as giving similar advice.

"magnanimous men" (1338b3)[37] who will rule in the best regime may be said to resemble philosophers in certain respects. They differ from philosophers in one very important respect. Whereas the philosopher as philosopher is necessarily concerned with accuracy, precision, or "proficiency" (*akribeia*), the magnanimous man—the "gentleman"—is characterized by a certain contempt for it.[38] It is more than doubtful that Aristotle would have required a public and hence universal education designed to impart proficiency in the theoretical sciences, even if proficiency in the sciences in question does not bring with it the illiberal effects attending proficiency in the liberal science of music.

It cannot be assumed that instruction in the theoretical sciences will take precedence over instruction in music in the three years following puberty. In fact, I think it must be assumed that music will be the central subject of education during those years. In Book VII, it will be recalled, Aristotle had distinguished three kinds of phases of education: education of the body, education of the irrational part of the soul, and education of the rational part of the soul. The first two represent an education in or through "habituation," and the third an education in or through "speech" or "reason." Now it is true that, as compared with the gymnastic education of the first period of education, the education in music is an education operating through or by means of "thought" (*dianoia*) (cf. 1341b6-7): music education is indeed, like the education in theoretical science, a dianoetic education. But there can be little doubt that the music education of the period following puberty must be understood as an education of the soul—more precisely, of the irrational or desiring part of the soul—rather than of the mind, and as an education in habits rather than an

37. Consider 1328a9-10 and context (1327b23-28a16)—an explicit response to the Platonic notion of the "philosophic" guardian (*Republic* 375b-76c).

38. Consider 1337b15-17 in the light of *Eth. Nic.* 1122b8, *Met.* 995a8-12, Plato *Gorgias* 487c7 (cf. *Laws* 818a1-2).

education in reason (cf. 1338b4–5). As will appear shortly, the music education of the young serves to habituate them to correct or noble enjoyment by affecting the quality or the character of their souls (1339a23–25, 40a16–18, 41a35–39). Music education is above all an education in moral virtue. Taking into account the fact that the severe gymnastic of the years immediately preceding twenty-one seems designed to inculcate the virtue of endurance (if not of courage), one is forced to say that the education of the entire period from puberty to twenty-one must be understood as the education of the irrational part of the soul by way of habituation. It is an education in virtue rather than in thought (cf. 1337a38–39).

According to Aristotle, the education of the lower part of the soul in moral virtue must be undertaken "for the sake of" or "with a view to" the education of the higher part of the soul, or of the mind (*nous*), in reason (1334b15–16, 27; cf. 1336b37–40). But it is necessary to bear in mind that there are two divisions of the higher part of the soul, and two kinds of reason. If it is true that some instruction in the theoretical sciences is to be permitted in the years immediately following puberty, a training of this sort is justified by its contribution to a later and more rigorous education in "theoretical reason" or in philosophy. But the education of the period from puberty to twenty-one is not primarily a theoretical education, and it cannot be understood to prepare (except indirectly) for the later study of philosophy. Besides, it is to be doubted whether the study of philosophy on the part of mature citizens of the best regime will be anything other than a private pursuit. When Aristotle speaks of an education of the "mind" in "reason," he is evidently thinking of an education, not in theoretical reason, but in practical reason—in "practical wisdom" or "prudence" (*phronēsis*). And "prudence" as it is understood by Aristotle has more than a little to do with moral virtue.[39]

39. *Eth. Nic.* 1144b15–32, 1178a16–19. Although *nous* is sharply distinguished from *phronēsis* in *Eth. Nic.* 1142a23–30 (cf. 1140b31–41a8), it seems to retain much of its ordinary and practical sense in the *Politics* (where it

The remaining chapters of Book VIII as we now have it are
devoted to a discussion of music education in the best regime.
Our investigation of Aristotle's argument will pay particular
attention to the question of the relation between the music
education of the young and those later activities—or that later
"education"—for which it must be understood to prepare.
What is the higher education in prudence to which Aristotle's
argument appears to point, and what is its relation to that
musical enjoyment which belongs to the leisured pastime of
mature citizens of the best regime?

---

certainly includes *logos praktikos* or *phronēsis:* cf. 1334b17–28 with 1333a16–30);
and consider *Problems* 955b22 ff., a passage that reminds of the contrast between *phronēsis* and the dianoetic sciences of mathematics and geometry in
Eth. Nic. 1142a11–20 (cf. n. 12 above).

2

Music and Education

---

1. Music and Music Education

"As regards music, some of the problems connected with it were raised at an earlier point in the argument, but it will be well to take them up again and develop them, so that we may provide as it were a prelude to the arguments one might give in expressing an opinion on this subject" (1339a11–14). The opening sentence of Chapter 5 is of more than passing importance for the understanding of Aristotle's argument in the remaining chapters of the *Politics*. In the first place, it is clear that the discussion of music forms an integral part of Aristotle's discussion of education and more generally of the best life: it cannot be taken to represent an independent and systematic treatise.[1] That the treatment of music in the final chapters of the *Politics* is not intended to be systematic or comprehensive must be particularly emphasized. As Aristotle says, he will deal only with "some of the problems" connected with music; and the problems to be discussed are those that have already been raised in a general way in Chapters 2 and 3. Aristotle will deal

---

1. It has sometimes been identified with the treatises listed as *peri mousikēs ā* in the catalogues of Diogenes Laertius (no. 116) and Hesychius (nos. 104, 124); see the apparatus of the edition of Otto Immisch, *Aristotelis Politica* (Leipzig, 1909), on 1339a11. That Anderson (*Ethos and Education,* pp. 122–23) refuses to commit himself on this question points up the weakness of his analysis as a whole.

with music only in its relation to education, and in particular the education of the young.

But Aristotle's statement is also suggestive as regards the manner and purpose of his discussion. Aristotle's discussion is intended to be a kind of preface, "as it were a prelude" (*hōsper endosimon*). Now *endosimon* is a musical term, and although it is used elsewhere by Aristotle as a metaphorical equivalent for *prooimion*,[2] its meaning is inadequately represented by the translation "preface." It is properly an instrumental prelude which gives the key to a tune or provides for the striking of the key-note (*endosis*).[3] Aristotle's discussion is not meant to serve as the "preface" to a more comprehensive treatment of music or of the relation between music and education. It is intended rather to strike the key-note—to provide the model or "set the tune"—for "the arguments one might give in expressing an opinion [*eipeien apophainomenos*] on this subject"; it is intended, in other words, to supply advocates of music education who are insufficiently grounded in philosophy or in music with an informed and articulate discussion of their position.[4]

Aristotle had indicated earlier that most of his contemporaries believe that music and musical education are "for the sake of pleasure" (1337b28-29). As will appear shortly, it is exceedingly difficult to justify an active musical education for the young on the grounds of pleasure alone. If the majority of Aristotle's contemporaries believed both that music is for the sake of pleasure and that education in music is desirable, as it seems likely they did, their position was particularly vulnerable to attack. That it had been under attack in fact—at least by musicians or musical theorists of a certain kind—appears

2. *Rhet.* 1415a5-8.

3. *De Mundo* 398b26, 399a19; cf. *Suda* s.v. *endosimon*.

4. Barker's translation—"we may thus provide something in the nature of a preface to the considerations which would naturally be advanced in any full view of the subject"—fairly reflects what appears to be the general view of this sentence, but bears no tolerable relation to the original. *Apophainesthai* connotes the declaration of opinion or judgment rather than comprehensive or theoretical treatment (cf. 1333b12).

highly probable. That Aristotle's own discussion is to be understood as a calculated response to this attack seems equally probable.[5] Aristotle's counterattack could not hope to be effective, however, unless it succeeded in convincing contemporary readers that while music education may well be tolerated "for the sake of pleasure," it can only be justified by an appeal to something higher than pleasure. It is not sufficient to say that Aristotle intended only to remind his nonprofessional audience of the grounds of its belief in the desirability of a music education. Precisely the grounds of its belief had to be altered if music education was to be provided with reliable defenders.

The discussion of music begins as follows:

> For it is not easy to distinguish what power it has, nor for the sake of what one ought to partake of it—whether for the sake of play and relaxation, as one partakes of sleep and drink (for these are not in themselves serious things, but are pleasant, and "as well put cares to flight," as Euripides says; and this is why they put it in this category and employ all these things in a similar manner, sleep and drink and music, and they include dancing among these as well); or whether it is rather to be supposed that music is in some respect directed to virtue, and that just as gymnastic makes the body of a certain quality, so also music is capable of making the character of a certain quality, habituating it to be capable of right enjoyment; or whether it contributes in some respect to pastime and to prudence—for this is to be set down as the third thing we have spoken of. [1339a14-26]

Aristotle raises two distinct questions:[6] (1) what is the power

5. Cf. Koller, *Musse*, pp. 39–40. A papyrus fragment discovered early in this century contains what appears to be a critique of the views of Damon regarding the ethical or educative value of music; a date of about 390 B.C. is now generally accepted. See B. P. Grenfell and A. S. Hunt, *The Hibeh Papyri* (London, 1906), I, 45–48, and W. Crönert, "Die Hibehrede über die Musik," *Hermes* 44 (1909), 503–21. That several of the arguments answered by Aristotle are strikingly paralleled in the fragments of Philodemus' *On Music* suggests that the Epicureans were able to draw on an older tradition of unorthodox musical thought. See Abert, pp. 38–43; Anderson, *Ethos and Education*, pp. 147–76.

6. a14–15 *oute . . . oute.* The structure of the argument is correctly analyzed by Koller, *Musse,* p. 38.

(*dynamis*) of music? (2) why should one "partake of" music? The meaning of the second question will become apparent in the immediate sequel: the question whether to "partake of" music is the question whether the young are to receive an active education in music. This question was first raised, though in somewhat different terms and without explicit reference to music, in the discussion in Chapter 2 of the kind and extent of the studies of which it is proper for the young to "partake" (cf. 1337b7, 16). In Chapter 3, the question of the purpose of music education was explicitly introduced, and Aristotle there argued that while the young now "partake of" music for the most part "for the sake of pleasure" (1337b28–29), the ancients had originally introduced it in education for the sake of or with a view to "the leisure associated with a pastime"; it is this argument which is referred to at 1339a26. As regards Aristotle's first question, the question of the "power" of music, it is not specifically raised in the earlier discussion, but it is closely related to the question of the purpose of music education. Indeed, the two questions are so closely related that it is hardly clear whether Aristotle's subsequent enumeration is to be taken in connection with one rather than the other: although the enumeration is in formal apposition to the second question, it is at least as much a list of the possible "powers" (cf. a22 *dynamenēn*) as of the possible purposes of music. Since, at all events, the question of the purposes of music education necessarily depends on the question of the power of music, it is the latter which is the "first" or more fundamental question (cf. 1339b11–14).

Aristotle now proceeds to raise in more direct fashion the question of the purpose of an active education in music.

That the young are not to be educated for the sake of play is clear, for they do not play as they learn—learning is accompanied by pain. But neither is it fitting to assign a pastime [*diagōgē*] to these ages, since the end [*telos*] does not belong to anything incomplete [*atelei*]. And yet perhaps it might seem that the serious activity [*hē spoudē*] of children is for the sake of their play when they will have become mature and complete [*teleiōtheisin*] men. If this is the case, however, what would be the point in learning it themselves instead of sharing in the pleasure and the learning by means of the performances of others, like the kings of the Persians and the Medes? For those who have made this very thing their work and profession will surely perform better than those who have cultivated it only for the length of time necessary to learn it. [1339a26–38]

Aristotle here makes explicit what had been tacitly assumed in the earlier discussion: the music education of the young involves the "partaking" or active participation of the young in music; the "learning" connected with music education consists above all in the actual learning of the skills of singing and of playing musical instruments (cf. 1340b20–21). It is precisely for this reason that the education of the young cannot be understood to be "for the sake of play": although music in itself is naturally "pleasant" to the young and hence well adapted to the requirements of play or relaxation (cf. 1339a16–18 with 40b14–17), the learning of musical skills is not pleasant as such.[7] Does music education then perhaps "contribute something to pastime and prudence" (*pros diagōgēn ti symballetai kai pros phronēsin*)(1339a25–26)?[8] At first sight, the reasoning which is meant to dispose of play would seem to dispose of *diagōgē* as well, for pleasure was also said to be an

7. The apparent contradiction or tension between the present passage and 1340b14 (cf. Koller, *Musse*, p. 38, n. 116) disappears as soon as one realizes that the pleasure connected with music is not Aristotle's primary justification for a music education of the young.

8. Much difficulty has been felt over the coupling of *phronēsis* with *diagōgē*, and some scholars have wanted to read *euphrosynē* (comparing 1339b4–5). Newman (on 1339a26) defends the reading of the manuscripts, but his interpretation of *phronēsis* as "intellectual culture" (thus also Susemihl-Hicks) will not do. Aristotle uses *phronēsis* in a wider sense with reference to scientific knowledge; and in any event, it is difficult to see how the music education of the young would not contribute to their "intellectual culture." It is not an incapacity to assimilate "knowledge" simply that makes the young "incomplete"; it is precisely their inability to acquire *phronēsis* in the narrow sense—prudence or practical wisdom, which depends decisively on experience. Aristotle's argument points to an intimate connection between prudence in the precise sense and the "pastime" of mature men.

essential part of *diagōgē* (1338a1–11; cf. 1339b17–24). But Aristotle's rejection of *diagōgē* as a possible purpose of music education does not imply that the music education of the young cannot be understood to contribute to the pastime of adults. That the purpose of music education may have to be determined with reference to the activities of mature persons is a possibility that is considered only in the sequel.

2. *Music and Virtue* (I)

Having eliminated play and pastime as proximate goals of music education, Aristotle is left, or so it seems, with the single goal of "virtue." But Aristotle's argument takes a different turn. Evidently, there is another alternative: the "serious" education in music could be "for the sake of" the "play" of mature men. Without deciding for or against this solution, Aristotle goes on to discuss the problem it raises. If music education is to be justified solely by the pleasure it provides in later life, why should the young be compelled to learn music themselves—that is, to acquire musical skills? Granted that an appreciation of music in later life presupposes a certain education in music: why not an education that is limited to listening to the performances of others—like the education of the kings of Persia? An education of this kind would provide a kind of learning, and it would be entirely pleasant. What is more, it might well prove to be more satisfying even from the point of view of learning: the performances of professional musicians could be expected to instruct more effectively in an appreciation of music than the struggling attempts of the nonprofessional student.[9] Finally, Aristotle adds, "if it is necessary for

9. At this point Koller fails to follow Aristotle's argument: the juxtaposition of *mathēsis* and *hēdonē* in a36 in no way contradicts a28–29 (thus Koller, *Musse*, p. 40, n. 23; cf. p. 49, n. 159), since the point is precisely that education need not be accompanied by the pain of *Selberlernen*. Both Koller and Newman (on a33 and 1341a22) mistakenly assume that Aristotle is speaking of the "pleasure and learning" that the Persian and Median kings derived from music as mature men (hence also Richards' conjecture *anapausis* for *mathēsis*). In fact, there is no difference for him between Greek and oriental practice as regards the enjoyment of music by mature men.

them to practice [*diaponein*, cf. 1339a8] this kind of thing themselves, it would also be necessary to set them up in the trade of cooking; but that would be absurd" (1339a39–41).[10] If music, like cooking, serves pleasure and only pleasure, then the learning of musical skills is no less illiberal or banausic than the learning of culinary skills.

In fact, however, the same problem recurs if it is a question of ends other than pleasure or play:

> There is the same difficulty even if it is able to make the characters better; for why should they learn these things themselves instead of learning, by listening to others, correct enjoyment together with the capacity for correct judgment, as the Spartans do? For though they do not learn it they are still able, so they assert, to judge correctly of the goodness and badness of tunes. And the same argument holds as well if they are to use it with a view to enjoyment and the pastime of free men [*pros euēmerian kai diagōgēn eleutherion*]: why should they learn it themselves instead of enjoying the performances of others? [1339a41–b6]

Since the question of education to virtue is treated here for the first time, Aristotle's statement on the subject deserves particular attention. When Aristotle had first raised the possibility that music education may be directed to virtue, he had explained that on such an understanding music would have to be capable of "making the character of a certain sort, habituating it to be able to enjoy in a correct manner [*chairein orthōs*]" (1339a24–25). The "correct enjoyment" that music teaches is, it would seem, practically synonymous with the virtue that is inculcated in the young by way of habituation.[11] Because Aristotle reports the Spartans' claim to be good judges of what is good and bad in tunes, however, it has been generally assumed that the "judgment" of which he speaks here and elsewhere must be fundamentally a technical or aesthetic one.

10. Cf. Philodemus *On Music* IV.37.13 (31) Kemke, Sextus Empiricus *Against the Learned* VI.33.
11. Cf. *Eth. Nic.* 1104b8–13.

But regardless of the exact meaning of the Spartan claim,[12] it would be wrong to assume that Aristotle is bound by the authority of Sparta in matters concerning either music of morality. In fact, Aristotle has already indicated that the kind of education preferred by the Spartans might well be superior to a conventional Greek education in music from a purely aesthetic point of view (1339a36-38). Aristotle will defend the conventional music education not because it can produce good literary critics or can further an appreciation of what is technically or artistically beautiful in music (consider 1338a18-19 and context), but because "it can make the characters better" (1339a41-42). When Aristotle speaks of "enjoyment" and "judgment," he is speaking of the enjoyment and judgment not so much of music itself as of the "decent characters and noble actions" (1340a17-18; cf. a23-25) which music is able to represent.[13]

3. Aristotle, Homer, and the Ancients

It must be said, however, that Aristotle has not made matters easy for his audience. The chief difficulty is that the argument of Chapters 5 and 6 does not seem to have been adequately prepared by the earlier discussion. In spite of Aristotle's claim that he will only "develop" his previous analysis of the problems connected with music, a cursory inspection of the discussion of music education in Chapter 3 will reveal that the words "virtue" and "character" are not so much as mentioned there. The argument of Chapter 3 gives the impression that there are only two possible interpretations of the purpose of

12. According to Athenaeus (XIV.628b), the Spartans were agreed that "they are able to judge finely of the art."

13. Cf. also 1340b22-25, 35-39. Precisely what Aristotle means by "judgment" with respect to music, and to what extent it is to be distinguished from "enjoyment," is far from clear. "Judgment" would seem to be more directly associated with the musical activity of mature citizens, and is therefore perhaps more intellectual (consider the use of the word in the context of the discussion of prudence in *Eth. Nic.* 1143a8-30); but Aristotle may only have in mind the ability to distinguish between different tunes or harmonies.

music education: either it is "for the sake of" pleasure or play or relaxation, or it is "with a view to" *diagōgē*. Although Aristotle decides for the second alternative, he is so anxious to show that music education is in no way "necessary" or "useful" that he will not even describe it as being "for the sake of" *diagōgē:* the education in music must be understood as being "for its own sake" (1338a9–12 ff.). Since music is said not to be useful even with a view to "political actions" (1339a15–17), and since it can hardly be denied that virtue is useful with a view to a great many political actions, one is forced to wonder whether Aristotle's two accounts are finally even compatible.

The difficulty may be resolved, I think, if the practical intention of Aristotle's argument is kept in mind. Aristotle has indicated that the majority of his contemporaries regard an education in music and music itself as being for the sake of pleasure or play and hence as something not fundamentally serious. Aristotle's most important task, then, is to convince his readers of the true dignity or seriousness of music—of the important role that music plays, or can play, in social or political life as a whole. But the most effective way to persuade contemporary readers of an unpopular view is to invest that view with the authority of antiquity; and it is in accordance with this simple rhetorical principle that Aristotle appeals to Homer or to the society described by Homer. That Aristotle's appeal to the ancients is not free of rhetorical exaggeration has been seen. But it can also be shown that Aristotle's agreement with the view of the ancients is not as complete as might at first appear. If the ancients understood that music supplies the pastime of a noble leisure, it would seem that they failed to understand that music education can and should serve a moral or political purpose as well; they had not grasped the intimate connection between music and virtue or the character of the soul. It is no accident that the Homeric poems are entirely silent on the subject of music education. Of Homer's heroes only Achilles gives evidence of a knowledge of music, and he is the exception—his tutor was the "divine beast" Chiron—that proves the rule.[14] Like the old-fashioned Spartans, like the Zeus of the poets (1339b7-10)—indeed, like the progeny of barbarian kings[15]—the Homeric heroes did not themselves "learn" music. If the ancients regarded music education as being "for its own sake," they could do so because music education as they understood it did not involve the "pain" of learning to sing and to play musical instruments. They could do so, in other words, precisely because they did not make a radical distinction between music education and the subsequent enjoyment of music by mature men. Precisely because the ancients believed that music education should be conducted "with a view to" pastime rather than "for the sake of" virtue, they saw no reason to insist on the actual learning of musical skills by the young.

This is certainly not to say that pastime must be ruled out of consideration as a goal of the music education of the young. It is only to deny that the understanding of pastime possessed by the ancients is for Aristotle an adequate one. As Aristotle will indicate in the course of Chapter 5, the ancients mistook pastime as they understood it for pastime in the true sense because they failed to realize the inner dependence of their leisured activity on the occupations or the requirements of practical life: what they took to be pastime was in fact only a sophisticated form of play or relaxation (1339a31-42). Even the ancients did not understand the full "seriousness" of music and of the education in music. What must now be seen is

14. Cf. [Plutarch] *On Music* 1145e-46a: Homer may teach through the example of Achilles the proper "use" of music for one who is "idle" or at leisure; he does not teach the necessity of an early education in music. Achilles sings the deeds of heroes and accompanies himself on the phorminx (*Iliad* 9.185 ff.)—precisely the activity of the professional "singer" (*Odyssey* 1.155 ff., 8.73 ff., 22.330 ff.). Chiron teaches Achilles in the way that the Muses teach the singer: music is in a sense the preserve of divinity, and comes to humans only as a gift; it is true that Phemius is "self-taught," but he still depends on the inspiration of the god (*Odyssey* 22.347-48; cf. 8.62-64). Cf. Max Wegner, *Musik und Tanz, Archaeologia Homerica III* (Göttingen, 1968), pp. 30-31.

15. Compare 1339a33-38 with Aristotle fr. 160 Rose.

whether music can indeed provide pastime in the true sense, and if so, what the relation is between pastime so understood and virtue.

4. The Power of Music (I)

The argument of Chapter 5 continues as follows: "But perhaps these things should be considered later. What must be investigated first is whether music is to have a place in education or not, and what its power is in view of the three possibilities mentioned, whether education or play or pastime [*paideian ē paidian ē diagōgēn*]" (1339b10-14). Aristotle returns from his digression regarding the learning of music by the young to the first and more fundamental question, the question of the power of music. Only be resolving this question will it be possible to determine whether music belongs in education at all—that is to say, whether the young should be exposed to music in any form. And on the answer to this question depends in turn the resolution of the question regarding the learning of musical skills. Aristotle's summary restatement of the alternative interpretations of the power of music is also of some interest. Where Aristotle had previously spoken of music as being capable of "making the soul of a certain quality" (1339a21-24), he now speaks simply of "education." In so doing, he provides what is in a way a tacit answer to the aporetic discussion in Chapter 2 regarding the purpose of education as a whole: the education of the young is above all or most fundamentally education to "virtue." What remains to be seen is whether music—and it is necessary to keep in mind that Aristotle is now speaking not of music education but of music simply—has in fact an "ethical" or "educative" effect.

Aristotle continues as follows:

It may reasonably be assigned to all, and seems to partake of all. For play is for the sake of relaxation, and relaxation is necessarily pleasant (for it is a kind of healing of the pain that comes through exertion), and it is agreed that pastime ought to have not only the noble (*to kalon*] but also pleasure—for happiness is from both of these; but all of us assert that music belongs among the most pleasant things, both by itself and with melody (at any rate Musaeus says that "singing is sweetest for mortals," which is why they have reasonably taken it into social gatherings and pastimes as being capable of delighting), so that even from this one might suppose that the young ought to be educated in it. For such pleasures as are harmless are suitable not only with a view to the end but also with a view to relaxation; and since it happens that human beings rarely attain the end [en tōi telei gignesthai], but frequently relax and make use of play not only for a purpose but also just because of the pleasure,[16] it would be a useful thing to let them relax through the pleasures that derive from this. [1339b15-31]

Aristotle begins by arguing that the most manifest power of music is its capacity to provide pleasure. Since music belongs among "the most pleasant things," it is obviously suitable not only for play or relaxation but also for the pastime of leisure—for pastime must involve not only "the noble" but "pleasure" as well. The fact that music provides pleasure could seem by itself sufficient to justify a music education. The "harmless" pleasure afforded by music is well suited to the "end": music education must be justified above all by reference to the end—the "happiness"—supplied by pastime taken as a whole. But it is also well suited to relaxation, and the fact is that men very often relax and make use of play, whereas they do not very often realize the end.

5. Pastime and Play

"But it has happened," Aristotle continues,

that man make play the end. For the end too perhaps involves a certain pleasure, though not any chance pleasure; and while seeking the former they mistake the latter for it, since it has a certain similarity to the end of actions. For the end is choiceworthy not on account of anything that will be, and pleasures of this sort are not for the sake of what will be, but of what has been, as for example exertions and pain. One may

16. Newman's interpretation (on b29) of *ouch hoson epi pleon* is right, Barker's ("not so much with a view to something beyond") wrong.

reasonably suppose, then, that it is for this reason that they seek happiness in these pleasures, and that they have recourse to music not for this reason alone but also because it is useful with a view to relaxation, as it seems. [1339b31-42]

Aristotle had previously treated "play" and "relaxation" as synonymous terms. He now rather unexpectedly distinguishes them. The pleasure of relaxation is indeed a kind of "healing" of the pain of past exertion (cf. 1339b15-17), but it is also and more fundamentally a "recreation" or a restoration of the individual "for the sake of" or with a view to future exertion.[17] The pleasure of play, on the other hand, is not "for the sake of" any future results but only of present enjoyment and the forgetting of past cares. In the last analysis, play no less than relaxation is "for the sake of" the pain of past exertion, but it is of the nature of play to cause a forgetting of that pain and therewith of the purpose that play serves: the pleasure of play appears to serve no purpose beyond itself.[18] It is for this reason that the pleasure of play is so easily confused with the pleasure associated with the "end"—the pleasure provided by genuine *diagōgē*.

The precise bearing of this argument does not seem to have been generally appreciated. What might seem to be an exceptionally fine and not obviously necessary distinction is actually of central importance for Aristotle's analysis as a whole. At first sight, the argument regarding play appears to be something of a digression. In fact, it is closely linked with what has preceded. The distinction between a relaxation which serves the future and a play which serves no purpose beyond itself is anticipated in b29-30 (men "make use of play not only for a purpose but also just because of the pleasure"), a remark which must be understood in conjunction with the preceding remark (b27-28) concerning the infrequency with which men actually attain the end. This remark is, or should be, somewhat disconcerting. Has not Aristotle just indicated that the end—that combination

17. For the recreative function of pleasure consider *Rhet.* 1369b33-70a3.
18. Cf. *Eth. Nic.* 1176b6-11, b27-77a1.

of pleasure and nobility which is pastime—is attainable by all who are in a position to devote themselves to "social gatherings and pastime" (*synousias kai diagōgas*) of a certain degree of refinement? What Aristotle means to suggest would seem to be this: what ordinarily passes under the name *diagōgē*—the social pastimes and the entertainments of a refined society—is in reality not *diagōgē* at all. Pastime as ordinarily understood and practiced may be said to presuppose the element of nobility or refinement; it is not primarily directed to the fostering of nobility or refinement. It is primarily concerned to "cheer" or "delight" (cf. b24 *euphrainein*); it is directed, in short, to the fostering of pleasure. Pastime in the ordinary sense of the term consists precisely in the enjoyment of pleasures which seem to serve no purpose beyond themselves—the pleasures, in other words, of "play" in the precise sense of that term.[19]

Aristotle's implicit critique of *diagōgē* as ordinarily understood is in the first instance a critique of the aristocratic pastimes of "the ancients" as described by Homer.[20] As Homer's Odysseus himself puts it: the "good cheer" (*euphrosynē*) of the banquet is the "loveliest end [*telos*]" and the "noblest thing" for human beings. The opulent banquets of the Homeric heroes are designed to cheer or delight (cf. 1338a28–29 *euphrainomenōn tōn anthrōpōn*) rather than to edify. Banqueting, and the enjoyment of music within the context of the banquet, is what the ancients "suppose [*oiontai*] to be the pastime of free men" (1338a22–23); it is not truly the pastime of free men. The ancients mistakenly regarded music and the other activities of their leisure as the end or the source of happiness for human beings because they found these activities "most pleasant" (1339b20). Precisely the pleasure of leisured activity seduced them into the belief that leisured activity as

---

19. Consider *Eth. Nic.* 1176b9–11 ff. *Diagōgē* in the ordinary sense is the pastime not of those who are truly happy but of those who are "congratulated on their happiness" (*hoi eudaimonizomenoi*); "these things seem to belong to happiness because it is in this way that the powerful spend their leisure."
20. Cf. Aristoxenus fr. 122,11 Wehrli: *ta deipna kai tas synousias tōn archaiōn.*

they understood it is the end.[21] The ancients may have provided a model of the refined intercourse of aristocratic society; they did not provide a model of true *diagōgē*.

6. *The Power of Music* (II)

In view of the very general misapprehension as to the true nature of pastime, one might reasonably expect Aristotle to elaborate his understanding of pastime and of the precise relation between the two components of pastime—between "pleasure" and "the noble." At first sight, the sequel disappoints this expectation. Aristotle appears to turn rather abruptly from the discussion of pleasure or play to a discussion of the third power of music.[22] It is, as it seems, impossible to leave matters at distinguishing between relaxation and a play which serves no purpose beyond itself. Rather, one must investigate whether the twin purposes of play and relaxation are not "accidental" (*symbebēke*) to music, and

> whether it does not have a more honorable nature than that which accords with the need we have spoken of [*timiōtera d' autēs hē physis estin ē kata tēn eirēmenēn chreian*], and one ought to partake not only of the common pleasure deriving from it which is

21. *Odyssey* 9.6–7, 11. Cf. Newman on 1338a22. The Homeric passage (*Odyssey* 9.3–11) to which Aristotle had earlier appealed would actually be used by subsequent writers to support an Epicurean view of the best life (Heraclides Ponticus fr. 55 Wehrli, Lucian *The Parasite* 10–11). When Koller (*Musse*, p. 36) argues that "Homeric society represents . . . for Aristotle the ideal of the *eleutheroi* and *pepaideumenoi*, and Homer is the authoritative teacher of the model *chrēsis* of music as well as of morality generally," he fails to take account of such passages as *Eth. Nic.* 1116a10–b3 (cf. Plato *Republic* 386a–87b) and 1180a24–29. The attempts that were made in antiquity (consider Aristoxenus fr. 122 Wehrli, Athenaeus XIV.627e–28b) to save the authority of Homer or "the ancients" from the charge that they regarded music only as a source of pleasure may properly be described as tendentious.

22. As Koller puts it: "Since the higher effect of music is mentioned at 40a3–5 in contradistinction to . . . ordinary pleasure, he clearly has in mind the differentiated musical enjoyment of *diagōgē*, of the sort that befits only the *teleiōthentes* and *pepaideumenoi*. But what follows does not proceed in the direction one expects after 40a2–5, but the author begins to speak rather abruptly in 40a7 of the character-forming effect of music, which has yet to be treated" (*Musse*, pp. 47–48; cf. Susemihl-Hicks on a6).

perceived by all—for music has a certain natural pleasure, so that the use of it is congenial to all ages and all characters—but should try to see if it is not in some way directed to the character and the soul. This would be clear if we become qualitatively different in our characters on account of it. But that we do in fact become qualitatively different is evident from many other things and in particular, and not least, from the tunes of Olympus; for it is agreed that they make the souls inspired, and inspiration [*enthousiasmos*] is a passion of the character which concerns the soul. Further, when listening to imitations all experience the passions that are represented, even apart from rhythms and tunes themselves. [1339b42–40a14]

Strictly speaking, the pleasure provided by music is only an accident of its nature. Aristotle's answer to the question of the "power" of music is that what is most fundamental in music is its capacity to affect the character and the soul. The fundamental "power" of music is education.

This must not be taken to mean that the power of music is effective only in the education of the young. The question of the power of music is the question of the capacity of music to affect man as man. And, in fact, what Aristotle is anxious to prove is precisely that "we," that is, Aristotle together with his mature audience, "become qualitatively different" (1340a7–8) or are affected in character and soul by music. Aristotle is primarily interested in the effect of music on mature adults, and his choice of examples is deliberate: neither the "tunes of Olympus" nor, as we shall see, the nameless "imitations" of which he speaks are of particular relevance to the young or to music education properly speaking.[23]

To realize this, however, is to realize that Aristotle's apparent failure to continue or complete his discussion of pastime is indeed only an apparent failure. When Aristotle says that it belongs to the "more honorable nature" of music to affect the character and the soul, his statement must be understood to apply to the musical pursuits of adults no less than to the

23. The "tunes of Olympus" were auletic nomes in the Phrygian mode, and thus doubly unsuited to the education of the young (cf. 1341a18 ff., 1342a32–b3). Cf. Anderson, *Ethos and Education*, p. 125.

young—and hence, in particular, to musical pastime. If what is truly "honorable" in music is its ethical or educative effect rather than the simple production of pleasure, then it must be precisely this effect which supplies the truly serious or "noble" element of pastime properly understood. In the last analysis, it is only and precisely this effect which distinguishes pastime, or genuine pastime, from play. Genuine pastime will combine, as it seems, the pleasures of play with the benefit deriving from a continuing education of the character and the soul.

It has been customary to regard Aristotle's doctrine of *diagōgē* as constituting a fundamental break with the severely "ethical" views of Plato, and as anticipating the characteristically modern notion of an "aesthetic" experience of music and the arts. A recent critic has shown that the usual interpretation can be maintained only with serious qualifications.[24] I believe it should be abandoned altogether. The bearing of Aristotle's remark concerning the ethical or educative effect of music has been misunderstood because of a general failure to pay attention to its context—in the first place to its immediate context, but more importantly, to the context and character of Aristotle's argument as a whole. Its immediate context is the discussion of the difference between pastime and play, or rather between genuine pastime and pastime as ordinarily or traditionally understood. This discussion itself points back to—and compels a reconsideration of—the preliminary discussion of pastime in Chapter 3. In the light of the later discussion, the rhetorical character of Aristotle's appeal to "the ancients" becomes evident: the ancients, as it now

24. It is the chief merit of Koller's analysis to have stressed the continuity between *paideia* and *diagōgē;* that he does not go far enough is due in large part to his misinterpretation of Chapter 3 and Aristotle's relation to "the ancients" (see note 21 above). Typical of the older view is the remark of Abert: "The doctrine of *diagōgē* is the side of Aristotle's musical aesthetics which is closest to modern views of art" (p. 14). See further A. Busse, "Zur Musikästhetik des Aristoteles," *RHM* 77 (1928), 40-41; W. Vetter, "Musik," *RE* XVI, 839; R. Schäfke, *Geschichte der Musikästhetik* (Berlin, 1934), pp. 98 ff.; S. H. Butcher, *Aristotle's Theory of Poetry and Fine Art* (London, 1898), p. 115.

appears, did not know genuine pastime; what they supposed to be pastime was only a sophisticated form of play.

In later antiquity, the musical authority Aristides Quintilianus could write: "The philosophers of former times [*hoi palaioi*] saw in music the greatest moral corrective [*epanorthōsis*]; . . . they contrived to make it an orderly pastime accompanied by pleasure [*diagōgēn syn hēdonēi kosmion*], and from something useless they rendered it useful." Elsewhere, in a passage which closely reflects what appears to be Aristotle's argument in Chapter 5, the same authority provides a more explicit statement of the twofold character of musical pastime or of music rightly understood: "All pleasure is not blameworthy, yet neither is it the end of music; but entertainment is accidental to it, while the aim to be pursued is what is beneficial with a view to virtue."[25] Genuine pastime combines pleasure with the noble, enjoyment with benefit, entertainment with instruction. In the Horatian formula (which may well directly reflect Peripatetic doctrine), it mixes the "sweet" with the "useful." Aristotle's doctrine of *diagōgē* is so little a step in the direction of modernity that it appears to represent the original formulation of one of the great commonplaces of ancient literary criticism.

7. The Meaning of Mousikē

It is necessary at this point to address a question that is too often neglected or taken for granted in discussions of Aristotle's argument—the question of the precise meaning of *mousikē*. Most commentators have tended to assume that the word is employed by Aristotle in a sense that anticipates if it is not

25. Aristides Quintilianus II.4 (57, 11–12, 21–22) and 6 (60,29–61,3) Winnington-Ingram. For the identity of *hoi palaioi* cf. I.1 (1,1–7) and II.7 (65, 10–21). That Aristides knew Aristotle or Peripatetic writings seems clear, in spite of the attempt of Hermann Koller, *Die Mimesis in der Antike* (Berne, 1954) pp. 82 ff., to show that his teaching on musical ethos derives exclusively from pre-Platonic sources. See R. Schäfke, *Aristides Quintilianus Von der Musik* (Berlin, 1937), pp. 100–2; J. Croissant, *Aristote et les mystères* (Paris/Liège, 1932); G. F. Else, "Imitation in the Fifth Century," *CP* 53 (1958), 85.

identical with "music" in its modern sense.[26] Yet the latitude of the term in contemporary usage was considerable, extending not only to all forms of music proper but to most forms of poetry, including some that were not normally sung or even accompanied by music.[27] It is difficult to believe that Aristotle could speak of *mousikē* in the context of its traditional role in education without understanding it to include those forms of poetry which had always had a prominent place in traditional music education. If Aristotle appears to take little notice of poetry either in Chapters 5–7 or in Books VII and VIII as a whole, it must be remembered that the entire discussion is fragmentary in nature. Moreover, it is possible that Aristotle concentrates on the question of the educative power of music in the narrow sense precisely because it is more controversial than the question of the educative power of poetry—in other words, that he simply takes for granted the prominent place of poetry in music education. When Aristotle remarks, in the context under discussion, that "music" belongs among the most pleasant things "both by itself and with song" (*kai psilēn ousan kai meta melōidias* 1339b20–21), it seems most likely that the expression "music by itself"—literally, "music bare"—is meant to apply to poetry unaccompanied by music rather than to music unaccompanied by poetry.[28] There are not many occurrences of the word elsewhere that illuminate Aristotle's usage. In an

26. Thus Newman, I, 405, Susemihl-Hicks on 1339b20, Abert, p. 13, Koller, *Musse*, p. 1, n. 1.

27. Consider especially Plato *Phaedo* 61a–b and *Menexenus* 239b–c, where *mousikē* as distinguished from *logos psilos* (prose or a prose speech) includes "songs and the rest of poetry" (c6). That the recitation of epic poetry was regarded as a part of *mousikē* appears from *Ion* 530a.

28. Thus also G. M. A. Grube, *The Greek and Roman Critics* (Toronto, 1968) p. 67, n. 2. The normal way of referring to purely instrumental music would have been *psilē kitharisis te kai aulēsis* (Plato *Laws* 669e1–2; cf. Athenaeus XIV.637f) or *kitharistikē te kai aulētikē* (*Poet.* 1447a15, 24). It is more usual, however, to find "poetry by itself" (*poiēsis psilē* or *logoi psiloi*) distinguished from "music," as in Plato *Phaedrus* 278c, *Menexenus* 239b (cf. *Symposium* 215c7); Aristotle *Poet.* 1447a29; Aristides Quintilianus II.4 (56,12–13) Winnington-Ingram.

earlier passage in the *Politics* (1281b8–9), he speaks of "the products of the musical art and those of the poets" (*ta tēs mousikēs erga kai ta tōn poiētōn*). This seems to approach the modern distinction between poetry and music proper; but the exact meaning of the phrase is not certain.[29] Later in Book VIII (1341b23), he seems to say that *mousikē* "consists in tune-composition and rhythms" (*dia melopoiias kai rhythmōn ousan*). This remark is an ambiguous one, however, and is probably better taken to mean that *mousikē* merely depends on or presupposes tune and rhythm—that is to say, that it "consists" in poetry as well as tune and rhythm or music in the narrow sense.[30] In general, Aristotle seems to employ *mousikē* in this broad and inclusive sense. When he wishes to speak of music as distinguished from song or poetry, he regularly speaks not of "music by itself" but of "tunes" (*melē*) or "tunes and rhythms"—the potentially ambiguous word *melos* being clearly used in its technical sense rather than in the more popular sense of "song."[31]

If it is "music" in its comprehensive sense which must be understood to possess the power of affording pleasure, it is "music" in the same sense which possesses the more fundamental power of "education." But does the educative power

29. Since what is at issue is the ability of a collective body to make aesthetic judgments, Aristotle may well be thinking merely of lyric as distinct from epic or dramatic poetry. Cf. 1341b25–26 and chap. III n. 10 below.

30. Newman (on 1341b23) expresses some doubt as to the correctness of the translation usually adopted ("musicam in cantus modulatione et rhythmis consistere," in the version of Sepulveda), and wonders whether Vettori's "musicam exerceri colique et per cantus et per numeros" is not better. The decisive consideration in favor of the latter is that Aristotle speaks not of *melos* or *melōidia* ("cantus modulatio") but of *melopoiia* ("cantus inventio"). Cf. Aristoxenus *Harmonics* II.38 Meibom, Aristides Quintilianus I.12 (29,21–30,1) Winnington-Ingram.

31. Aristotle underlines his use of *melos* in the technical sense by speaking of *ta melē auta* (1340a13–14, 38–39), just as Philodemus speaks of *melos katho melos* (*On Music* IV.3.11 [65] Kemke) when he wants to make clear that he means a purely instrumental effect. For the double sense of *melos* consider Plato *Republic* 398c–d and Aristides Quintilianus I.12 (28,8–10) and 4 (5,4–10) Winnington-Ingram; cf. Abert 53–55.

of "music" depend for Aristotle on its properly musical element alone? Or does poetry too contribute to its capability to affect the character and the soul? An answer to this question is provided, it may be argued, in the immediate sequel to the passage just considered. Aristotle proceeds to offer two illustrations of his general proposition that "music" is capable of affecting the character and the soul. The first is "the tunes [*melē*] of Olympus," which "it is agreed make the souls frenzied." The second is the fact that "when listening to imitations all experience the passions that are represented, even apart from rhythms and tunes themselves" (*akroōmenoi tōn mimēseōn gignontai pantes sympatheis, kai chōris tōn rhythmōn kai tōn melōn autōn*) (1340a8–14). What precisely does Aristotle have in mind? Do these illustrations refer to a single phenomenon, or to two distinct kinds of experiences? To begin with, Aristotle regularly uses the word *melos,* as was indicated above, to designate the purely musical or melodic aspect of *mousikē,* and by extension purely instrumental music: the "tunes" of Olympus were not "songs" but auletic nomes, solo pieces for the flute.[32] Secondly, it is one thing to say that "tunes" or purely instrumental music affect the character and the soul; it is something else—something requiring an extended argument—to say that they "imitate" the character and the soul, or human action generally. It is only in the sequel (1340a18 ff.) that Aristotle takes up the question whether and in what sense tunes and rhythms are in fact imitations. Accordingly, the imitations of which he proceeds to speak here would seem to be something other than imitations by means of tunes and rhythms simply. Rather, as Aristotle plainly indicates, they must be separable from tunes and rhythms, and yet at the same time susceptible of combination with them. The imitations to which Aristotle appeals are, in short, poetic imitations.[33]

32. [Plutarch] *On Music* 1132f, 1133d–f, 1137b. Cf. Susemihl-Hicks, pp. 621–22.
33. The commentators have not known what to do with this passage. Susemihl-Hicks find no difficulty in taking *chōris* adverbially, though

Aristotle would appear to be thinking particularly of epic poetry and tragedy. As Plato had made clear in his account of poetry in the *Republic,* the effect of tragedy (and of the Homeric epic which inspired it) depends largely on the "sympathetic" experience of an audience presented with characters who "imitate" its own passions and sentiments. Poetry can affect the character and the soul—it can very powerfully affect the character and the soul—even without the accompaniments of music in the narrow sense of the term.[34] As Aristotle himself makes clear in the *Poetics,* tragedy, like epic, can have its proper effect even in the absence of dramatic performance, through reading alone.[35] In any event, what Aristotle seems most interested to show in the argument of Chapter 5 is precisely that the ethical or educational effect of "music" is rooted simultaneously and independently in music in the narrow sense and in poetry.

8. Music and Poetry in the Poetics

It may be helpful to glance briefly at Aristotle's treatment of the definition and the nature of poetry in the *Poetics.* In the first

---

Susemihl also suggested the emendation *kai chōris<tōn logōn dia>tōn rhythmōn kai tōn melōn autōn* on the basis of a lacuna in several manuscripts (in which he is followed by Anderson, pp. 186–88); but as the sentence then does little more than repeat the point already made with reference to the (instrumental) music of Olympus, it would seem to be out of place—Susemihl-Hicks transpose it after a23, and emend *eti* to *epeidē.* Newman's defense of the received text through an interpretation of *mimēseis* as "imitative sounds" (adopted in Barker's translation) is rightly rejected by Anderson, p. 187. The rendering of Gigon—"when we listen to musical representations, even without dance and song"—must equally be ruled out in view of Aristotle's consistent use of *melos* in the sense of "tune." Grube (p. 67, n. 2) comes closer in taking *mimēseis* as "speeches in prose."

34. Consider particularly Plato *Republic* 605c–d: "for the best of us, when listening to Homer or some other of the tragic poets imitating one of the heroes in grief . . . , do you not know how we enjoy this, and giving ourselves over to it follow along experiencing the passions represented [*hepometha sympaschontes*]?" Cf. *Ion* 535e, *Gorgias Helen* 9 (fr. B11 Diels-Kranz).

35. *Poet.* 1462a11–18.

place, it may be observed that music and song are no less a part of "poetic art" (*poiētikē*) as Aristotle understands it than poetry is of *mousikē:* "poetic art" includes the composition both of dithyrambic (as well as comic and tragic) songs and of instrumental music for flute and lyre (*Poetics* 1447a8-16, 23-25). On the other hand, *mousikē* as it is understood in the *Politics* is not simply coextensive with *poiētikē* as it is understood in the *Poetics*. According to the *Poetics*, there is a branch of the poetic art which has remained "unnamed up to the present days": it is that which uses "only speech or verse by itself" (*monon tois logois psilois ē tois metrois*, 1447a28-b9), and which therefore includes both the "Socratic speeches" and epic poetry.[36] The "bare verse" of epic poetry may be a part of *mousikē* as that term is used in the *Politics;* the "bare speech" of a Platonic dialogue is clearly no part of it. The single occurrence in the *Poetics* of the word *mousikē* suggests that Aristotle's conception of it there excludes the spoken portions of tragedy, but includes the choral songs.[37] As in the *Politics,* Aristotle goes a certain way, but by no means all the way, in the direction of establishing a clear distinction between "music" and "poetry."

If there is a fundamental agreement between the *Poetics* and the *Politics* as regards the definition of "music," there appears to be a direct conflict between them as regards its nature. To judge from the *Politics,* the pleasure provided by poetry is only an accident of its true nature—of its capacity to affect or to educate the character and the soul. To judge from the discussion of Chapter 4 of the *Poetics,* poetry is indeed capable of educating in a certain sense, but it is not capable of educating the character and the soul: poetic imitation affords pleasure in

36. I follow the text and interpretation of G. F. Else, *Aristotle's Poetics: The Argument* (Cambridge, Mass., 1963) pp. 29-31, 38.

37. Cf. Else, *Aristotle's Poetics,* pp. 36-38. *Mousikē* in 1462a16 would seem to include both the instrumental accompaniment of tragic "verses" (something Aristotle alludes to nowhere else in the *Poetics*) and "song-composition" (*melopoiia*), i.e., the composition both of the words and the music of choral lyrics (thus Else, pp. 236-37).

a kind of "learning" which is indistinguishable from a purely intellectual comparison between imitation and thing imitated (1448b5-17). It is true that the discussion of Chapter 4 has no discernible relation to Aristotle's subsequent treatment of the various kinds of poetry, but in the absence of other direct evidence it appears to represent the position of the *Poetics*. According to a widely shared interpretation, Aristotle's view of poetry as a whole is a decidedly "intellectualized" one.[38]

This line of reasoning rests, I think, on a manifest misinterpretation of Chapter 4 of the *Poetics*. In fact, what Aristotle discusses in that chapter is not the nature of poetry but the natural causes which "generated poetic art." He is there interested only and precisely in the efficient causes of poetic composition (cf. 1448b22 ff.); he is not at all interested in the formal or final causes of poetry, or—except incidentally—in the effect of poetry on its audience. The argument of Chapter 4 is intended to show only that poets first came to exist because imitation and the delight in imitation are natural to human beings (1448b5-9) and because harmony and rhythm are natural to human beings (1448b20-21);[39] it is not intended to show that poetry can or should provide to its audience only the pleasure that is connected with imitation. It is no accident that Aristotle speaks of the delight in imitation as a pleasure that is shared by "all" (1448b8-9; cf. 13-14). If the delight in imitation is an intellectual pleasure, it is evidently an intellectual pleasure of a rather low order; and in any event it is not simply an intellectual pleasure.[40] The delight in imitation of which Aristotle speaks in the *Poetics* is precisely what he calls in the *Politics* the "common" or "natural" pleasure in music which is "perceived by all"—the pleasure that makes music "congenial to all ages and all characters" (1340a2-5). It would be better to say that the delight in imitation is one part of the common or

38. See, for example, Else, *Aristotle's Poetics,* pp. 128-30.
39. For the dispute as to the two causes see Denis de Montmollin, *La Poétique d'Aristote* (Neuchâtel, 1951), p. 79; I follow Else, *Aristotle's Poetics,* 127.
40. The aesthetic pleasure to which Aristotle alludes in 1448b17-19 cannot be supposed to be exclusive of the pleasure in learning. Cf. *Pol.* 1339a36-38.

natural pleasure which all men experience in listening to music, for it is also the case that "all delight in rhythm and tune" "by nature."[41] We have learned from the *Politics* that the common experience of the natural pleasure deriving from music is not the only experience associated with it, and that music has in fact a "more honorable nature." Not only does music or poetry cause men to delight in imitations; it causes them to share the experience, to "experience the passions" (*sympaschein*) of the persons imitated; and because it affects the passions, it affects the character and the soul. If the ethical or educative power of poetry is nowhere explicitly discussed in the *Poetics*, it is equally true that it is nowhere explicitly disavowed. And Aristotle certainly speaks explicitly of the effect on the spectator of "pity and fear"—the "passions" most directly engaged by the experience of tragic poetry.[42]

9. Music and Virtue (II)

The argument of Chapter 5 continues as follows:

> Since music happens to be one of the pleasant things, and since virtue concerns correct enjoyment and correct loving and

41. [Aristotle] *Problems* XIX.38.920b29–31.

42. In 1460b22–26, Aristotle indicates that "correctness" in imitation may be violated in order to attain "the end of the art" or to have a "more stirring" effect. He could seem to suggest that the imitation of things which are real or possible is not an indispensable requirement of poetic art because the "end" of poetic art is something other than the pleasure in "learning" through the comparison of an imitation with its known or real original, or in other words that the "stirring" of the passions is in some way the "end" of poetic art. Aristotle also tells us, however, that "the end of the art" has "already been spoken of," which is certainly not the case—unless by "the art" Aristotle here means tragedy, for the "end" as well as the "work" (*ergon*) of tragedy had been discussed (1450a22–23, 30–35), and the "work" of tragedy was said to be effected by those parts of the plot by which tragedy "particularly moves the soul [*psychagōgei*]." The expression "the work of the art" is used elsewhere (1462b12, cf. b15 *telos*) with clear reference to tragedy. Still, it would be a mistake to assume (as does Else, *Aristotle's Poetics*, p. 573) that other forms of poetry, and in particular epic, must be considered incapable of affecting the passions: Aristotle insists that the essential features of tragedy were already employed in Homeric epic (1459b8–13).

hating, it is clearly necessary to learn and to become habituated
to nothing so much as to correct judgment and enjoyment of decent characters and noble actions; and there are likenesses that
are particularly close to the genuine natures in rhythms and
tunes of anger and gentleness, and again of courage and
moderation and all their opposites, as well as of all other things
pertaining to character—as is clear from experience, for we are
changed in soul when we listen to such things; but the habituation to feel pain and enjoyment in like things is near to being
disposed in the same way as regards the reality. [1340a14–25]

"Virtue" and "music" belong together. Just as music "happens to be" or is "by accident" (*symbebēke*) one of the pleasant
things while possessing a "nature" that is capable of affecting
the character and the soul, so is virtue inseparable from "enjoyment" or from a correct attitude toward pleasures and
pains. Music is, then, ideally suited to providing an education
in virtue. It is ideally suited to providing an education in that
"correct judgment and enjoyment" which appears to be an integral part of the leisured pastime of mature citizens.

Of fundamental importance for the understanding of Aristotle's argument as a whole is the transition which occurs at
1340a18. *Mousikē* as used at a14 is not synonymous with
rhythmoi kai mele in a19 and subsequently; it continues to be used,
and is used throughout, in its comprehensive sense. When
Aristotle urges the necessity of a music education in virtue, he
is not speaking only of the music education of the young, and
he is thinking at least as much of poetry as of music in the narrow sense. But the fact that Aristotle discusses in the sequel the
question of the effect of music in the narrow sense—of
"rhythms and tunes"—does not mean that he is thinking only
of the effect of music on the young. Aristotle takes up the question of music in the narrow sense precisely because the ethical
or educative effect of "rhythms and tunes" is much more questionable than the ethical or educative effect of poetry. But it is
true that Aristotle is particularly concerned with rhythms and
tunes insofar as they affect the young. Because the study and
practice of music in the narrow sense makes up a considerable

part of the conventional music education of the young, an education of that kind could never be justified if it were the case that the ethical or educative power of ''music'' resides in its ''poetry'' alone.

It will not be necessary to follow in detail the argument of the remainder of Chapter 5. Something should be said here, however, regarding Aristotle's understanding of the notion of ''character'' (*ēthos*). In spite of the fact that the argument of the latter part of Chapter 5 is primarily intended to prepare an answer to the question of whether the young are to receive a conventional education in music, Aristotle's defense of the ethical or educative value of rhythm and tune is conceived in the broadest possible spirit. When Aristotle speaks of the likenesses in rhythms and tunes of ''anger and gentleness, and again of courage and moderation and all their opposites, as well as of all other things pertaining to character [*tōn allōn ēthikōn*],'' he gives us to understand that the educative power of rhythm and tune is not limited to a capacity to affect character or to form virtuous habits simply.[43] Rhythms and tunes contain likenesses not only of the virtues and vices or of character in the narrow sense, but also of what only ''pertains'' to character—for example, ''anger and gentleness.'' Rhythms and tunes represent passion no less than character (1340a6). Rhythm and tune no less than music as a whole are capable of arousing passion in the soul or of causing men to ''experience the passions'' which it represents (1340a8–13).

At the same time, however, it is necessary to observe that Aristotle does not make a clear verbal distinction between ''character'' and ''passion.'' What Aristotle means when he speaks of ''things pertaining to character'' (*ēthika*) is exactly what he has in mind when he speaks somewhat later (1340a29,

43. ''The entire remainder of the chapter is concerned with the possibility and the principles of character formation through music'' (Koller, *Musse,* p. 48). Richards' conjecture *ēthōn* for *ēthikōn* in a21 (accepted by Ross) is of interest only as evidence of the misunderstanding to which the argument is here exposed.

33, 39) of "characters" (*ēthē*) simply;[44] and when he describes the passion aroused by the tunes of Olympus as a "passion of the character as it pertains to the soul" (*pathos tou peri tēn psychēn ēthous*) (1340a11-12), it is evident that the word *ēthos* must have more senses than one. In the strict sense, *ēthos* is "moral character"—the sum of the fixed dispositions or states (*hexeis*) with respect to virtue and vice.[45] In the larger sense, *ēthos* is "character" simply—the sum both of an individual's dispositions or virtues and of his characteristic passions; it is "character as it pertains to the soul," or simply "the character of the soul" (*to tēs psychēs ēthos*).[46] To speak of the effect of music on *ēthos* in the strict sense is to speak of the formation of moral character in the young by way of habituation. To speak of the effect of music on *ēthos* in the larger sense is to speak also and indeed primarily of its effect on the passions of adults—of those whose moral character has already been formed if not completely determined by a past education. The proof that rhythms and tunes contain likenesses of all that pertains to character is

44. As appears from the fact that the "signs of characters" in the visual arts are said to be manifested *epi tou sōmatos en tois pathesin* (1340a32-35), and that at least some of the musical harmonies described as providing "imitations of charcters" (a39) manifestly represent and affect the passions (1340a42, b4-5; cf. 1342b1-3).

45. Cf. *Eth. Nic.* 1105b19-6a6. It seems also to be used on occasion with reference to individual *hexeis* or virtues (*Eth. Nic.* 1144b4).

46. *Pol.* 1337a39, 1340b1-12; cf. *Rhet.* 1386b9-12, 33, 1388b31. Susemihl's objections (pp. 622-24) to the reasonable view of A. Döring, *Die Kunstlehre des Aristoteles* (Jena, 1876), pp. 355 ff., are not easy to understand. He seems to argue that there is no need to assume that Aristotle uses the term *ēthos* in a wider sense because for Aristotle there is no fundamental distinction between *ēthos* and *pathos* or because each virtue is always accompanied by an appropriate passion. This is to forget that virtuous dispositions may be overcome by the passions—the phenomenon Aristotle calls *akrasia*, "moral weakness" or "incontinence" (*Eth. Nic.* 1145b8 ff.); nor are the "passions of a good character" necessarily good in all respects (cf. *Rhet.* 1386b9-12 with 1354a16-26, 1390a18-23). Cf. A. Kahl, *Die Philosophie der Musik nach Aristoteles* (Leipzig, 1902), p. 27. For the different senses of *ēthos* see W. J. Verdenius, "The Meaning of *ēthos* and *ēthikos* in Aristotle's *Poetics*," *Mnem.* 12 (1945), 241-57; E. Schütrumpf, *Die Bedeutung des Wortes ēthos in der Poetik des Aristoteles*, Zetemata XLIX (Munich, 1970), pp. 1-46.

precisely that "we are changed in soul" by listening to them (1340a22): Aristotle appeals now, as he had appealed earlier (1340a7-8), to an experience of mature persons.

The implications of Aristotle's argument for understanding the history of what has come to be called the idea of "musical ethos" are fundamental; they will be considered at length in an appendix.

10. The Music Education of the Young

Aristotle's description of the effect of various musical modes or harmonies (1340a40-b5) may be most conveniently considered at a later point. After indicating that rhythms possess and therefore affect character in a manner analogous to the tunes or harmonies, Aristotle proceeds to draw his conclusion:

> From all these things it is evident, then, that music is capable of making of a certain quality the character of the soul; and if it is able to do this, clearly the young should be exposed to it and educated in it. And the teaching of music is suited to the nature of those of this age; for the young are unable to endure anything that is unsweetened [anēdynton] on account of their age, and music belongs by nature among the sweetened things (tōn hēdysmenōn]. [1340b10-17]

Aristotle's argument proves and is intended to prove the "ethical" power of music in its broadest sense: music is capable of affecting "the character of the soul." His final remark fully accords with this conclusion. Music belongs "by nature among the sweetened things"[47] because the pleasure connected with music is in the last analysis only an attribute or accident of its "more honorable nature"—of its power to affect character most broadly understood.

Chapter 6 begins as follows:

> Whether they should themselves learn how to sing and play instruments or not—the problem discussed earlier—must now be

47. Bywater's conjecture hēdysmatōn (accepted by Ross) should certainly be rejected in favor of the reading of the manuscripts. Poet. 1450b16 is not a relevant parallel, and hēdysmenōn is plainly meant to echo anēdynton (cf. Newman on 1340b16).

decidcd. It is, then, hardly unclear that it makes a great difference with regard to becoming of a certain quality if one participates in these activities oneself [*ean tis autos koinōnēi tōn ergōn*]; for it is impossible or very difficult to become good judges [*kritas spoudaious*] without participating. [1340b20-25]

The argument of Chapter 5 had decided only the question of whether the young are to receive an education in music; it had not decided the question of whether they are to receive a conventional music education involving the learning of musical skills. It is this second question which is here addressed, and rather quickly disposed of.

One could wish that Aristotle had not so quickly disposed of it, for in fact it is not clear why the learning of musical skills makes a great difference with regard to "becoming of a certain sort"—that is, with regard to the acquisition of virtue. But Aristotle's thought can perhaps be reconstructed with the aid of some later Peripatetic material. In the nineteenth book of the *Problems,* the question is raised "why all delight in rhythm and tune and generally in consonances." The answer given is that "we delight by nature in motions that are according to nature," as appears in particular from the fact that "children delight in these things from infancy." At the same time, however, it seems that "it is through habituation that we delight in the varieties of tunes [*tropois melōn*]."[48] It makes sense to connect the distinction here implied with the distinction between merely "listening" to music and actively "learning" musical skills. On the one hand, there is a natural delight in musical "motions"—in "tunes" as well as in rhythms—that is experienced by "all" (hence in particular by children) just by "listening" to music. On the other hand, there is a delight in the "varieties of tunes"—a delight, that is, not in "tunes" as such but in individual modes or harmonies—that is experienced only by those who have been properly "habituated"; and such habituation is most effective, it would seem, in and through the active learning of music. It is above all by actually

48. [Aristotle] *Problems* XIX.38.920b29-32.

learning to play and sing compositions in a certain mode that the student comes to enjoy or to delight in that mode—and in the ethos which it represents. It is by actually learning to play and sing compositions in the mode or modes which best represent the moral virtues that the young are most effectively habituated to delight in the moral virtues or to acquire what Aristotle has called the "capacity for right enjoyment" (1339a24-25). It is precisely for this reason, it would seem, that the perception or the enjoyment of musical ethos is not available to all in the way that the perception of ethos is available to all in poetry (cf. 1340a12-13) and in the visual arts (cf. 1340a28-32).[49] It is not sufficient to say that correct enjoyment indeed presupposes education, but may be achieved through an education in "listening" to music or to certain musical modes. Such an "education" is available in greater or lesser degree to all, and it is evidently insufficient.[50] The correct enjoyment of musical ethos depends on a special "habituation" (cf. 1340a23) which is effected above all by the acquisition and practice of musical skills.

11. Music and Liberal Education

After remarking that education is of practical use also in occupying and absorbing the energies of the young (1340b25-31), Aristotle proceeds as follows:

49. I do not see any necessity for reading $<ou>$ pantes in 1340a31-32 with Müller and Ross. The fact that the representation of character in the visual arts is slighter than in music does not mean that the perception of visual ethos is necessarily more restricted than that of musical ethos, since the nature of the representation or imitation is in each case very different. Aristotle seems to anticipate—and is perhaps the source of—the distinction between autophyēs aisthēsis and epistēmonikē aisthesis in the musical treatise of Diogenes of Babylon (Stoicorum Veterum Fragmenta III, frs. 57 and 61 = Philodemus On Music IV.1B,25-2,15 [62-63] Kemke); cf. Koller, Musse, pp. 44-46; A. J. Neubecker, Die Bewertung der Musik bei Stoikern und Epikureern (Berlin, 1956), pp. 11-18. Aristides Quintilianus contrasts mousikē with "painting and all such arts partaking of the beauty connected with sight" which are "easily apprehended by all" (pasin eukataleptoi), I.1 (1,19-21) Winnington-Ingram.

50. Consider Libanius For the Dancers 89: "Thus the learner ridiculed the nonlearner, and one who did not know how to put his hands to the lyre was

That there is to be an education in music of a kind that will include actual participation [*houtos hōste kai koinōnein tōn ergōn*] is clear from such considerations; and it is not difficult to distinguish what is fitting and unfitting for each age and decide it, with a view to answering those who assert that the occupation is a bánausic one. To begin with, since it is for the sake of judging that they should take an actual part, they must therefore actively engage in it when young, but when they become older leave off the activity itself and be capable of judging the noble things and of enjoying correctly as a result of the learning that took place in their youth. [1340b31-39]

In the first place, it should be observed that Aristotle does not say that the education in music is to be an education in musical skills simply. He says only that music education must "include" an active training. Secondly, Aristotle's argument follows strictly from his proof (1340a1-14) of the power of music to affect "the character and the soul," and from its corollary (a16-18): "it is necessary to learn and to be habituated to nothing so much as to correct judgment and enjoyment of decent characters and noble actions." It must be stressed again that the purpose of music education in general, and of the musical training of the young in particular, cannot possibly be understood to be the training of "good judges" in the sense of "good literary critics." If a proper appreciation of modes and rhythms were the purpose of the music education of the young, one would suppose that the young must be expected to become familiar with all the varieties of modes and rhythms. In fact, however, Aristotle soon makes it clear that the young will only learn and practice one musical mode—the Dorian. As was indicated earlier, the actual learning of musical skills by the young does not greatly contribute to an "aesthetic" appreciation of music in later life (1339a36-38). There is no reason to suppose that correct "aesthetic" judgment of the (technical)

---

mocked; but if there were no difference between learning and casual listening and it affected souls in the same way, the theater in those times would have made all the same, since the listening was common to all."

goodness or badness of musical compositions is directly proportionate to—or even at all dependent upon—the ability to sing
and play musical compositions. For, indeed, "the many" may
be just as capable—they may be more capable—of correctly
judging "the works of music" than the educated few
(1281b7–8).[51] The "correct judgment" which the music education of the young prepares must be understood as a moral judgment of "noble things" rather than an aesthetic judgment of
"beautiful things" as such. In what immediately follows,
Aristotle proceeds to confront the question of whether the learning of musical skills by the young is an illiberal occupation.

> As regards the accusation brought by some that music makes
> them banausic, it is not difficult to resolve the question by in-
> vestigating to what point those who are being educated with a
> view to political virtue should participate in the activity [*tōn
> ergōn koinōnēteon*], what sort of tunes and rhythms they should
> partake of, and, finally, what instruments are to be used for learn-
> ing—for it is likely that this too makes a difference. The
> response to the accusation lies here, for there is nothing that
> prevents music from having such an effect if it is used in certain
> ways. It is evident, then, that the learning of it should neither
> interfere with their later activities nor render the body banausic
> and useless in regard to military and civic training—in regard
> to the uses now, or in regard to the learning later [*pros men tas
> chrēseis ēde, pros de tas mathēseis hysteron*]. [1340b40–41a9]

Aristotle's concluding remark (a7–9) is of some importance for
what is to follow, although it is widely regarded as unintelligible in
the form it appears in our manuscripts.[52] Aristotle's argument, I
believe, is this. As the citizens of the best regime are being
educated with a view to political virtue rather than with a view to

---

51. Cf. Newman on 1340b22. Diogenes of Babylon (Philodemus *On Music*
I.16,7–11 [8–9] Kemke) seems to compare music with painting, which
teaches the sight "to judge finely of many visible things"—it does not teach it
only or even primarily to judge the work of the art.

52. Bojesen's transposition of *chrēseis* and *mathēseis* is adopted by Susemihl
and Ross; the transposition of *ēde* and *hysteron* was suggested by Spengel.
Newman's attempt (on 1341a7) to defend the received text by taking *chrēseis* to
refer to bodily and *mathēseis* to intellectual activity founders on the fact that the
whole phrase is in apposition to a7 *mēte to sōma poiein banauson*.

technical (or even critical) virtuosity, and early music education must be allowed to interfere neither with the (political or civic) activities that the young will have to engage in when they are mature, nor with the preparations they must make with a view to those activities when they are still young. What are the preparations, the "military and civic training" (*polemikai kai politikai askēseis*), to which Aristotle refers? Since Aristotle makes it clear that he is here concerned solely with the effect of a study of music on "the body," I think it must be assumed that he is referring to the entire program of gymnastic education in the best regime. When Aristotle speaks of "the uses now" and "the learning later," he is speaking of gymnastic education from the point of view of the music education of the years immediately following puberty. The education in music can be permitted to interfere neither with the "uses"—with the continuing practice—during the years of music education itself of the gymnastic lessons learned in the period before puberty, nor with the "learning" that will accompany the severe Spartan gymnastic of the period immediately following the years devoted to an education in music.

The desired result would be achieved, Aristotle continues,

> if they did not labor at [*diaponoien*] the kinds of things that belong to technical contests or the extraordinary feats and superfluous accomplishments which have now come into the contests and from the contests into education—though what is of this sort should be studied too[53] to the point that they are able to enjoy noble tunes and rhythms and not merely the common element in music, which even some other animals enjoy as well as the multitude of slaves and children. It is also clear from this what instruments are to be used. For neither flutes nor any other technical instrument should be brought into education—the cithara, for example, or any other of this sort—but only those that will make them good hearers either of music education or of the other. [1341a9-21]

In accordance with the necessities of an education that is in the service of "political virtue," Aristotle rigorously excludes from the music education of the young everything of a merely "technical" nature. It is manifest that the music education of

53. Reading *alla kai ta toiauta* in 1341a13 with Dreizehnter.

the young is not calculated to prepare the competent "judging" of technical or virtuoso performances.

Aristotle approves for the purposes of "education" only those instruments which will make the young "good hearers either of music education or of the other." The "other" education of which Aristotle speaks would seem to be the gymnastic education alluded to earlier. More precisely, it seems to be the gymnastic education of the period immediately preceding twenty-one: Aristotle is still looking ahead from the music education of the years after puberty, and he thinks of the education that immediately follows it. But is the "music education" of which Aristotle speaks, then, just the music education of the years following puberty? It is possible that he is thinking of the nonmusical elements of this education—of the learning of poetry. But Aristotle uses the future tense (*poiēsei* a20) with reference to both kinds of education; and when he speaks of "hearers" or "listeners" (*akroatai*) of music education, one is reminded of his earlier distinction between an education by way of "habituation" and an education by way of "listening" (1332b10-11; cf. 1340a12, 22, 42a3-4). Aristotle may be indicating that the education of the young in music is a preparation not only for the gymnastic education, the "military and civic training" (cf. 1341a9), of late adolescence, but also for a continuing music education which operates through (mere) "listening" rather than through the actual learning of musical skills and the habituation accompanying or effected by it. The music education of the young may have to be understood as at once an education in virtue and a preparation for the music education of mature citizens.

That the music education of the best regime does not end with youth or with the formation of moral character properly speaking—that the education in musical skills is only part of a larger music education "with a view to political virtue" (1340b42-41a1) which extends through the years of maturity— is a suggestion for which Aristotle's audience cannot be wholly unprepared. In Book VII, Aristotle had repeatedly indicated that education will not be limited to the formation of character or to "habituation" to moral virtue, but will extend to include an education of the "mind" in "reason," an education which cannot be expected to begin before the age of twenty-one; and he had indicated that it is necessary to distinguish between an education in "theoretical reason" and an education in "practical reason." That Aristotle's education in practical reason could be an education in music in the narrow sense is extremely unlikely. As I have tried to show, however, when Aristotle speaks of "music" he means to speak not only of "tunes" and "rhythms" but also of poetry. It is, it would seem, not accidental that Aristotle's final objection to the use of the flute in the education of the young is that it prevents the simultaneous use of "speech" (*logos*): the education in flute-playing is not an education "with a view to thought" (1341a24–25 ff., b6–7).

The possibility of a higher education in music has been overlooked in the second place because it is assumed as a matter of course that the musical activity appropriate to the mature citizens of the best regime, which Aristotle has called "pastime" (*diagōgē*), is fundamentally if not wholly an "aesthetic" activity which can have nothing to do with education. I have tried to show that Aristotle's argument is reduced to incoherence by such an assumption. Aristotle's proof that the "more honorable nature" of music is its power to educate or to affect the character and soul is at the same time a proof that the "more honorable" activity of *diagōgē*—that *diagōgē* rightly understood—is a fundamentally "ethical" or "educative" activity. The element of beauty or nobility (*to kalon*) which it is generally agreed *diagōgē* should possess (1339b17–19) appears to consist for Aristotle at least partly in the activity of "judging the noble things" (1340a38). The "judgment" which music education is intended to form is not an aesthetic judgment—even if one that presupposes a certain moral education. Though indeed operating in and through the imitations supplied by music or poetry, it is a judgment not of those imitations as imitations but rather of the things they imitate—of "decent characters and noble actions" (1340a17–18). While the exact nature of the "judgment" of which Aristotle here speaks is not made clear in the *Politics* as we have it, it is at least plausible to connect it with that judgment which he appears to treat elsewhere an indispensable element of "practical wisdom" or "prudence" (*phronēsis*).[54] This would help to explain, at any rate, Aristotle's earlier suggestion that the ultimate justification for an active music education in youth may lie in its contribution to the "pastime and prudence" (*diagogē kai phronēsis* 1339a25–26) of mature citizens. Whether such an interpretation receives additional support in the text of *Politics* VIII must remain to be determined.

54. *Eth. Nic.* 1143a6–10, 19–35. Cf. 13 above.

3

Music and Catharsis

1. Music and the Best Regime

Because of its intrinsic interest as well as its numerous and perplexing difficulties, the final chapter of the *Politics* has received more attention and been treated in greater detail than any other part of Book VIII. It is fair to say that these efforts have so far failed to establish a generally satisfactory interpretation of Chapter 7 as a whole; and if a measure of agreement has been reached with regard to the more important questions, and particularly the question of catharsis, it is too often an agreement proceeding from the exhaustion of the contending parties rather than a genuine resolution of the difficulties involved. This state of affairs is due in large part to a general tendency to treat Chapter 7 in isolation from the argument of Book VIII as a whole. In some cases the difficulties of Aristotle's argument are treated merely as textual problems. Even when an appeal is made to the discussion of Chapters 5 and 6, the interpretation of the argument there is perfunctory at best, and usually presupposes that interpretation of Chapter 7 which it is intended to support. The most serious obstacle in the way of an adequate interpretation of the chapter, however, is the prevailing confusion regarding Aristotle's understanding of catharsis. Without pretending to resolve this endlessly disputed question, I think it is possible at least to define it with greater precision than is generally done.

Because it has been doubted whether Chapter 7 actually formed an integral part of the original version of Book VIII,[1] it will be well to begin by observing its close connection with what has preceded. In the first place, of course, the chapter itself is an artificial division, and corresponds to no real break in Aristotle's argument: its opening is the apodosis of a sentence which had originated some ten lines earlier.[2] After concluding his discussion of the instruments to be employed in the education of the young, Aristotle had continued thus:

> Since we reject technical education—education, that is, with a view to the contests[3]—as regards both the instruments and the practice of it (for the one who is engaged in this kind of education undertakes it not for the sake of his own virtue but for the sake of the pleasure of his listeners, and a vulgar pleasure at that, so that we judge the practice of it to be rather menial in character and unsuited to free men; indeed, it has the effect of rendering them banausic, for the object with a view to which the end of their activity is determined is a bad one, for the vulgarity of the spectator usually causes the music itself to change, so that the artisans, who practice it with a view to the spectator, are themselves qualitatively changed, and their bodies too are affected on account of the motions), we must next investigate harmonies and rhythms. . . . [1341b8–19]

Aristotle's argument presupposes and follows strictly from his earlier statement (1340b31–41a9) concerning the matters still to be treated in Book VIII. The question which has been under discussion in Chapter 6, and which will continue to be kept in view in the "investigation" of Chapter 7 (cf. *skepteon* 1341b19 with *skepsamenos* 40b41), is the question whether music makes men banausic (1340b34–35, 40–41). By the end of Chapter 6, two of the matters that Aristotle had promised to investigate

1. Busse, pp. 42 ff. Busse's argument for the "lateness" of Chapter 7 rests entirely on its supposed contradictions with the earlier part of Book VIII.

2. *de* in 1341b19 is bracketed by Susemihl-Hicks and Ross, perhaps rightly.

3. I follow Newman (on 1341b10) in beginning the parenthesis after *agōnas:* the parenthesis is intended to explain the rejection of *technikē paideia,* not Aristotle's use of that term.

106

have been dealt with: Aristotle has resolved (1341a9–17) the question of the kind or extent of the instruction of the young in music (*mechri posou tōn ergōn koinōnēteon* 1340b42; cf. 41b9), and he has resolved (1341a17–b8) the question of the proper use of musical instruments in that instruction (*en poiois organois tēn mathēsin poiēteon* 1341a2–3; cf. 41b8–9). What remains to be treated, then, is the question of the tunes and rhythms that are to be employed (*poiōn melōn kai poiōn rhythmōn koinōnēteon* 1341a1–2).

Chapter 7 begins as follows:

> We must next investigate harmonies and rhythms, and whether all harmonies and all rhythms should be used with a view to education or a distinction should be made, and then whether we shall set down the same distinction for those who are actively engaged in education or some other third distinction is needed [*tois pros paideian diaponousi poteron ton auton diorismon thēsomen ē triton dei tina heteron*]. [1341b19–23]

This sentence has puzzled the commentators, and has been variously emended.[4] The reading of the manuscripts clearly suggests that when Aristotle promises to investigate the harmonies and rhythms to be used "with a view to education," he cannot be thinking of the education of the young, for he also promises to investigate the harmonies and rhythms to be used by "those who are actively engaged in education" or in the learning of musical skills—that is to say, precisely the young.[5] But Aristotle had seemed earlier to indicate that the music education of the best regime can be understood to encompass not only the learning of musical skills by the young but an

4. The beginning of the chapter is discussed at length by Hermann Bonitz, *Aristotelische Studien* III (Vienna, 1868), 95–99. Susemihl-Hicks and Newman (III, 127) follow Bonitz in bracketing *kai pros paideian* in b20 and marking *triton dei tina heteron* as corrupt. Susemihl-Hicks suggest *tina heteron, triton de . . .; triton* alone is bracketed by Ross. Dreizehnter, however, lets stand the text of the manuscripts.

5. Cf. 1341a18–21. Susemihl-Hicks understand *tois pros paideian diaponousi* to refer to "those whose work is teaching" music; but Aristotle is clearly thinking of the "learning" of music by the young (cf. 1341a9–11, 1339a4–8, 31–40).

education of mature citizens in and through listening to music, and that the end of music education as a whole is (political or civic) "virtue."[6] At the end of Chapter 6, he had stressed the incompatibility of "technical education" and an education that is "for the sake of virtue," and had seemed to indicate that the banausic effects of a concern for technical virtuosity will be felt by professional musicians no less than by the young. It is hardly surprising, then, that the discussion of harmonies and rhythms in Chapter 7 will not be limited to a discussion of their effect on the young. If mature men can be "qualitatively" changed,[7] if they can be rendered illiberal in character and soul, by a concern for technical virtuosity, it is necessary to consider whether they will not be similarly affected by certain harmonies and rhythms. In fact, Aristotle will decide that certain harmonies are only fit for a "vulgar" audience, an audience composed of the noncitizen classes of the best regime (1342a18-29). When these considerations are taken into account, the first sentence of Chapter 7 constitutes an intelligible if not perfectly satisfying link in Aristotle's argument.[8]

Aristotle's argument continues as follows:

> Since we see that music depends on tune-composition and rhythms [*dia melopoiias kai rhythmōn ousan*], and since one ought

6. The beginning of Chapter 7, as indeed the chapter as a whole, can leave no doubt that the "investigation" announced in 1340b41 ff. is not restricted to the question of the young, and that the expression "those being educated with a view to political virtue" (which must be taken with 1341a1-2 *poion melon kai poion rhythmōn koinōnēteon* as well as with *mechri te posou tōn ergōn koinōnēteon*— as is indicated by the *te*) is meant to apply to mature citizens as well as to the young (cf. 1340b31-32).

7. There is no reason to emend *poious tinas* in 1341b18, as has been suggested by Susemihl and others. The phrase may be applied without difficulty to the body as well as to the character or soul (cf. 1339a23).

8. The three "distinctions" involved in the passage are, then, that between the musical activities of the citizens and those of the noncitizens, between the music "education" of the citizens and their other musical activities, and between the musical "learning" of the citizens when young and their musical education or culture generally. If the text is felt to be intolerably abrupt, the simplest solution would seem to be to assume a lacuna following *rhythmous* in 1341b19.

not to be ignorant of the power which each of these possesses with regard to education, nor whether one should prefer music with good tune to music with good rhythm, believing as we do that these matters have for the most part been adequately treated by some of the current experts in music and by those in philosophy who have experience and familiarity with music education, we shall refer to them anyone who is seeking a detailed account of particulars, and limit ourselves to distinguishing, as it were, in a legal manner, and speak of these things only in a general way. [1341b23-32]

Two points may be made. In the first place, it is necessary to stress once again that "music" is not to be identified with "harmonies and rhythms." As was argued earlier, Aristotle's remark need not mean, as it is usually taken to mean, that *mousikē* "consists in tunes and rhythms," but would seem to mean only that it "depends" on them, that it exists or is realized by means of them.[9] It is also of some interest to learn that "music" does not depend on or presuppose tune and rhythm equally, that some kinds of "music" favor one of these elements over the other.[10] In the second place, it is important to observe both that Aristotle relies on the authority of others, and that he does not rely on it completely. Since the matters to be discussed have "for the most part been adequately treated" by philosophers and by musical experts, Aristotle can dispense with a thorough and detailed treatment; but his general discussion cannot for that reason be assumed to be wholly derivative. In fact, as I shall try to show, Aristotle deviates from the teaching of his predecessors in one important and indeed fundamental point: Aristotle's doctrine of catharsis will prove to be wholly new.[11]

9. See Chapter II, sec. 7 above.

10. The discussion of the question "whether one should prefer music with good tune to music with good rhythm [*tēn eumelē mousikēn ē tēn eurhythmon*]" is missing from the text as we have it. If the interpretation of the meaning of *mousikē* offered here is correct, it seems not improbable that the discussion concerned whether lyric or epic poetry is to be preferred in the education of the young (cf. 1340b7-10 with *Poet.* 1459b34-60a1)

11. As to the identity of Aristotle's authorities, the fact that the musical doctrine of the *Republic* will come in for criticism (1342a32 ff.) does not

2. The Uses of Tunes or Harmonies

In the sequel, Aristotle turns to the question of "tunes" or "harmonies." A general remark may be in order regarding Aristotle's terminology. "Tune" and "harmony" are imperfect translations of *melos* and *harmonia*. *Harmonia* is properly the tuning of a musical instrument, and hence the musical mode determined by a particular instrumental tuning. *Melos* is properly the melodic realization of a particular *harmonia*, and may accordingly refer either to an individual tune or to a kind of tune; in the latter sense, it seems to have been used almost interchangeably with *harmonia*.[12] Aristotle appears to use the term in both senses (cf. 1341b35–36 with 42a9–10).

Aristotle's argument begins as follows:

> Since we accept the distinction of tunes as distinguished by some of those in philosophy, who set down some as expressive of character [*ēthika*], some of action [*praktika*], and some of inspiration [*enthousiastika*]—and they set down the natures of the harmonies as being related to each of these, one harmony to one kind of tune—and since we assert that music should be used not for the sake of one sort of benefit but for the sake of many (it is for the sake both of education and catharsis—as to what we mean by catharsis, we will now speak of it simply, but again and more clearly in our discussion of poetic art—and third with a view to pastime, release and the relaxation of strain), it is evident that all the harmonies are to be used, but that all are not to be used in the same way, but with a view to education those that

---

necessarily mean that Plato must be ruled out of consideration. The fact that Aristotle speaks of "current experts in music" would seem to rule out Damon, although not his school. Aristotle almost certainly relied extensively on the expertise of his pupil Aristoxenus, and I shall argue that he adopts Aristoxenus' view of musical scales; but there is no evidence that the threefold distinction of types of harmonies ascribed in the immediate sequel (1341b32–36) to "some of those in philosophy" derives specifically from Aristoxenus. For Aristoxenus' relation to Plato consider particularly fr. 82 Wehrli; the relation of both to Damon as well as to Aristotle is treated at length in the Appendix.

12. Cf. Anderson, pp. 25–29, 34–35.

are most expressive of character, and with a view to listening to the performances of others those expressive of action and inspiration as well. [1341b32–42a4]

When this passage is read, as it is usually read, with a view primarily to the question of catharsis rather than in the context of Aristotle's argument as a whole, an interpretation of the following sort invariably results. Aristotle has hitherto concerned himself mainly with the uses of music in the formation of character or the moral education of the young; in Chapter 7, he broadens his inquiry to include possible uses of music which have nothing to do with character, with the young, or with education. Aristotle distinguishes between "ethical" tunes which serve the purposes of education on the one hand, and "practical" and "enthusiastic" tunes which are reserved for the enjoyment of older men on the other. Despite the complication that "ethical" tunes appear to be prescribed for older men as well as for the young,[13] there is little difficulty in identifying the purposes served by the musical "listening" of mature men. Because Aristotle will proceed to discuss the purgative or cathartic effect of certain kinds of enthusiastic music, the enthusiastic tunes may confidently be connected with "catharsis." Whether catharsis is to be understood as an end in itself or whether it should be connected with "pastime" or "relaxation" (cf. 1342a14) is not altogether clear; but catharsis surely has nothing to do with education. As regards "practical" tunes, Aristotle appears to forget about them; if they are discussed (reading *praktika* for *kathartika* at 1342a15), they must be connected with "relaxation," and particularly the pleasure or relaxation of the noncitizen class of the best regime.[14]

13. As Aristotle says that "the most ethical" are reserved for "education," it is natural to take *kai tais praktikais kai tais enthousiastikais* (1342a4) as meaning "the practical and enthusiastic as well," i.e., in addition to ethical tunes generally (cf. Susemihl-Hicks).

14. Cf. Susemihl-Hicks and Newman on 1341b40. The tendency of more recent interpretation, however, has been to link catharsis more closely with pleasure and "play" (thus, for example, Franz Dirlmeier, *"Katharsis pathēmatōn,"* Hermes 68 [1940], 82–87, who attempts to argue that "catharsis"

It is true that Aristotle distinguishes in the present passage between the musical "education" of the young and the musical "listening" (*akroasis*) of older persons. At the beginning of Chapter 7, however, Aristotle had appeared to indicate that the question of the uses of harmony and rhythm "with a view to education" is by no means identical with the question of the uses of them by those who are engaged in acquiring musical skills, that is, by the young (1341b21–23). It cannot simply be assumed that practical or enthusiastic—to say nothing of ethical—tunes will have nothing to do with "education" in the wider sense of the term. In the discussion of Chapter 5, it will be recalled, Aristotle had argued that music possesses in its very nature the power of education—that it is intrinsically capable of affecting the character and the soul; and he had indicated that this power can be operative not only in the education of the young but in the pastime of mature persons as well. What is more, Aristotle had there adduced as one of two proofs of the ability of music to affect the character and the soul precisely the example of the "enthusiastic tunes" of Olympus (1340a6–12). It is this passage particularly which must be kept in mind in attempting to understand Aristotle's later remark, frequently cited as evidence of the incompatibility of "education" and "catharsis," that "the flute expresses not so much character as frenzy [*ouk estin ho aulos ēthikon alla mallon orgiastikon*], so that it is to be used on those occasions when the looking is productive of catharsis rather than learning [*hē theōria katharsin mallon dynatai ē mathēsin*] [1341a21–24]."[15] In the first

---

in the enumeration of 1341b38–41 replaces "play" in the enumeration of 1339b13–14), and supporters of this view have found it more convenient to retain the reading of the manuscripts at 1342a15.

15. "This separation of *katharsis* from *paideia* is so compellingly clear that one has difficulty grasping how, after the hundreds of years that clear-thinking men have concerned themselves with this, anyone can continue to bring Aristotle's musical-poetic *katharsis* into connection with ethics" (Wolfgang Schadewaldt, "Furcht und Mitleid," *Hermes* 83 [1955], 153). Thus also Susemihl-Hicks on 1341a23 and Ernst Howald, "Eine vorplatonische Kunsttheorie," *Hermes* 59 (1919), 194. Cf. Rostagni, p. 51.

place, Aristotle has been arguing for the exclusion of the flute as well as other "technical" instruments from the education of the young; in spite of the elliptical phrasing (*theōria* belongs only with *katharsin*—it supplies, in effect, another reason for the unsuitability of the flute), the *mathēsis* of which he speaks is certainly the musical learning of the young.[16] In the second place, the flute is not "frenzied" simply; it is only "rather [*mallon*] frenzied than ethical." In fact, Aristotle plainly states that the frenzy (*enthousiasmos*) inspired by the (flute) melodies of Olympus is an experience affecting "the character of the soul" (*to peri tēn psychēn ēthos*) (1340a11–12). We have seen that *ēthos* is an ambiguous term. The adjective *ēthikon* is no less ambiguous: the fact that flute music or the cathartic effect associated with it does not contribute to the formation of character in the young does not mean that it is in no sense "ethical" (cf. 1340a21). Whether or in what sense its effect on "the character and the soul" is truly a kind of education must of course remain to be seen.

3. Tunes or Harmonies in the Politics *and the* Problems

What, then, is the precise distinction among "ethical," "practical," and "enthusiastic" tunes or harmonies? Apart from the later evidence of Chapter 7 itself, two passages are of particular importance for Aristotle's understanding of the different tunes or harmonies. The first occurs in Chapter 5, in Aristotle's general discussion of the "ethical" nature of harmony and rhythm. "There are," he argues,

> imitations of characters in tunes themselves, as indeed is evident; for the natures of the harmonies were distinct at the outset and such as to dispose the listeners in a certain way, and a different way with regard to each of them—some, for example the so-called Mixed Lydian, affect them with grief and apprehen-

16. Newman (on 1341a22) assumes that the reference is to mature persons; but Aristotle invariably applies the term *mathēsis* to the learning of the young. Newman's interpretation of 1339a34–36, to which he appeals in this connection, is mistaken, as is his interpretation of 1341a8–9 (cf. 1340b36–39).

sion; others, the relaxed modes, with a softness or effeminacy of spirit; another, with a moderate and settled feeling, as the Dorian alone of the harmonies is thought to do; and the Phrygian is thought to make them inspired [*enthousiastikous*]. [1340a38–b5]

Aristotle's opening remark should be emphasized. All the modes described here are "imitations of character"—all are "ethical" in the broad sense of that term. This phrase could seem to suggest, however, that the "ethical" tunes which in Chapter 7 are distinguished from other kinds of tunes (and in particular "enthusiastic" tunes) must be taken as "ethical" in the narrow sense—that is, as tunes expressive only of moral character or of virtue and not at all of "passion"—and must be identified with the Dorian tunes which Aristotle prescribes for the education of the young (1342a28–32). At the same time, however, Aristotle speaks of the Dorian (and of harmonies that may be found similar to it) as the "most ethical" of the harmonies (1342a3); and he definitely implies that ethical harmonies will not only be used in the education of the young. Is the term used, then, in still another sense?

That it is so used is confirmed by a passage in Book XIX of the *Problems* which seems to presuppose the distinction of harmonies adopted by Aristotle in the last chapter of the *Politics*. The following translation incorporates my own reconstruction of the text, which is at one point obviously corrupt; although deviating considerably from the solutions usually adopted, I think something like it can be shown to be necessary.

> Why is it that choruses in tragedy sing neither in the Hypodorian nor the Hypophrygian mode? Is it because these harmonies are least melodious, which is most necessary to the chorus? Hypophrygian has an active character [*ēthos praktikon*], which is why the sortie and the arming in the *Geryone* were composed in it; Hypodorian has a character marked by magnificence and stateliness [*megaloprepes kai stasimon*], so that of all the harmonies it is best suited to the lyre. Both are unsuited to the chorus, and more appropriate to those on the stage. For these imitate heroes, and in ancient times only the leaders were

heroes, while the people—it is of these that the chorus is composed—were mere human beings. For this reason a mournful and inactive [goeron kai hesychion] character and tune is suited to it; for these are merely human. Now the other harmonies have these—the Hypophrygian least of all, < the Hypodorian and Dorian (?) to a greater extent, but the Mixed Lydian has them above all. Even the Phrygian has them, > since it is enthusiastic and bacchic. This mode affects us with passion, but the passionate are the weak rather than the powerful, so that it too is suitable for choruses. But the Hypodorian and Hypophrygian stir to action, which is inappropriate to the chorus; for the chorus is an interested yet inactive onlooker, providing only goodwill to those who are present.[17]

If the supplement I have provided is essentially correct, the author of this passage identifies the Mixed Lydian "tune" as the harmony most appropriate to a tragic chorus, argues that the Phrygian harmony is also suited to it, and implies that other harmonies, at least insofar as they partake of the ethos exemplified in Mixed Lydian, are suitable as well. What is otherwise known of the music of tragedy would appear to confirm this analysis. Aristoxenus speaks of Mixed Lydian as "a passionate mode [pathētikē tis], suiting tragedies." He claims that it was invented by Sappho, that it was learned from her by "the tragic poets," and that "they took it over and joined it with Dorian; for the one provided magnificence [to megaloprepes] and the other passion [to pathētikon], and tragedy is a mixture of these."[18] A late source seems to refer to it as the tragikos tropos, the musical mode most characteristic of tragedy.[19] Plato speaks of Mixed Lydian and of the older or "strained" Lydian as

17. [Aristotle] Problems XIX.48.922b10-27. For a full discussion of this passage and possible emendations, see Carnes Lord, "A Peripatetic Account of Tragic Music," Hermes 105 (1977), 175-79.

18. [Plutarch] On Music 1136c = Aristoxenus fr. 81 Wehrli.

19. Suda s.v. Aríōn. I have argued elsewhere ("Aristotle's History of Poetry," TAPA 104 [1974], 316-17) that the tragikos tropos which the author of this notice claims as the invention of Arion is most probably the Mixed Lydian mode, and that it was brought by him from Lesbos and employed in a primitive form of tragedy. Euripides is represented as composing in the Mixed Lydian mode by Plutarch, The Right Way of Listening 46b.

"threnodic" harmonies.[20] And, as we have seen, Aristotle cites it as an example of the kind of harmony which affects its listeners with "grief and apprehension" (*odyrtikoterōs kai synestēkotōs*).[21] But Mixed Lydian was not the only tragic mode, even for choruses. Aristoxenus testifies to the central importance of Dorian music in tragedy, and when he says that "tragic laments were at one time set to the Dorian mode,"[22] he suggests that its use was not limited to the songs of "heroes." Taking into account the evident similarity between the Dorian and Hypodorian modes—both, it seems, were "magnificent and stately" in character[23]—it is a reasonable supposition that one or both of these modes were mentioned by the author of the *Problems* as sharing with Mixed Lydian, though to a lesser extent, that "mournful and inactive character" which is particularly suited to the songs of a tragic chorus. Finally, Aristoxenus also informs us that it was Sophocles who first "made use of Phrygian tune-composition in his own songs" or who introduced the Phrygian mode into tragedy.[24]

There can be no doubt that the distinction adopted by Aristotle in the last chapter of the *Politics* was also present to the author of the *Problems*. Two of Aristotle's categories are expressly named. The Hypophrygian and Hypodorian harmonies, those most expressive of the action appropriate to the heroes of tragedy, are distinctly (if in different degrees) "prac-

20. *Rep.* 398e1–2.
21. For the adverbial form *synestēkotōs*, *LSJ* cites only this passage, translating "in a constrained way"; Susemihl-Hicks render "with restraint, oppressively"; D. B. Munro (*The Modes of Greek Music* [Oxford, 1894], p. 12) "depressed"; Newman (on 1340a42) compares the Stoic idea of the "compression" or "contraction" of the mind through pain. The meaning is, I would suggest, rather different. *Synistasthai* may mean "be drawn up in a battle line, be at odds with" (*LSJ* B.II.1–2), and derivatively "be at odds with oneself, be troubled, uneasy, apprehensive" (B.VI; cf. *systasis* B.I.1). For a clear use of the perfect participle in this sense consider Menander *Perikeiromenē* 291 Körte.
22. [Plutarch] *On Music* 1136e = Aristoxenus fr. 82 Wehrli.
23. Compare *Problems* 922b14–15 with Aristoxenus fr. 81 Wehrli and *Pol.* 1342b12–13. Cf. Abert, pp. 82–83.
24. *Life of Sophocles* 23 = Aristoxenus fr. 79 Wehrli.

tical"; the Phrygian harmony is "enthusiastic and bacchic"; and Aristotle's third category is, I think, unmistakably implied. Although the author chooses to emphasize less the distinctive character of the harmonies that are mournful and inactive than what they share with the other harmonies, it is clear that they form a separate group; and although Mixed Lydian rather than Dorian is presented as most characteristic of this group, "ethical" would seem an appropriate designation. Both Dorian and Mixed Lydian are expressive of character in the sense that both represent the character of the soul in an immediate or direct way (rather than through its reflection in action or in the distorting medium of frenzy). Mixed Lydian indeed represents passion rather than character properly speaking, but passion is a constituent element of the character of the soul broadly understood.

It is misleading, then, to connect Aristotle's distinction of the kinds of tunes, as is frequently done, with the distinction of the objects of poetic imitation—*ēthos, pathos, praxis*—that is suggested at one point in the *Poetics*.[25] The distinction adopted in the *Politics* is a conventional one, and it cannot be assumed that it is one with which Aristotle was entirely satisfied; what is more, Aristotle also distinguishes in the *Poetics* between *praxis* and *ēthos* simply.[26] In the account of tragic music in the *Problems*, the category of "ethical" modes evidently embraces both the "ethical" Dorian and the "passionate" Mixed Lydian. And while it is true that the enthusiasm characteristic of Phrygian music is treated as a "passion," it is equally true that the connection is not regarded as self-evident: the suitability of the Phrygian mode for tragic choruses (and by that fact its resemblance to the Mixed Lydian) stands in need of argument. That the category of enthusiastic music does not embrace the passionate modes generally—that the Phrygian mode is the on-

25. *Poet.* 1447a27–28. Thus Newman on 1341b32, Susemihl-Hicks on 1341b34, Busse, p. 44, Rostagni, pp. 49–50.
26. Consider *Poet.* 1450a16 ff. Aristotle also distinguishes between *ēthikē* and *pathētikē tragōidia* (1455b32–56a1; cf. 1459b7–9).

ly properly enthusiastic mode—is confirmed by the account of the *Politics*. No mode apart from the Phrygian is described as "frenzied" or as capable of "making men enthusiastic"; and, indeed, Aristotle plainly indicates that the effect of Phrygian music, like that of Dorian, is unique or unparalleled (1340b4–5; cf. 1342b1–3). It is true that the Phrygian mode has something in common with the Mixed Lydian mode or with ethical-passionate music generally. But it is also true that all the harmonies have something in common with music of that kind, including the "practical" harmonies. For "actions," as we learn from another passage in the *Problems,* are "signs of character."[27] As we have learned from the *Politics,* all music is fundamentally ethical in the broad sense of that term.

Aristotle's distinction of the kinds of tunes presupposes, then, something like the following distinction among harmonies. The Phrygian harmony corresponds to the category of "enthusiastic" tunes. To the category of "practical" tunes belong the Hypophrygian (or Ionian) and the Hypodorian (or Aeolian) harmonies. To the category of "ethical" tunes belong, finally, both the Dorian harmony and the harmonies of the Lydian group—the relaxed or soft Lydian (clearly referred to by Aristotle, though not named, in the account of Chapter 5: cf. 1340b2–3 with 42b20 ff.), the strained or threnodic Lydian (implicitly referred to in connection with Mixed Lydian, 1340a42–b1), and the Mixed Lydian. The last category, obviously, is the least homogeneous, and it is necessary to distinguish further between the properly ethical—the "most ethical"—Dorian harmony and the "passionate" harmonies of the Lydian group.[28]

27. *Problems* XIX.27.919b36–37; cf. 29.920a5–7.
28. The view taken here of the categorization of the harmonies is in essential agreement with that of Abert (pp. 96–97), except that he is inclined to include the relaxed or "sympotic" Lydian in the category of "enthusiastic" harmonies. Susemihl-Hicks (pp. 630–31) place Mixed Lydian as well as the strained or threnodic Lydian in the "enthusiastic" class; but they are correct in pointing out that the related Lydian must be considered an "ethical" rather than "enthusiastic" mode.

4. The Catharsis Question

In the sequel, Aristotle proceeds to the promised discussion of catharsis. His explanation is as follows:

> For the passion that strongly affects some souls is present in all, but differs by greater or less, for example, pity and fear, and again enthusiasm; and there are some who come to be possessed by this motion, but by means of the sacred tunes, when they use the tunes that put the soul in a frenzy, we see them settling down as if obtaining a cure and a catharsis. This same thing, then, the pitying and the fearful and in general those gripped by passion must also experience, and others insofar as each is affected by such things, and for all there must be a certain catharsis and a feeling of relief accompanied by pleasure. [1342a4–15]

This passage represents Aristotle's most extended utterance on the subject of catharsis. As such, it is of central importance in any interpretation of the doctrine (if it can be called a doctrine) of tragic catharsis in the *Poetics*. Unfortunately, the relation between tragic poetry and the catharsis of pity and fear of which Aristotle speaks here is quite obscure. Especially since Aristotle appears to refer his readers to a fuller discussion of catharsis in the (no longer extant) second book of the *Poetics*, it is difficult to believe that the catharsis of pity and fear can be anything other than the tragic catharsis of the *Poetics*. On the other hand, it is necessary to keep in mind that Aristotle is engaged in a discussion, not of poetry, nor even of "music" in a general sense, but rather of "tunes and harmonies." And if there is one thing that is clear from the discussion of tragedy in the *Poetics*, it is that the effect of tragedy does not depend on its music or indeed on any of the accompaniments of actual tragic performances: according to Aristotle, the effect of tragedy is primarily if not entirely the work of its poetry and in particular of its plot.[29] There is, in

29. *Poet.* 1450b15–19, 1453b3–8, 1462a9–18. Cf. Else, *Aristotle's Poetics,* pp. 440–41, Croissant, p. 58. Susemihl-Hicks (on 1342a7) find it "more than probable" that the catharsis of Chapter 7 is a musical catharsis which has nothing to do with tragedy. It must be said that the difficulty has not often been seriously faced.

addition, the problem of the exact relation between the cathar-sis of pity and fear and the catharsis of enthusiasm. If it is in-deed tragedy which is here meant, is tragedy, or tragic music, fundamentally "enthusiastic" in character? Is tragedy altogether analogous in its nature and effect to enthusiastic music or enthusiastic poetry? That Aristotle intends such an analogy could seem to be suggested by the fact that, according to the teaching of the *Poetics,* tragedy originated in perfor-mances of dithyrambic poetry, a kind of poetry that Aristotle will characterize as "frenzied" or "passionate" and hence as the poetry best suited to a musical accompaniment in the Phrygian mode (1342b1–12).[30] On the other hand, it has to be admitted that Aristotle gives no hint in the *Poetics* of a substan-tive similarity between tragedy and dithyramb, and is com-pletely silent as to the possible cathartic effect of poetry of this sort. As for the question of music, we have seen that the Peripatetic author of the *Problems,* while admitting and even stressing the propriety of the use of Phrygian or enthusiastic music in tragedy, leaves no doubt that the ethical and practical modes have and should have the dominant position.

In the general eagerness to find some solid ground for an in-terpretation of tragic catharsis, the particular difficulties posed by the context of Aristotle's argument have usually been brushed aside, or else very inadequately treated. In what has now become the received interpretation, the catharsis of pity and fear is understood to be precisely analogous to the catharsis of enthusiasm. Both enthusiastic music and tragic poetry provide catharsis and a feeling of pleasure to "all." Both enthusiastic music and tragedy purge the passions that they arouse or stimulate by means of those passions themselves; they purge the passions in and through arousing them or through arousing

30. *Poet.* 1449a9–11. ". . . tragedy retained from its origins the general character [of dithyramb], the use of the flute and of the Phrygian and Hypophrygian modes" (Croissant, p. 61). In fact, the Phrygian mode was not employed in tragedy before Sophocles, according to Aristoxenus (fr. 79 Wehrli = *Life of Sophocles* 23).

them to a fever pitch. Further, they purge altogether the passions in question. Like enthusiasm, pity and fear are passions which resemble if they are not indistinguishable from "diseases"; they are wholly unsalutary, and require not moderation or "purification" but healing, "evacuation," or "purgation." In spite of the fact that the "healing" (*iatreia*) of enthusiasm takes place in a context of religion or ritual, catharsis as Aristotle conceives it is best understood not as a kind of religious purification but as a kind of medical cure. Catharsis is analogous if not identical to the practice of homoeopathic treatment in medicine. Indeed, it may be necessary in the last analysis to understand pity and fear as well as enthusiasm less as passions of the soul than as diseases in the precise sense, as disorders which are at least as much physiological as psychological in character and origin.[31]

This is not the place to undertake an investigation or even an adequate review of the theory and practice of catharsis prior to Aristotle. In any event, I doubt whether such an investigation can be of more than limited usefulness in determining Aristotle's own position. It seems much more likely that Aristotle's

31. This is in brief the interpretation of Jacob Bernays, *Grundzüge der verlorenen Abhandlung des Aristoteles über Wirkung der Tragödie* (Breslau, 1857) = *Zwei Abhandlungen über die aristotelische Theorie des Drama* (Berlin, 1880), pp. 1–117. Though Bernays' emphasis on the strictly medical character of catharsis, and in particular his understanding of catharsis as simple purgation (*Entladung*), have not gone unchallenged (see, for example, Rostagni, pp. 15–16, Croissant, pp. 64–68, Pierre Boyancé, *Le culte des Muses chez les philosophes grecs* [Paris, 1936], pp. 186, 197–98, Rudolf Stark, *Aristotelesstudien* [Munich, 1954], p. 40), his interpretation is still the prevailing one. In recent scholarship there has been a tendency to understand catharsis and the passions affected by it in more strictly physiological terms; see in particular Schadewaldt, pp. 129 ff., Helmut Flashar, "Die medizinischen Grundlagen der Lehre von der Wirkung der Dichtung in der griechischen Poetik," *Hermes* 84 (1956), 19 ff. Summaries of the controversy and of more recent work may be found in Flashar, pp. 12–18, Else, *Aristotle's Poetics*, pp. 225 ff., and D. W. Lucas, *Aristotle's Poetics* (Oxford, 1968), pp. 278 ff. The study of Alexandre Nicev, *L'énigme de la catharsis tragique dans Aristote* (Sofia, 1970), rejects most of the assumptions of Bernays and his followers (see particularly pp. 5–15) and develops an alternative interpretation which, while unpersuasive in many respects, points in what I shall try to show is the right direction.

use of the term catharsis is unprecedented than that it can be explained as the borrowing or residue of a particular doctrine, tradition, or practice. As was pointed out earlier, Aristotle does not promise in Chapter 7 that his reliance on authority will be in all respects complete; and the very fact that so much of the subsequent discussion is taken up by an explanation of the phenomenon of catharsis—an explanation, it should be added, which Aristotle himself admits to be less than adequate—suggests strongly that in the matter of catharsis Aristotle's authorities can have provided little help. An unprejudiced examination of the relevant material—something which, as far as I am aware, is very much lacking—will yield, I think, the same conclusion. The remarks that follow can do no more than prepare such an examination.

5. Catharsis in Greek Culture

There is, to begin with, the question of catharsis and medicine. That the catharsis of which Aristotle speaks in the last chapter of the *Politics* must be understood to be in some sense a medical cure will be disputed by no one. But it is an entirely different matter to assert that a satisfactory explanation of Aristotelian catharsis is to be sought in the theory or practice of Greek medicine. There is an obvious and serious difficulty with such an interpretation, though it is one not often discussed in the literature on this subject. The catharsis of which Aristotle speaks is manifestly a homoeopathic cure. But it is more than doubtful whether catharsis in the medical sense is homoeopathic, or indeed whether Greek medicine even recognized the principle of homoeopathic treatment. Aristotle seems only to reflect the consensus of the earliest medical writers when he remarks that "cures [*iatreiai*] come about by nature through opposites."[32]

At first sight, a more promising source for Aristotle than scientific medicine would seem to be Pythagoreanism. Although the evidence is sparse and in some cases of very

32. *Eth. Nic.* 1104b17–18. Compare Hippocrates *On Winds* 1, *On the Sacred Disease* 21, *On the Nature of Man* 9; cf. *Aphorisms* II.22.

doubtful value, it seems that the early Pythagoreans recognized in theory and used in practice a "catharsis" of the passions or the soul by way of music; and it has been argued that it is this doctrine, adapted and in certain respects possibly distorted, which appears in the discussion of music in the *Politics*. But it is relatively easy to see that the apparent similarities between Pythagorean catharsis and Aristotelian catharsis are indeed only apparent. The Pythagoreans, unlike Aristotle, rejected for the purposes of catharsis not only the flute but every variety of enthusiastic music. Unlike Aristotle, they regarded musical catharsis as an essentially private or individual therapy designed to "tame" or subdue the passions and thereby to prepare the soul for a life devoted to contemplation.[33]

33. The argument for a Pythagorean origin of Aristotelian catharsis has been made chiefly by Rostagni (pp. 65-70) and Hermann Koller (*Mimesis*, pp. 68-69, 98-119, 132). The most complete account of Pythagorean practice is that of Iamblichus (*Life of Pythagoras*, 64-68, 110-14, 224 Deubner); see also Plutarch *On the Moral Virtues* 441e, *On Isis and Osiris* 384a, Theon of Smyrna 12 Hiller, Porphyry *Life of Pythagoras* 35 Nauck. Rostagni attempts to distinguish between two kinds of musical therapy recognized by the Pythagoreans: (allopathic) *katartysis* or *hēmerōsis*, the "taming" of the soul in preparation for philosophy, and (homoeopathic) *katharsis*. As appears, however, from Iamblichus *Life of Pythagoras* 68, *katharsis* and *katartysis* are synonymous, and Rostagni's interpretation of 224 *epiteinontes kai anientes achri tou metrou* seems certainly wrong: the phrase refers not to the homoeopathic effect of one kind of music but to the allopathic effect of different kinds of music. Rostagni's use of Iamblichus *On the Mysteries* III.10 is vitiated by the fact that this passage seems to betray at least as much Peripatetic (or Neoplatonic) as Pythagorean influence (see Croissant, pp. 125-28). Koller's attempt to show that a Pythagorean doctrine of homoeopathic catharsis with respect to enthusiasm is reflected in a passage of Aristides Quintilianus (III.25) overlooks the fact that Aristides earlier (II.19) speaks of Pythagorean catharsis as a cleansing effected by the measured music of the lyre of pollution caused by the "irrational" music of the flute. Cf. Kahl, p. 22, Busse, p. 49, Croissant, pp. 49-56, Stark, p. 45. In an important passage to which Nicev (pp. 283 ff.) has called attention recently, Olympiodorus (*Commentary On Plato's First Alcibiades* 145-46 Westerink) distinguishes a "Pythagorean mode" of catharsis from, among others, an "Aristotelian mode." His brief description of the former—a mode "which is unreliable, making one taste the passions with a fingertip, just as doctors do in administering 'a little of the worse'" (*hos kai sphaleros, akrōi daktylōi poiōn apogeuesthai tōn pathōn, hōi kai hoi iatroi chrōntai tōi 'smikrōi cheiron' paralambanontes*)—suggests a prophylactic treatment rather than any form of cure or therapy.

The origin of a notion of homoeopathic catharsis is to be sought, I believe, not in scientific medicine nor even in the pseudo-science of the Pythagoreans, but rather in certain magical and religious beliefs which science had from the beginning consciously opposed.[34] The scientific view that diseases are cured by their opposites must be understood in the light of the prescientific view that it is precisely the cause of a disease or an evil which supplies the most efficacious remedy against it. If it is Dionysus who visits men with the madness of bacchic frenzy, it is also Dionysus who can best release men from that madness: Dionysus Baccheios and Dionysus Lysios are aspects of the same godhead.[35] The cure of religious ecstasy or "enthusiasm" in and by means of a bacchic or ecstatic ritual is the phenomenon to which Aristotle appeals when he attempts to explain the nature of catharsis. At the same time, however, it is necessary to distinguish carefully between the popular understanding of the working of bacchic and corybantic ritual and Aristotle's understanding of it. In the popular view, the "catharsis" effected by rites of this kind is in the first place, and above all, a ritual purification. It is not primarily a psychic or psychological catharsis; and, in fact, the ritual in question appears to have been inseparable from the actual excitement of bacchic frenzy.[36] It is only secondarily and as it were acciden-

34. Consider particularly Heraclitus fr. B5 Diels-Kranz: "they are purified [kathairontai] by polluting themselves with other blood, just as if one were to wade into mud in order to cleanse oneself of mud." According to a Hippocratic author, it is ignorance and superstition which induce men to rely on the "easy method of healing" by way of "purifications [katharmoisin] and charms" (On the Sacred Disease 1).

35. Dionysus is also called Iatros (Athenaeus I.22e, 36b). See Erwin Rohde, Psyche, 8th ed. (New York, 1960), pp. 286–87 and n. 21; E. R. Dodds, The Greeks and the Irrational (Berkeley, 1966), p. 273 and n. 19.

36. Cf. Euripides Bacchae 72 ff. This is one of two passages cited by Dodds (p. 76 and n. 78) as evidence that the social function of early Dionysiac ritual was "essentially cathartic, in the psychological sense." The other is Servius Commentary on Vergil's Georgics I.166: "the sacred rites of father Liber were aimed at the purgation of the soul." That Servius is speaking of a "psychological" purgation is rendered highly doubtful, however, by another passage not cited by Dodds: "In all the sacred rites of Liber there are these

tally that bacchic or corybantic rites can be understood to be "cathartic" in the psychological sense. For a catharsis of this sort would evidently be needed or wanted, not by their votaries as such, but only by persons who happened to be genuinely "possessed" by a divinely visited madness—a madness of an entirely different order than the "frenzy" temporarily induced by the ritual itself.[37]

Finally, to the extent to which the genuine or psychological "healing" (*iasis*) of madness actually practiced in these cults was understood to be a kind of catharsis, it was understood to be effected by religious means, by ritual purification, rather than by music or dance as such.[38] Aristotle's understanding is, of course, quite different. For him, the "cure" (*iatreia*) of enthusiastic madness is effected not by ritual purification but by

---

three kinds of purgation: either they are purged by pitch and sulphur, or cleansed by water, or fanned with air" (*Commentary on Vergil's Aeneid* VI.741). Dodd's position is a peculiar one in that he himself stresses that *ekstasis* was the "aim" of the Dionysian cult (p. 77). Cf. Croissant, pp. 9–11.

37. In spite of the objection raised by Susemihl-Hicks (p. 647, n. 1), Döring is correct in pointing out (p. 252) that the ritual itself cannot have been considered the source of the pollution which demanded ritual cleansing. If there was a cure for ordinary bacchic excitement, it was external to the ritual itself and allopathic in character—the "catharsis of enthusiasm" practiced by the Pythagoreans (cf. Iamblichus *Life of Pythagoras* 112 Deubner and n. 33 above). Iamblichus clearly distinguishes between the "excitement" and the "healing" of enthusiasm in the ritual (*On the Mysteries* III.9 *empoiein ē iatreuein ta pathē tēs paratropēs*), and he seems to distinguish a homoeopathic and an allopathic method of healing (III.10 *tēn tou homoiou katadochēn kai tēn tou enantiou aphairesin iatreian tina pherein*). Theophrastus speaks of music as "healing severe excitations of the mind [*tas epi makron gignomenas tēs dianoias ekstaseis*]" (fr. 88 Wimmer).

38. Melampus was said to have cured the madness of the daughters of Proteus "by secret sacrifices and purifications [*katharmois*]" (Pausanias VIII.18.3; cf. Apollodorus II.2.2). When Dionysus himself was struck with madness he went to Phrygia where he was "purified . . . and learned the rites" (Apollodorus III.5.1); cf. Plato *Phaedrus* 244d–e. For the character of the "purifications" in question see Rohde, p. 287 and nn. 25 and 26. In the extended discussion of *Laws* 790d–91a, Plato describes the religious curing of madness not as *katharsis* but as *ta tōn Korybantōn iamata* or *hai tōn ekphronōn baccheiōn iaseis*.

the music accompanying it. Accordingly, he uses "catharsis" to signify not the ritual purification but the musical "cure" itself. In the last analysis, Aristotle uses catharsis in a sense that is appropriate less to religious discourse than to the rational language of scientific medicine. He uses it nevertheless in a sense that is peculiar to him.

6. Enthusiasm, Pity, and Fear

Is the catharsis of pity and fear of which Aristotle speaks in fact precisely analogous to the catharsis of enthusiasm? There are good reasons, I think, for believing that it is not. When Aristotle first introduces the subject of catharsis, he remarks: "as to what we mean by catharsis, we will now speak of it simply [haplōs], but again and more clearly in our discussion of poetic art" (1341b38-40). To judge from the manner in which the subsequent argument has been interpreted, Aristotle is usually understood to say that he will speak of catharsis by itself, in essence or essentials, without elaborate explanations; that the discussion might lack a certain clarity is only the consequence of the intrinsic difficulty of a notion of musical or poetic catharsis. And yet Aristotle had announced at the very outset that he would not provide an "accurate treatment of particulars" but would instead distinguish "in a legal manner" and speak of "the general types" (1341b30-32). Aristotle speaks not "simply" but "generally." His account of catharsis will be a general account which dispenses with the "distinctions" that would be required in an accurate or clear account of particulars.[39]

That there is indeed a fundamental "distinction" between the catharsis of pity and fear and the catharsis of enthusiasm appears from the following considerations. According to Aristotle, the catharsis of pity and fear is effective not only in the case of the pitying or the fearful or the "passionate"

39. Haplōs "can also be that which is spoken in a simple and universal sense, as opposed to a more accurate definition of a thing" (Hermann Bonitz, Index Aristotelicus [Berlin, 1870], 77a52-55). Consider especially Magn. Mor. 1185a38.

generally but also in the case of "others insofar as each is affected by such things": the "certain catharsis" (*katharsis tis*) of which Aristotle speaks here is a catharsis which affects "all" (1342a14). As for enthusiasm, Aristotle says only that it is a "passion" (*pathos*) which affects "every soul" in some degree, and that "certain people" (*tines*) who come to be "possessed" (*katokōchimoi*) by it are to obtain a healing and catharsis by listening to a certain kind of enthusiastic music, the "sacred tunes."

Now it is almost certain that the "sacred tunes" of which Aristotle here speaks are to be identified with the tunes of Olympus he had mentioned previously.[40] What is the effect of the tunes of Olympus generally speaking? Aristotle had earlier told us that "it is generally agreed that they make the souls inspired" (*homologoumenōs poiei tas psychas enthousiastikas* 1340a9–11). In the present passage, he describes the sacred tunes as "tunes arousing the soul to frenzy" (*tois exorgiazousi tēn psychēn melesi* 1342a9–10).[41] The tunes of Olympus were flute melodies primarily in the Phrygian mode; but the flute and Phrygian music alike are "frenzied and passionate" (*orgiastika kai pathētika* 1342b3). Generally speaking, the tunes of Olympus affect men precisely by *making* them "enthusiastic." Unlike the catharsis of pity and fear, the catharsis of enthusiasm does not affect all; it is not a necessary consequence of the experience of enthusiastic music. It would rather seem that enthusiastic music (or enthusiastic music of a certain kind) effects a catharsis of enthusiasm only in the case of those who were "possessed" by the passion of enthusiasm prior to and independently of any experience of enthusiastic music.

40. Or those compositions of Olympus which were in the Phrygian mode (cf. Susemihl-Hicks, pp. 621–22). Plato has Alcibiades remark of the auletic pieces of Olympus that "they alone make men possessed and, through being divine, reveal those who are in need of the gods and the rites" (*Symposium* 215c). Cf. *Minos* 318b and Proclus *Commentary on Plato's Republic* I.62,5–9 Kroll, where the Phrygian character of "the tunes of Olympus" is taken for granted.

41. For the meaning of *exorgiazein* compare Philodemus *On Music* III.65 (49,8–10) Kemke: *exorgiazousi kai pros baccheian agousi.* Cf. Croissant, p. 4.

Properly speaking, as it seems, the tunes of Olympus, and Phrygian or enthusiastic music generally, make men "enthusiastic" only in a qualified sense. Enthusiasm properly speaking is not aroused by enthusiastic music or by any other kind of music.[42] Genuine enthusiasm is, indeed, not so much a passion as a pathological disorder or disease;[43] it is a mental disturbance, a kind of madness. While it is true that a certain disposition or susceptibility to enthusiasm exists in all men, genuine enthusiastic "possession" is an experience which affects only a few; it is qualitatively different from the common experience of enthusiasm which is induced by religious rituals of a certain kind. While most men are susceptible in greater or lesser degree to ritually induced enthusiastic excitement, the susceptibility to enthuastic "possession" is abnormal. In the last analysis, it appears to be determined by a particular physical condition, an abnormal or unnatural preponderance of black bile. "Melancholics" are particularly susceptible to enthusiastic possession because they are "qualitatively different in character" from most men.[44]

The tunes of Olympus have, then, a double effect. In the case of most men, they arouse or stimulate frenzy or enthusiastic passion. In the case of those who are already

42. A good deal of confusion has surrounded this point. Boyancé (pp. 196-97) cites Cicero *On Divination* I.50.114 as proof that the *kinēsis* of which Aristotle speaks (1342a8) is a *kinēsis* of enthusiasm by means of music. In fact, the passage shows just the opposite: Cicero's phrase *ardore aliquo inflammati* applies to enthusiasm induced in the activity of divination; it is only compared to musically induced enthusiasm (*ut ii qui sono quodam vocum et Phrygiis cantibus incitantur*).

43. Cf. Susemihl-Hicks, p. 642.

44. The crucial text is *Problems* XXX.1 (on its authorship see Croissant, pp. 74-79). Croissant (pp. 46-47) points to 954b20 *pasi memiktai ti tēs dynameōs* as proof that there is only a difference of degree between those who are melancholic by nature and most men. But she fails to pay attention to the immediate sequel: "but those who have it in the extreme are qualitatively different in their characters . . .; those who share in this mixture to a slight degree are the average sort, but those who have a quantity of it are dissimilar to most men." Aristides Quintilianus implicitly distinguishes between normal enthusiasm and "unmixed" (*akratos*) enthusiasm (II.5-6; consider particularly 58,21-28 Winnington-Ingram).

"possessed" by the disease of enthusiasm or who are suffering the temporary derangement of enthusiastic madness, they calm or exhaust frenzy by effecting a catharsis of enthusiasm. However, one may have to understand the enthusiastic "passion" which is stimulated by Phrygian music generally, it seems clear that the catharsis effected by the sacred tunes is very precisely the healing of a disease or a pathological disorder, and that the disease in question has its roots if not its origin in the body. Whether or to what extent the catharsis of enthusiasm may have been conceived by Aristotle as a physical or strictly medical cure is not easy to say. To judge from the account in the *Politics,* the cure is of a psychic rather than a physical nature, though it may well have to be understood as a cure of the (psychic) symptoms of enthusiastic madness rather than of its permanent (physical) causes. What can perhaps be said is that the catharsis of enthusiasm is a cure which, while temporary, is radical or complete. If enthusiastic possession is indeed a kind of madness, it makes no sense to speak of a moderation or purification of the excesses of enthusiasm, or of a transformation of excessive or unhealthy enthusiasm into normal or healthy enthusiasm: the "melancholic" enthusiasm recognized by Peripatetic writers is clearly a manic-depressive disorder which by its nature excludes a healthy mean.[45]

45. Boyancé's attempt to distinguish between a normal or healthy passion of enthusiasm and a disease of enthusiastic madness (pp. 189-90) rests on a misreading of *Problems* XXX.1. The phrase "natural mixture" (*physikē krasis*) does not refer to a normal or healthy admixture of black bile but rather, as is clear from the immediate context (954a27–34), to a natural preponderance of black bile. The author is distinguishing between those in whom such a preponderance is natural and permanent (*hosois en tēi physei synestē krasis toiautē* a28–29) and those in whom it arises from a temporary cause (*nosēma ti melancholikon*) but one that does not affect their character, while the former are "qualitatively different in character," and are either actually mad or susceptible to seizure by "mad or enthusiastic diseases" (*nosēmata manika ē enthousiastika*), "when they arise not in the manner of a simple disease but through a natural preponderance" (*hotan mē nosēmati genontai alla physikēi krasei*). There are, in other words, two kinds of enthusiastic disease, a temporary or simple disease arising in otherwise normal people and not affecting character, and a chronic condition arising in those who suffer from a permanent preponderance of black bile and are

Let us now consider how matters stand with regard to pity and fear. In spite of some recent attempts to interpret *eleos* and *phobos* in Aristotle's usage or in the Greek understanding generally less as passions than as physical or pathological symptoms of certain psychic states,[46] it remains true that Aristotle distinguishes between passions that are normal and passions that are diseased.[47] Whereas diseased passions are simply unsalutary or contrary to nature, normal passions, like the virtues, permit of "excess and deficiency" and hence of a mean which is not only not harmful but which may even be salutary. "For example, in fearing [*phobēthēnai*], feeling con-

---

thus affected in their character. This is why "all melancholics are exceptional not through disease but through nature" (955a40); the natural, healthy, or normal condition is that of most men, who have only a small share of such a mixture (954b25–26). Helmut Flashar, *Melancholie und Melancholiker* (Berlin, 1966), pp. 60–67, detects in this passage an implicit theory of the mean: when the excess of bile is neither overheated nor overcooled, there exists that "normale Abnormalität" which is characteristic of philosophic, political, and poetic genius; when it is overheated, enthusiasm and madness result. It can only be said that the relation between genius on the one hand and enthusiasm on the other is left quite obscure.

46. The view of Schadewaldt and Flashar; see also Max Pohlenz, "Furcht und Mitleid? Ein Nachwort," *Hermes* 84 (1956), 49 ff. Schadewaldt speaks of "seelisch-leibliche Elementaraffekte," arguing that "pity" and "fear" and their modern equivalents inadequately express the Greek notions *eleos* and *phobos,* which he renders respectively as "Jammer" or "Rührung" and "Schauder" or "Schrecken." Aristotle does not deny that the passions have a certain physical existence, or even that physical expressions of the passions are to a certain extent involuntary (cf. *De An.* 403a5–24); but if the passions may be said to exist "in matter," they remain for Aristotle "arguments in matter" (*logoi enhyloi, De An.* 403a25), which is to say essentially congruent with reality and therefore useful for man.

47. Compare *Eth. Nic.* 1136a8–9 with 1148b15–49a20. Aristotle appears to use the term "natural passion" (*pathos physikon*) of an abnormal passion caused by a natural or physical deformity of some kind, though abnormal passions caused by "habituation" may also be included; consider particularly the description of pathological fear (1149a4–9). He uses the term "human passion" (*pathos anthrōpinon*) of those normal passions which are least blameworthy when carried to excess (cf. 1147b20–48a11, 1149b4–11). Cf. *Eth. Eud.* 1228b35–37.

fidence, desiring, pitying [*eleēsai*], and in being pleased or pained generally there is a greater and less, and neither is good.''[48]

A distinction between normal and diseased passions, between passions and pathological states, is clearly present to Aristotle in the passage under consideration. Pity and fear, like enthusiasm, can come to exist in certain individuals in extreme or pathological forms, while existing normally, if to a greater or lesser degree, in all. Pathological enthusiasm, as has been seen, is susceptible to cathartic healing by music of a certain kind. ''This same thing,'' Aristotle now asserts, can happen in the case of those who experience pathological pity and fear—and indeed, as it seems, all passions that can exist in a pathological state. It can also happen, he proceeds to add, to ''others insofar as each is affected by such things,'' or to normal men insofar as each is normally affected by pity or fear or similar passions. The result is that for all there is ''a certain catharsis'' as well as ''a feeling of relief accompanied by pleasure.''

It is far from clear how close an analogy Aristotle is attempting to establish among the catharsis of pathological enthusiasm, the catharsis of pathological pity and fear, and the catharsis of normal pity and fear. In spite of his explicit statement that ''this same thing'' occurs in each case, the fact that he applies the expression ''a certain catharsis'' rather than ''catharsis'' simply to the case of pity and fear generally suggests that the catharsis of pathological pity and fear and the catharsis of normal pity and fear are not in all respects identical. It suggests, in other words, that the catharsis of enthusiasm and of similar pathological conditions is not simply the model for the catharsis of pity and fear in and through the experience of tragic poetry.

That the catharsis of enthusiasm and the catharsis of normal pity and fear are different kinds of catharsis employed for different purposes and effected by different means is fully confirmed, I believe, in the sequel. The decisive evidence is provided by the brief remark that follows directly on Aristotle's ac-

48. *Eth. Nic.* 1106b16–25; cf. 1108a30–b6.

count of the catharsis of pity and fear. After indicating that "a certain catharsis and a feeling of relief accompanied by pleasure" will be experienced by all, he goes on to say: "In a similar way the cathartic tunes too provide harmless delight to human beings" (*homoiōs de kai ta melē ta kathartika parechei charan ablabē tois anthrōpois*) (1342a15–16).

This sentence has puzzled the commentators, who generally resort to one of two equally unsatisfactory expedients: either *praktika* is read for *kathartika,* or Aristotle is understood to distinguish between the effect of cathartic "tunes" and the effect of cathartic "harmonies."[49] But apart from the fact that Aristotle had spoken previously of cathartic tunes of a certain kind (it need hardly be added that there is no evidence of textual corruption), the meaning of the sentence, taken in its context, is perfectly intelligible. When Aristotle spoke of the catharsis of enthusiasm which is effected by the sacred tunes, he did not suggest that music of this kind is pleasant either in itself or for those who are actually healed by it. When he speaks of the catharsis of pity and fear, however, he leaves no doubt that it is an experience "accompanied by pleasure," and that catharsis and pleasure alike are experienced by all. When he argues, then, that the cathartic tunes in a similar way provide pleasure or delight to human beings, what he means to say is that the sacred tunes, the tunes of Olympus, not only provide a catharsis to those who are possessed by enthusiasm but also give pleasure to ordinary men—just as the music that effects

49. The emendation *praktika* for *kathartika,* first proposed by Sauppe, has been widely accepted (cf. Susemihl-Hicks on 1342a15 and pp. 639–40, Ross on 1342a1, Busse, p. 45; Koller, *Mimesis,* p. 72, agrees that the sentence is "no longer intelligible in its current form"). Those who keep *kathartika* usually understand a distinction between cathartic "tunes" and cathartic "harmonies" (Newman, I.366; Howald, p. 195; Rostagni, p. 54; Dirlmeier, p. 81, n. 5), though Newman also suggests (on 1342a15) that the distinction is between "sacred tunes" and "cathartic tunes." Schadewaldt distinguishes the effect of cathartic "songs" from catharsis "in the events of life described previously" (p. 155; cf. Bernays, *Zwei Abhandlungen,* pp. 8–9). But Aristotle has been speaking of music in general, not of medicine, and of "tunes" in particular, not of "harmonies." A (partial) distinction between "tunes" and "harmonies" appears only in the sequel.

the catharsis of pity and fear also provides a pleasure experienced by all. What makes the similarity remarkable, however, is precisely the more fundamental difference between the two types of catharsis. For what the sacred tunes provide to human beings or to ordinary men is pleasure and only pleasure. By the same token, what they provide to those who are possessed by enthusiasm is catharsis and only (or primarily) catharsis—for it is not to be expected that a medical treatment or cure will be essentially pleasant. The sacred tunes bring catharsis only to those few who are "strongly affected" by enthusiasm or whose suffering is pathological in character; they do not bring catharsis to "others insofar as they are affected by this kind of thing" (cf. 1342a5 with 12-14). As we have seen, the normal effect of the sacred tunes—their effect, that is, on normal men or on human beings generally—is precisely to "heighten frenzy in the soul" (1342a9-10), to "make the souls enthusiastic" (1340a10-11). But the "enthusiasm" that most men are capable of experiencing is far removed from that pathological enthusiasm which borders on madness. Normal enthusiasm, the enthusiasm aroused by the cathartic tunes, is "harmless." The cathartic tunes provide, in addition to catharsis, "harmless delight" (*charan ablabē* 1342a16). The excitement of enthusiasm by the sacred tunes or by enthusiastic music generally is an experience that is both harmless and delightful for the great majority of men.

Aristotle's argument makes excellent sense, then, if one takes the expression "cathartic tunes" to refer, not to music that is cathartic of pity and fear, but to music that is cathartic of enthusiasm, that is, to the "sacred tunes" discussed in the previous sentence. As appeared earlier, the music associated with enthusiasm—tunes in the Phrygian mode—is quite distinct from the music associated with tragedy. Keeping in mind Aristotle's initial distinction between "ethical," "practical," and "enthusiastic" tunes as well as the argument of *Problems* XIX. 48, we may reasonably assume that Aristotle is here implicitly distinguishing between "cathartic" or "enthusiastic" tunes and the tunes proper to performance of tragedy. These would include, though perhaps without being limited to, "practical" tunes. Even if one retains the reading of the manuscripts at 1342a15, then, one is not compelled to suppose that the category of "practical tunes" has inexplicably dropped out of the argument. As to whether "practical tunes" must then be understood as the primary motor of catharsis within the tragic performance, we here note only that Aristotle seems to go out of his way to avoid linking the catharsis of pity and fear directly with a particular type of music, or indeed with music altogether.

By way of summary of the foregoing interpretation, it may be helpful to provide a paraphrase of the crucial passage (1342a4–16) treating enthusiasm and catharsis. Aristotle argues, I believe, as follows. Pity, fear, and enthusiasm are passions which exist in greater or lesser degree in all men, but which are also susceptible to pathological development—involving, that is, a difference of kind not degree—in some few men. In the case of enthusiasm, the corresponding pathological state can be cured by a quasi-medical treatment centered on the use of a certain kind of music—a kind of music which stimulates enthusiastic passion in normal men, but in pathological cases acts as a homoeopathic purgative or catharsis, releasing the sufferer completely from the symptoms if not the underlying causes of his condition. The same thing occurs in the case of men who are pathologically affected by pity, fear, or similar passions. Something similar also occurs in the case of men who are normally affected by pity, fear, or similar passions in greater or lesser degree. For all such men, there occurs some kind of catharsis together with a feeling of relief accompanied by pleasure. In a similar way, the cathartic tunes too—the tunes which effect the catharsis of pathological enthusiasm—provide pleasure to normal individuals. They do not indeed provide catharsis to normal individuals, but the enthusiastic passion they stimulate is itself "harmless" or non-pathological in character.

7. The Character of Tragic Catharsis

If the interpretation offered here is correct, what conclusions can be drawn regarding the specific character of tragic catharsis? Is the catharsis of pity and fear, or of normal pity and fear, to be understood as a total purgation or a partial purification? In the first place, whatever the similarities or differences between the operation of catharsis in the case of enthusiasm and the pathological forms of pity and fear, there is no reason to suppose that Aristotle takes his bearing from the abnormal or pathological as such. The spectators of tragedy must be assumed to be, at least in the very great majority, normal individuals who are subject to passions such as pity and fear in normal if varying degrees. What kind of catharsis can be supposed to be appropriate under such circumstances?

The tendency of recent interpretations of catharsis has been to blur this issue, and to treat pity and fear as passions which, if not actually pathological, are in some degree abnormal and hence simply undesirable. Yet Aristotle elsewhere makes it perfectly clear that pity and fear are for him fully normal or natural passions, and hence potentially beneficial. Pity, Aristotle tells us, is a passion "belonging to a good character" (ēthous chrēstou); it is closely allied with a sense of justice.[50] As regards fear, "there are some things one ought to fear and where it is noble to fear, and others where it is not base, for example loss of reputation; for the one who is afraid is a decent man and moved by shame, while the one who is not afraid is shameless."[51] Indeed, not even the fear of death or suffering is wholly devoid of practical benefit.[52] It is, to say the least, implausible that Aristotle could have been satisfied to recommend a total purgation of passions which he regarded as being not only not necessarily harmful but even potentially beneficial

50. *Rhet.* 1368b8–15.
51. *Eth. Nic.* 1115a12–14; cf. 1108a30–35.
52. Compare *Rhet.* 1382b29–83a3 with *Pol.* 1334a22–28: those who are not exposed to the fear of death or suffering tend to become bold, disdainful and "criminally arrogant" (*hybristai*).

both to the individual and to the city.[53] It would be one thing if Aristotle had recommended a catharsis of pity and fear for those who are strongly affected by or excessively prone to these passions, or in whom these passions are in danger of becoming diseased. In fact, however, he recommends the catharsis of pity and fear for "all."

One may grant that the language of Aristotle's account suggests a fundamentally "medical" view of catharsis without at the same time committing oneself to the interpretation of catharsis which is at present generally accepted. For, indeed, even the medical usage of catharsis is fundamentally ambiguous. The phrase *katharsis tinos* may well mean "complete purgation [evacuation] of a certain thing" (genitive of separation); but it may equally mean "partial purgation [purification] of a certain thing" (objective genitive). And, in fact, it is the second meaning which corresponds most closely to the cor-

53. Music is described by Theophrastus (fr. 89 Wimmer) as a "movement of the soul involving a release of the evils that are caused by the passions" (*kinēsis tēs psychēs kat' apolysin ginomenē tōn dia ta pathē kakōn*). "*Pathos* is therefore a *kakon*," says Dirlmeier, and argues that such a view—Theophrastus' "*apolysis*-theory"—is central to Aristotle's conception of catharsis (pp. 90–91; cf. Flashar, "Die medizinische Grundlagen," p. 13). The inference is of course a non-sequitur, and it is wholly unwarranted. According to Seneca, "Aristotle stands as a defender of anger and forbids it to be cut out of us" (*stat Aristoteles defensor irae et vetat illam nobis exsecari*); "Aristotle says that certain passions can serve as arms if one uses them well" (*Aristoteles ait affectus quosdam si quis illis bene utatur pro armis esse*) (*On Anger* III.3.1, I.17.1; cf. Philodemus *On Anger* 31–32 [65–67] Wilke). According to Cicero (*Tusculan Disputations* IV.19–20), "the Peripatetics say that those perturbations which we think should be eliminated are not only natural but provided by nature to be useful . . . , and they say that the other sorts of passions are useful as well. Pity is useful for getting us to render assistance and alleviate the misfortunes that men suffer undeservedly . . . ; if one were to remove fear, all carefulness in life, which is greatest among those who fear the laws, the magistrates, poverty, ignominy, death, or pain, would be eliminated. In arguing thus they admit that these passions need to be pruned back, but assert that they neither can nor need be uprooted entirely, and suppose that in almost all things a mean is best" (*Peripatetici perturbationes istas, quas nos extirpandas putamus, non modo naturales esse dicunt sed etiam utiliter a natura datas . . . , reliquas quoque partes aegritudinis utiles esse dicunt, misericordiam ad opem ferendam et hominum indignorum calamitates sublevandas . . . , metum vero si qui sustulisset, omnem vitae diligentiam*

rect or technical medical usage.[54] When Aristotle speaks in the *Poetics* of tragedy as "effecting through pity and fear the catharsis of passions of this sort" (*di' eleou kai phobou perainousa tēn tōn toioutōn pathēmatōn katharsin*), it is conceivable that *tōn toioutōn pathēmatōn* is to be taken as a genitive of separation, and that Aristotle is to be understood to say that tragedy effects a complete purgation or evacuation of pity and fear.[55] But it is not, I think, very likely. In view of Aristotle's explicit statements regarding the nature of the human passions, and in particular of the passions of pity and fear, the burden of proof surely rests with those who assert rather than those who deny that Aristotle can have believed that tragedy, or tragedy at its best, substantially conflicts with the requirements of moral or political life. On the other hand, there seems little reason to assume that the

---

sublatam fore, quae summa esset in eis qui leges, qui magistratus, qui paupertatem, qui ignominiam, qui mortem, qui dolorem timerent. haec tamen ita disputant ut resecanda esse fateantur, evelli penitus dicant nec posse nec opus esse et in omnibus fere rebus mediocritatem esse optimam existiment). It seems likely that this represents the doctrine of Theophrastus' *peri pathōn* (consider fr. 72 Wimmer). The same doctrine appears to figure in Aulus Gellius XIX.12, where Herodes Atticus is reported to have argued in opposition to the Stoics that the passions "should be moderated . . . and intelligently and carefully purged" (*moderandos esse . . . et scite consideratique purgandos*). Cf. Bernays, *Zwei Abhandlungen*, pp. 66, 113-14, Rostagni, pp. 10-11.

54. For the first meaning consider particularly *Gen. An.* 738a27-28 *katharsis tōn perittōmatōn ha tou nosein aitia tois sōmasin.* Aristotle frequently uses *katharsis* as a technical term for menstruation (*Hist. An.* 583a31). In medicine, however, expressions like *katharsis cholēs* or *katharsis haimatos* refer to purification rather than evacuation; the technical term for the latter was *kenōsis.* According to Galen (*Commentary On Hippocrates' On Humors* V.12 [XVI, 105] Kühn), "Hippocrates was accustomed to speaking of evacuation when all the humors are evacuated indiscriminately, and of catharsis when the bad are evacuated according to their quality." See Susemihl-Hicks, pp. 648-50, and H. Siebeck, *Aristotles*, 4th ed. (Berlin, 1922) pp. 95 ff. (cf. Stark, p. 40).

55. Dirlmeier, p. 91, Flashar, "Die medizinischen Grundlagen," pp. 12-17, 48; cf. Max Kommerell, *Lessing und Aristoteles* (Frankfurt, 1940), pp. pp. 265 ff. Bernays saw the difficulties in this view more clearly than some of his followers, but his own solution—the complete purgation of pity and fear in tragedy, since it is only temporary, effects over time a purification or moderation of these passions (*Zwei Abhandlungen*, pp. 66-67)—is hardly satisfactory.

catharsis of enthusiasm of which Aristotle speaks in the *Politics* is anything other than a complete purgation. In short, catharsis is a "general" term, and there is every indication that tragic catharsis is of a very different character than the properly therapeutic catharsis associated with pathological enthusiasm (or even an analogous catharsis applied to the pathological forms of pity and fear).

8. *Theatrical Music and the Citizen Class*

"Accordingly," Aristotle continues,

> it is to be set down that those undertaking contests in theatrical music must use harmonies of this sort and tunes of this sort. But as there are two kinds of spectator, the one free and educated, the other vulgar and drawn from the mechanics and laborers and others of this sort, contests and spectacles are to be permitted for this sort as well with a view to relaxation. And just as their souls are distorted from the condition that is according to nature, so too are there deviations among the harmonies, and tunes that are strained and highly colored; and what is most akin by nature provides pleasure to each kind of man. Accordingly, permission is to be given to those who compete before this sort of spectator to use this particular variety of music. [1342a16–28]

The best regime as it has been outlined by Aristotle in Books VII and VIII of the *Politics* consists fundamentally of two classes or kinds of men: the citizen class properly speaking, and the class of farmers, laborers, and mechanics, slaves or serfs who are lacking in education as well as the leisure that is necessary both for the acquisition of virtue and for the enjoyment of genuine happiness (cf. 1328b33–29a2). What Aristotle now argues is this: because there are two distinct classes in the best regime, and indeed two different ways of life, a fundamental distinction must also be made with regard to the music that is to serve as the entertainment or the leisured activity of those classes. Just as the best regime consists fundamentally of two classes of men, so will it require two fundamentally different kinds of music which serve two distinct purposes. One kind of music will be permitted the "vulgar" spectator of the non-citizen class; it will be a music that serves the purpose of "relaxation" (*anapausis*). Another kind of music will be reserved for the citizen class. Although Aristotle does not here explicitly identify its purpose, there can be no doubt that the music in question is intended to supply the leisured "pastime," the *diagōgē*, of the mature citizens of the best regime.

What are the two kinds of music? Aristotle's argument is elliptical, but the main points, I think, are relatively clear. To begin with, it is necessary to realize that Aristotle is no longer concerned with "tunes" or "harmonies" alone. When Aristotle speaks of the "theatrical music" that is reserved for the citizen class, and of the "type of music" that will be permitted the noncitizen class, he is thinking not only of music in the narrow sense but of poetry as well, that is, of "music" in its most comprehensive sense. It would seem that he has been thinking of "music" in that sense for some time. Since it is not necessary to assume that "the cathartic tunes" which Aristotle mentions (1342a15) refer to anything other than "the tunes of Olympus," it is not necessary to assume that the catharsis of pity and fear of which he speaks (1342a11-15) is a catharsis effected only by "tunes" or by music in the narrow sense. In fact, it is not necessary to assume that it is a catharsis effected by music at all. While Aristotle had made clear that the catharsis of enthusiasm is effected by music of a certain kind, he fails completely to indicate the agency or instrument of the catharsis of pity and fear. Precisely because Aristotle's account of catharsis is "general" in nature, there is no good reason for believing that it contradicts the account of catharsis provided in the *Poetics*. To judge from the account in the *Poetics,* the catharsis of pity and fear has nothing to do with music in the narrow sense. There is no reason why the catharsis of pity and fear should not be understood, in the *Politics* as in the *Poetics,* to be effected by tragic poetry. It is certainly true that Aristotle's earlier account of the effect of the various harmonies leaves the definite impression that the musical mode most appropriate to tragedy is no

139

more essentially "cathartic" than the mode appropriate to enthusiastic music. Just as the tunes of Olympus and Phrygian music in general normally serve to "make" men enthusiastic (1340a9–11, b4–5), so the effect of the Mixed Lydian mode is precisely to make its hearers *more* receptive to grief or pity as well as to a certain uneasiness, apprehension, or fear (1340a42–b1).

In the immediate sequel, Aristotle says all that he will say explicitly about the music that is to constitute the *diagōgē* of mature citizens: "In a similar way the cathartic tunes too provide harmless delight to human beings. Accordingly, it is to be set down that those undertaking contests in theatrical music must use harmonies of this sort and tunes of this sort" (1342a15–18). Since "cathartic tunes" must be understood to refer only to enthusiastic tunes of a certain kind composed in the Phrygian mode, "harmonies of this sort and tunes of this sort" must plainly have a wider reference. The reference, I think, is precisely to the tunes and harmonies of tragedy, of the "theatrical music" par excellence. Implicit in Aristotle's argument is his view that "tune-composition is the greatest of the pleasant things" connected with tragedy, but has nothing to do with tragic catharsis.[56] The tunes and harmonies appropriate to tragedy, like the sacred tunes and the harmony appropriate to them, may be allowed in the theatrical music of mature citizens because they afford harmless delight to human beings.

Whether the sacred tunes as such, the "tunes of Olympus," must be supposed to form a part of the theatrical entertainment of the citizens of the best regime is not easy to say. I am inclined to think that Aristotle means only that "tunes of this sort" and the harmony appropriate to them are to be permitted within tragedy itself. It will be recalled that the author of the *Problems* insists on the suitability of the Phrygian mode for the songs of the tragic chorus. And one must wonder whether performances of purely instrumental flute music would be

56. *Poet.* 1450b15–18; cf. 1450a33–34.

altogether in keeping with the educational program of the best regime. One of Aristotle's objections to the use of the flute in the education of the young was that it precludes the use of "speech" and hence in no way contributes to "thought" (1341a24–5, b6–7). It is certainly possible that he would object on much the same grounds to its employment in the musical pastime of mature citizens. Solo flute music could seem to have too much the character of entertainment, of mere play.

9. *The New Music and the Old*

But if tragic as well as enthusiastic music is reserved for the citizen class of the best regime, what kind of music does Aristotle allow to the noncitizen class? The most important clue is provided by Aristotle's remark that "there are deviations among the harmonies, and tunes that are strained and highly colored [*tōn melōn ta syntona kai parakechrōsmena*]" (1342a24–25). It is, to begin with, significant that a distinction is drawn between "harmonies" and "tunes," a distinction evidently prepared by the reference to "harmonies" as well as "tunes" in 1342a16–17. This distinction must be understood with reference to the fact that in Greek musical practice the character of a particular tune depended not only on its "harmony" but also on its "scale" (*genos*). There were three basic types of scale, enharmonic, diatonic, and chromatic; of these the latter two admitted of a number of varieties which were called "colorings" or "shadings" (*chrōmata*). Now the use of the chromatic scale and of musical coloring in general had sharply increased in the later fifth and in the fourth century in connection with a widespread revolution in musical practice—a revolution caused, at least in the view of its opponents, by an undue attention to the requirements of a "vulgar" audience. Those who championed the older music as against the new—its greatest defender was Aristoxenus, a student of Aristotle and almost certainly his chief musical authority—regarded the chromatic scale as "unmanly, vulgar, and illiberal," and advocated a return to the "solemn, noble,

141

simple, and pure'' enharmonic.[57] When Aristotle recommends to the ''vulgar and illiberal'' class of the best regime ''tunes that are strained and highly colored,'' he is certainly thinking of the chromatic and ''colored'' music that had become popular in his own time.[58]

Considerations of this kind also serve to clarify Aristotle's view of the theatrical music of the nonvulgar class. It is no accident that the new music was itself primarily a theatrical music: Aristotle himself stresses the corrupting effect of theatrical performance on the character of the music performed as well as on the performers themselves (1341b15–16).[59] In fact, it is precisely to avoid this danger that Aristotle insists on distinguishing, and separating, vulgar and nonvulgar spectators. And it is because he does this that Aristotle is able at the same time to remove the new music from the theater, and to restore the older music to its rightful place of honor. That such a restoration is indeed contemplated by Aristotle is suggested, I believe, in the following way. When Aristotle had spoken of the theatrical music of the citizen class, he had appeared to distinguish between the harmonies proper to it and the tunes proper to it. In the light of the subsequent argument, it would seem to be the consideration of scale which underlies this distinction. It is true that Aristotle does not explicitly describe the tunes proper to theatrical music in the way that he describes the tunes proper to the music of the noncitizen class. But if, as would seem to be the case, ''tunes of this sort'' (1342a17) refers primarily to ''cathartic tunes'' (1342a15), we gain an important clue as to what Aristotle may have in mind. The cathartic tunes are, I

57. Philodemus *On Music* IV.2,15–25 (63–64) Kemke; cf. Grenfell and Hunt, *The Hibeh Papyri*, I.13.22 *oute chrōma deilous oute harmonia andreious poiei.* Compare Aristoxenus frs. 70, 76, and 124 Wehrli. Proclus (*Commentary on Plato's Timaeus* 191e–f) characterizes the enharmonic scale as ''educative'' (*paideutikon*).

58. Consider Aristoxenus *Harmonics* I.23 Meibom. For the pejorative sense of *parakechrōsmena* cf. Plutarch *Convivial Questions* III.1.1.

59. Cf. Plato *Laws* 700d, Aristoxenus frs. 76 and 124 Wehrli. Only professional musicians could play compositions in the chromatic scale, according to Aristides Quintilianus I.9 (16,10–13) Winnington-Ingram.

have tried to argue, the tunes of Olympus. According to Aristoxenus, Olympus was the originator of the enharmonic scale, the embodiment of every musical virtue.[60]

If we are correct in suggesting that Aristotle recommends not the tunes of Olympus as such but rather the employment in tragedy of "tunes of this sort," what he argues would seem to be this: those undertaking theatrical music should make use both of the harmonies characteristic of enthusiastic (as well as tragic) music and of the tunes characteristic of the compositions of Olympus. They should employ both the Phrygian mode (as well as the other modes specifically associated with tragedy) and the enharmonic scale. If this is indeed Aristotle's argument, it has a point. Tragedy in its classic phase seems always to have avoided the chromatic scale and the musical "coloring" associated with it.[61] In the modern tragedy of Agathon and his successors, however, the influence of the new music had made itself felt: tragedy too had been corrupted by a music of "unnatural colorings" (*parachrōseis*).[62]

10. Citizen and Vulgar Harmonies

What, then, of the harmonies? It seems possible to distinguish without too much difficulty the harmonies that are appropriate to the theatrical music of the citizen class. They are just the harmonies normally used in the composition of tragic music. The Phrygian harmony is clearly indicated; as for the rest, the testimony of the *Problems,* though not in all respects satisfactory, is sufficient for present purposes. The tragic mode par excellence, the harmony best adapted to the laments of the tragic chorus, is the Mixed Lydian. For more animated scenes and in particular for the songs of heroes, Hypophrygian and Hypodorian are most appropriate. Finally, Dorian should not be excluded as a harmony of choral lyric. It will be seen that

60. [Plutarch] *On Music* 1134f = Aristoxenus fr. 83 Wehrli.

61. [Plutarch] *On Music* 1137e. The one surviving piece of tragic music from the classical period employs an enharmonic scale in the Phrygian mode (Karl von Jan, *Musici Scriptores Graeci* [Leipzig, 1895], pp. 110–12).

62. Plutarch *Convivial Questions* III.1.1.

this result agrees with Aristotle's earlier indications. Aristotle had announced that every variety of harmony, the "ethical" as well as the "practical" and the "enthusiastic," would be used "with a view to listening to the performances of others" (1342a3–4); and each variety is or may be suitably employed in tragedy. Of the "ethical" harmonies there is the Mixed Lydian (and possibly the Dorian), of the "practical" the Hypohrygian and Hypodorian, and there is the "enthusiastic" Phrygian.

As regards the harmonies appropriate to the music of the noncitizen class, Aristotle limits himself to remarking that "there are deviations [*parekbaseis*] among the harmonies" (1342a23–24). The meaning of this expression is clarified to some extent by a passage occurring in Book IV of the *Politics* in which Aristotle discusses the question whether all other regimes can be understood as derivations or variant forms (*parekbaseis*) of oligarchy and democracy. It appears that music offers a certain parallel:

> It is, some assert, the same with harmonies as well; for there too they set down two kinds, the Dorian and the Phrygian, and the other systems they call either Doric or Phrygic. This is a particularly common assumption, then, regarding regimes. But the distinction we have made is truer and better, that one or two are well constituted while the rest are deviations—deviations on the one hand from the well blended harmony [*tēs eu kekramenēs harmonias*] and on the other from the best regime; and these will be oligarchic when they are more "strained" [*syntonōteras*] and more despotic, and democratic when they are "relaxed" and "soft" [*aneimenas kai malakas*]. [1290a19–29]

What Aristotle does in this passage is to replace a technical distinction with a moral one. Whether the other harmonies must be understood as variant forms of Dorian or Phrygian is immaterial: the important distinction is between the "one or two" properly constituted harmonies and the harmonies that "deviate" from or are inferior to them. Which of the harmonies, then, are properly constituted? At first sight, Aristotle would seem to be thinking only of the Dorian harmony, which he will expressly describe as forming "the mean between extremes'' (1342b14–16). On the other hand, the ''extremes'' as he describes them here unmistakeably recall two harmonies in particular—the ''strained'' or threnodic Lydian and the ''relaxed'' or ''soft'' Lydian (cf. 1340b2–3); and since Aristotle leaves open the possibility that there is more than one well-constituted harmony, it seems likely that he thought of Mixed Lydian as a mean between the extremes represented by the other Lydian harmonies. The very name ''Mixed Lydian'' is sugestive of a mixture or ''blend'' of musical elements—it will be recalled that the author of the *Problems* speaks of it as being at once ''mournful'' and ''inactive'' or ''calm'' (*hēsychion*)—and Aristotle may have had this fact particularly in mind.[63] If the ''best regime'' is in the strictest sense the way of life of the class which rules in the well-constituted city, it is entirely appropriate that the well-constituted harmonies should be reserved for the music which contributes to the formation of that way of life. If the music education of the citizens of the best regime is in its earliest stage an education in and through Dorian music, it would seem to be in its later stage an education dominated by Mixed Lydian music.

However this may be, it makes excellent sense to assume that the two ''extreme'' Lydian harmonies are the deviant harmonies that will be set aside for the use of the noncitizen class. The soft or ''relaxed'' (*aneimenē*) Lydian would seem ideally suited to the requirements of a music which is intended to provide ''relaxation [*anesis*] and a relief from tension.'' It was the mode characteristically associated with feasting and drinking, with the relaxed atmosphere of the banquet.[64] As for the threnodic Lydian, its strained character would seem to agree well with a taste for ''tunes that are strained'' or high-pitched. It seems to have been used primarily in funeral celebrations, though dirgelike music in the Lydian mode was evidently per-

63. Cf. R. P. Winnington-Ingram, *Mode in Ancient Greek Music* (Cambridge, 1936), p. 28, who suggests it may originally have been a mixture of Lydian with Dorian or Aeolian (Hypodorian).

64. Cf. 1342b23 ff. and Plato *Republic* 398e.

formed at festivals.[65] Since Aristotle is thinking of publicly established musical performances, it is probably to be assumed that he intends both harmonies to be used in religious festivals specially established for the noncitizen class.

Finally, there are "the tunes that are strained and highly colored." These must be assumed to be distinct from, or at least not completely identical with, tunes composed in the "extreme" Lydian harmonies. What Aristotle has in mind, it would seem, are chromatic or "colored" tunes in the Phrygian mode. I would suggest that he is thinking particularly of the music what was used to accompany the dithyrambic poetry of his day, the "new" dithyramb of Melanippides, Timotheus, and Philoxenus. In the sequel, Aristotle will mention Philoxenus in connection with his argument that the Phrygian mode is the only mode truly suited to dithyrambic poetry (1342b3–12). But if Philoxenus' experiment with a Dorian dithyramb was unsuccessful, the innovations of Philoxenus and others in regard to the scales of dithyrambic music had been only too successful, and the new dithyramb enjoyed a wide if undeserved popularity.[66] Since it is only the noncitizen class of the best regime that is to be exposed to music of this kind, it is inaccurate to say that Aristotle wished to rehabilitate it simply. But Aristotle's acceptance of the new dithyramb surely represents his greatest concession to "vulgar" pleasure.

11. The End of the Politics

It will not be necessary to follow in detail Aristotle's brief and straightforward discussion of the harmonies to be used in the education of the young. Although Aristotle declares his willingness to follow the advice of musical experts, it is clear that of existing or recognized harmonies the Dorian is the only one

65. [Plutarch] On Music 1136c = Aristoxenus fr. 80 Wehrli.
66. Consider especially [Plutarch] On Music 1135c–d; cf. 1141c ff. = Aristoxenus fr. 76 Wehrli. A general account may be found in A. W. Pickard-Cambridge, Dithyramb, Tragedy and Comedy, 2nd ed. (Oxford, 1962), p. 38–59.

that is to be employed in "education" properly speaking. As regards the final section of Chapter 7 (1342b17–34), I join with the majority of recent commentators in considering it an interpolation.[67]

At the beginning of Chapter 7, Aristotle had announced his intention to investigate the uses of harmonies and rhythms in the best regime both generally and "with a view to education"; and he had indicated that it may be necessary to distinguish between the harmonies and rhythms to be used in the education of mature citizens and those to be used in the education of the young. The subsequent discussion of harmonies clearly accords with this program. Although the term *paideia* itself is reserved for the education of the young, the more fundamental distinction is plainly that between the musical education or culture of the citizen class of the best regime and the musical entertainment of its noncitizen class, between a music that serves the leisured pastime (*diagōgē*) of mature citizens and a music that serves the relaxation (*anapausis*) of the vulgar.[68] I have attempted to show that the theatrical music prescribed as the education or pastime of mature citizens must be understood to include not only the tunes or harmonies associated with tragedy but even and precisely tragedy—tragic poetry—itself. This suggestion is surely not implausible in itself. Still, it is difficult to believe that Aristotle would have been satisfied to allude in so vague and even cryptic a fashion to matters of such obvious importance. If Aristotle was thinking of tragedy, why does he not say so? Why is the question of poetry not explicitly discussed?

67. The interesting question of Plato's understanding of the character and educational role of Phrygian music cannot be pursued here. A somewhat fuller treatment, as well as a discussion of the authenticity of the final paragraph of the *Politics,* appears in the Appendix.

68. The phrasing of 1342a18–22 could seem to suggest that *anapausis* is the aim of the musical activity of the educated as well as the vulgar; but the sequel shows that it is necessary to distinguish the "pleasure proper" to the diagogic enjoyment of the educated from that proper to the relaxation of the noncitizens (a25–28; cf. 1339b31 ff.).

The answer, I think, is that the question of poetry *was* explicitly discussed, in the no longer extant portion of Book VIII. If my interpretation of the sense of the term *mousikē* as it is employed in Book VIII is correct, there is every reason why it should have been discussed. And I believe some confirmation is provided by two forward references in the text of the *Politics* itself. The first, which has not been sufficiently noticed, occurs toward the end of Book VII. After discussing the harmful effects of obscenity or scurrility (*aischrologia*) in "imitations," and the necessity of preventing the young from becoming spectators of iambic recitations or performances of comedy, Aristotle goes on to remark:

> This argument we have made now only in passing [*en paradromēi*]; at a later point it will be necessary to deal with these matters more fully and with greater precision [*hysteron d' epistēsantes dei diorisai mallon*], discussing first whether or not there should be regulations in these matters, and how they should be regulated; for the present we have touched on them only so far as is necessary. [1336b24–27]

Aristotle here seems to announce a later treatment of the question of the moral effect of poetry or of certain kinds of poetry.[69] The second passage occurs in Chapter 7 of Book VIII, immediately following Aristotle's first mention of the term catharsis. "As to what we mean by catharsis," he says there, "we will speak of it now in a general way, but again and more clearly in the treatment of poetic art [*palin d' en tois peri poiētikēs eroumen saphesteron*]" (1341b38–40).

The clearer discussion of catharsis promised by Aristotle at the end of the *Politics* is generally assumed to have been provided in the *Poetics* (*peri poiētikēs*), Aristotle's treatment of, or treatise on, "poetic art." The difficulties involved in such a view are, however, notorious. Unless one is prepared to assume a large lacuna following the brief mention of tragic catharsis in Chapter 6 of the *Poetics,* the missing discussion

69. Cf. Eduard Zeller, *Die Philosophie der Griechen,* 4th ed. (Leipzig, 1921) II², 736 ff.

must be located in a lost second book of the *Poetics*. Assuming such a book indeed existed, it would seem to have dealt with comedy and epic poetry. Yet there is no direct evidence that Aristotle recognized a catharsis effected either by comedy or by epic, and it seems very unlikely that he did.[70] Further, if catharsis was discussed there, it is certainly strange that some reference to that discussion should not be made when the subject of catharsis is introduced in Chapter 6.

One solution, suggested many years ago and usually rejected out of hand, is worth reconsidering in the light of the analysis offered here. It is that Aristotle's expression "in the treatment of poetic art" refers not to a separate Aristotelian treatise but to a later and lost discussion within the *Politics* itself. Analogous expressions appear a number of times in the *Rhetoric* with reference to material found elsewhere in that work (and occasionally within the same book), and the same is arguably true of the *Politics* itself.[71] While in itself impossible of proof, the suggestion that Aristotle discussed catharsis in a lost section of *Politics* VIII gains greatly in plausibility if the reading of the argument of *Politics* VIII proposed here is essentially correct. Such a discussion would be wholly in place in the context of a discussion of the moral or political uses of poetry or of music generally—the discussion which Aristotle appears to promise toward the end of Book VII.

A further clue as to the structure and scope of the argument of the missing portions of Book VIII can perhaps be gathered

70. See chap. IV, n. 56 below. The promise of a later discussion of comedy and epic occurs at *Poet.* 1449b21–22.

71. The suggestion was made by Georg Finsler, *Platon und die aristotelische Poetik* (Leipzig, 1900), pp. 3–8, citing *Rhet.* I.10.1369b14–15 (referring to II.2 ff.), 1369b29–30 (referring to I.6–8), II.1.1378a18–19 (referring to II.2 ff., and in particular to 4); cf. 1373b36–37, 1391a19–20, 1393a11–12. Compare in addition *Pol.* 1260b12–13 *en tois peri tas politeias* (referring to III ff.?) and particularly 1335b4–5 *mallon lekteon en tois peri tēs paidonomias, typōi de hikanon eipein kai nyn* (apparently referring to a dicussion following VIII—cf. 1272a23–26, 1336b24–27 and context, 1338a30–34). Cf. H. Otte, *Neue Beiträge zur aristotelischen Begriffsbestimmung der Tragödie* (Berlin, 1928), pp. 62–68.

from a forward reference in Chapter 3. Aristotle had there promised (1338a30–37) to return later on to the question of the number and nature of the "liberal arts" which should form part of the education of the best regime; this promise is unfulfilled in the *Politics* as we have it. The context of that earlier discussion had appeared to suggest that Aristotle might have been thinking of "liberal arts" other than music, and in particular of scientific or philosophical studies. If that is indeed the case, it is a plausible hypothesis that the argument of the missing chapters of Book VIII developed along the lines suggested by Aristotle's preliminary discussion of education in Book VII. If the extant portion of Book VIII treats primarily of music in the narrow sense and of education to virtue, the missing portion may have contained an account both of the education in "practical reason" by way of poetry (or music in the wider sense) and of the education in "theoretical reason" by way of science or philosophy.

More important than the question of where Aristotle discussed catharsis, of course, is the question of whether he indeed discussed it, or could have discussed it, in the terms I have suggested. What role can Aristotle have expected tragic catharsis, or poetry generally, to play in a civic or political education?

4

Poetry and Education

1. Poetry and Education

The suggestion that tragedy and comedy were intended to provide a moral or political education to the citizens of the best regime is exposed to the objection that Aristotle cannot have been so authoritarian or Platonizing as to believe that mature men are seriously in need of an education of this kind, nor so philistine as to require the highest forms of classical art to serve any purpose other than that of aesthetic or "cultured" enjoyment. This objection, or rather these closely related objections, seem a more accurate reflection of the preoccupations of Aristotle's modern interpreters than of anything Aristotle himself says or is likely to have said. It has been the fashion for some time to smile at the backwardness of an age which saw in tragedy as it is interpreted by Aristotle what Jacob Bernays once called a "moral reformatory."[1] But not even the age of historical scholarship can boast a freedom from typical prejudices, and there is reason to wonder whether the view of Lessing is not after all truer than the view of Bernays. In Book VIII of the *Politics,* Aristotle explicitly denies that the end of

1. *Zwei Abhandlungen,* p. 3. Bernays emphasizes "how thoroughly alien to Aristotle is the idea of the last century that the theater is a kindred and rival institution to the church, a kind of moral reformatory, and how relentlessly he insists on preserving its character as a place of entertainment for the different classes of the public" (p. 9). Cf. Albin Lesky, *Greek Tragedy* (New York, 1965), pp. 5–6.

music or poetry is enjoyment, whether the simple enjoyment associated with "relaxation" or the cultured enjoyment associated with "play." In Book VII, he indicates unmistakably that "education" in the best regime will not be limited to the education of the young; and Book VIII contains what I have tried to show are allusions to the "music education" of mature citizens.

But even granting that traces of a doctrine of this sort may be discovered in Books VII and VIII, is it not also true that Books VII and VIII of the *Politics* are demonstrably "early?" Do *Politics* VII and VIII not in fact present the spectacle of a Platonizing doctrine *in statu evanescendi?* Is it not hazardous to use *Politics* VII and VIII as a guide to the thought of the mature Aristotle? Is it not particularly hazardous to use the information provided by the *Politics* as a guide to the interpretation of tragic catharsis in the *Poetics?*

Although the questions treated in the last two books of the *Politics* are not explicitly discussed by Aristotle in those works which are generally agreed to be "late" (or indeed in any other work now extant), the evidence of those writings would seem to confirm rather than to contradict the argument of the *Politics*. In an earlier chapter, some attempt was made to indicate the compatibility of the teachings of the *Politics* and the *Poetics* as regards the question of the nature or purpose of "music." While Aristotle does not pronounce explicitly on this question in the *Poetics* as we have it, there can be little doubt that according to the teaching of the *Poetics* the measure of excellence in poetry, or at any rate in tragic (as well as epic) poetry, is neither its beauty nor the pleasure it provides but rather its capacity to move the passions or to affect "the character and the soul."[2]

As regards the question of education, there is a certain plausibility to the view that Aristotle recognized to a greater extent than Plato what one may call the moral autonomy of the mature individual, and that he would have regarded any at-

2. A good demonstration of the central importance of poetry's capacity to move the passions may be found in Döring, pp. 93 ff.

tempt to legislate or inculcate morality—excepting, presumably, the necessary education of the young—as destructive of morality itself.[3] At the same time, however, there is a passage in Book X of the *Nicomachean Ethics* which suggests what would seem to be quite a different view.

2. *Education and Law in the* Nicomachean Ethics

In the final chapter of Book X of the *Ethics,* Aristotle concludes his account of the good life by asking the question "how men become good."[4] As appears from Book VII of the *Politics* (1332a38–b11), the question "how men become good" is very nearly synonymous with the question of "education." Aristotle answers that question as he answers it in the *Politics:* men become good by nature, by habit, and by "teaching" (*didachē*) or "reasoned speech" (*logos*). He then proceeds to argue that reasoned speech is not sufficient for converting men to a life of "nobility and goodness" or "gentlemanship" (*kalokagathia*); that it is necessary to acquire in youth an education in "habit" that will dispose the soul to enjoy or delight as well as hate in a noble manner and thus render the character "somehow akin to virtue" (*pōs oikeion tēs aretēs*); and that the training and practices of the young must be supported by suitable laws. "But it is perhaps not enough," he continues,

> that they receive correct training and supervision when they are young, but as they must practice and be habituated to these things[5] when they are mature, we would need laws for this too,

3. Thus D. J. Allan, "Individual and State in the *Ethics* and *Politics,"* in *La "Politique" d'Aristote,* Entretiens Fondation Hardt XI (Geneva, 1965), pp. 55 ff. The more conventional view appears in Ernest Barker's remark that "Plato and Aristotle perhaps treated their contemporaries too much as if they were 'always children'" (*The Politics of Aristotle* lii; cf. Barker, *The Political Thought of Plato and Aristotle* [London, 1906], pp. 424–25, 430–31).

4. *Eth. Nic.* 1179a35–b21. That the final chapter of the *Nicomachean Ethics* is early has been argued by Stark, *Aristotelesstudien,* pp. 16–17; but cf. R. A. Gauthier and J. Y. Jolif, *L'Ethique à Nicomaque* (Louvain, 1958), III, on 1180a21–22.

5. Reading *auta* with the manuscripts as against the conjectural *atta* adopted by Gauthier-Jolif (on 1180a3). Throughout this passage Aristotle stresses the

and generally for the whole of life; for the many [*hoi polloi*] obey necessity rather than reasoned speech [*logos*], and punishments rather than the noble. Accordingly, there are some who think that legislators ought to exhort and persuade to virtue for the sake of the noble, and that they will be heeded by those who are adequately grounded in decent habits, while those who are disobedient and naturally inferior ought to be chastised and punished, and the incorrigible banished; for decent men who live with a view to the noble will allow themselves to be ruled by reason, while baser men who aim at pleasure ought to receive painful punishments as if they were beasts of burden. . . . If, then, as was said, the one who is going to be good must be well trained and habituated, and then live the same kind of life in accordance with decent practices and without doing anything base either unwillingly or willingly, he must live according to a kind of intelligence and a correct order possessing force . . . ; but law has the power of compulsion, being a form of reasoned speech based on a certain prudence and intelligence [*logos ōn apo tinos phronēseōs kai nou*].[6]

Apart from the fact that it is not clear to what extent Aristotle is speaking in this passage in his own name, one is inclined at first to think that the argument for the necessity of law or of a continuing education in virtue rests entirely on the defective nature of ordinary men or of "the many." And yet the passage as a whole shows clearly enough that "those who are adequately grounded in decent habits"—decent or virtuous men, educated "gentlemen"—are no less in need of a continuing "habituation" to virtue than are the vulgar.[7] The only difference is that gentlemen are to be habituated primarily by reasoned speech while the many are to be habituated primarily by force or compulsion. Nor can there be much doubt that the view Aristotle appears to ascribe to others is in fact, if one discounts the ex-

---

continuity between the "practices" required of the young and those required of older men (cf. a2–3 *epitēdeuein kai ethizesthai* with a14–16).

6. *Eth. Nic.* 1180a1–18.

7. For the relation between "law" and "habit" consider *Pol.* 1268b22 ff., and particularly 1269a20–21: "law has no strength with a view to persuasion apart from habit."

treme statements regarding the proper treatment of non-gentlemen, his own view.[8]

Aristotle had indicated when speaking in his own name that the early education in habit is an education not so much "in" virtue as "with a view to" virtue. An early education in habit serves to render the character "somehow akin to virtue": it is not a complete or final education in virtue. The complete education in virtue is an education in "reason" as well as "habit." Education as a whole requires the cooperation, not to say the most perfect agreement or the most perfect harmony, between an early education in habit and a later education in reason.[9] Or as Aristotle also puts it, virtue in the full sense cannot be attained without "right reason," "prudence," or practical wisdom (*phronēsis*).[10]

In the passage we have been considering, Aristotle is concerned to establish the necessity of law rather than the necessity of education. Still, it is easy to see that law by itself cannot provide the education in virtue that Aristotle appears to require. The law or the legislator can "exhort" to virtue; how persuasive will such an exhortation be? To what extent is the "speech" represented by law indeed "reasoned speech," and to what extent merely peremptory command?[11] If it is true that

8. Allan is embarrassed by this passage. He is "disposed to think either that it is of early date, or that Aristotle owing to literary reminiscence (to be more precise, because he is here following Plato's *Protagoras*) has allowed himself to be shifted from his proper ground" (p. 73). He is satisifed that a14 ff. betrays "the language of someone resuming his own deliberation after an excursion into the opinions of others" (p. 76). But a14 ff. in fact affirms the opinion which has just been discussed, at least insofar as it bears on the education of "gentlemen": *epitēdeumasin* in a16 echoes *epitēdeuein* in a2–3 (cf. note 5 above and *Pol.* 1333a11–16), and the sentence as a whole (*houtōs* in a16 as well as the apodosis in a17–18 is omitted from Allan's paraphrase) admits and even stresses the necessity of a "supervision" (cf. a25 ff.) not only of the practices of the young but of those of mature gentlemen. As regards the Platonic reference, Aristotle seems to be "following" *Laws* 862d–63a at least as much as *Protagoras* 325a–b.

9. Compare *Pol.* 1334b6–12 with Plato *Laws* 653b–c and 659d.

10. *Eth. Nic.* 1144b15–32.

11. Cf. Plato *Laws* 719c–23d.

law is necessarily based on "a certain prudence and intelligence," is it not also true that the prudence or intelligence
embodied in law is necessarily partial and limited? There is indeed a sense in which morality cannot be legislated: whereas
moral action, and in particular prudent action, is concerned
with particulars, law is necessarily general. In fact, what is
most characteristic of the "decent man" (*ho epieikēs*) is precisely
his ability to correct the law, or justice as defined by law, in the
light of particular circumstances which the law is unable to
foresee. "Decency" properly speaking—that is to say, "equi-
ty" (*epieikeia*)—is higher than law.[12]

3. Moral Weakness

It would be wrong to distinguish in too absolute a fashion between an early education by way of "habit" and a later education by way of "reason," between an early education to virtue
and a later education to practical reason or prudence. It is clear
from the account of the *Ethics* that there is a sense in which the
later education in "reason" is no less an education by way of
"habituation" than is the education of the young. And it is also
clear that there is a continuity between the aims or objects of
the earlier and those of the later education. The training of the
young has as its object the inculcation of moral virtue; but
"mature men must also be trained and habituated" to the
practice of moral virtue.[13] The aim of both educations, the aim
of education as a whole, is moral virtue. Prudence or practical
wisdom is so far from being independent of moral virtue that it
is in the service of moral virtue. An education in prudence
would necessarily involve a continuous strengthening of moral
habits as well as the development or deepening of moral
awareness. If it is the task of the early education to render the
character "somehow akin to virtue," it is the task of the education in prudence to translate a settled disposition to virtue into
principled and intelligent moral action.

12. *Eth. Nic.* 1136a31 ff.; cf. 1180a34 ff.
13. *Eth. Nic.* 1180a2–3.

Still, there would seem to be important differences between an education directed to the formation of the habits of virtue in the young and an education designed to preserve and strengthen moral character and to ensure moral behavior in mature men. The element of intelligence, the practical knowledge necessary to translate moral dispositions into moral action, is surely peculiar to the later education, since it is to a great extent dependent on experience. But lack of knowledge or lack of experience is not the only obstacle in the way of becoming a truly virtuous man. An early education in virtuous habits can be expected to culminate in the formation of what Aristotle calls "moral choice" (*proairesis*), a settled disposition to choose or to prefer virtue and the actions that accord with virtue. But the fact of possessing a correct moral choice does not infallibly guarantee that a man's actions will always be guided by it. There are men who are in certain cases and even habitually prevented from acting in accordance with their moral choice by the force of their passions. This is the phenomenon which Aristotle calls "incontinence" or "moral weakness" (*akrasia*). According to the teaching of the *Ethics,* a morally weak man cannot be fully prudent or morally "serious" (*spoudaios*), though he may well possess a highly developed practical intelligence in the form of "cleverness," a quality which is easily mistaken for prudence.[14]

That Aristotle distinguishes implicitly between "character" and the "character of the soul"—between moral character properly speaking and the complex of virtues and passions which constitutes character in a general sense—was argued at an earlier point.[15] In what may be a reflection of Peripatetic doctrine, Aristides Quintilianus speaks explicitly of a public "therapy" or "cure" by way of music for citizens afflicted by an excess of "passion," and considers musical therapy of this sort a form of "character education" (*ēthikē paideusis*).[16] Accord-

14. *Eth. Nic.* 1152a6–14.

15. See chap. II, sec. 9 above.

16. Aristides Quintilianus II.5–6 (58,6–59,7), 9 (68,22–28) Winnington-Ingram.

157

ing to Aristotle, the susceptibility to excessive passion which manifests itself in "moral weakness" is indeed "curable," at least where it is the result of habit rather than of nature.[17] If it will be granted that not even the strictest of early educations can be expected to eradicate all susceptibility to excessive passion,[18] it is surely plausible to assume that the higher education of Aristotle's best regime is intended in the first place to counter or to forestall the development of the "habit" of moral weakness by providing a kind of therapy for the passions and hence for the "character of the soul." To the extent to which a susceptibility to excessive passion is incompatible with prudence strictly speaking, there is no difficulty in understanding a therapy of this sort as the necessary accompaniment of an education in "practical reason."

A musical therapy of the passions appears to have been practiced by the Pythagoreans as a preparation for or accompaniment to an education in philosophy. The Pythagorean term for this kind of therapy was *katharsis*. In spite of the differences between catharsis as understood by the Pythagoreans and catharsis as understood by Aristotle, the precedent is an important one. If Aristotle's notion of catharsis derives from scientific medicine or from religious ritual of a certain kind, the fact that Aristotle can extend the application of cathartic therapy in the way he does, from the diseased or the abnormal to the healthy, from pathological conditions to the passions of ordinary human beings, would seem to argue the influence of Pythagoreanism. And the Pythagoreans certainly supply the only precedent for a catharsis effected by poetry rather than by music alone, if reliance can be placed on the report that they employed selected passages from Homer and Hesiod "with a view to the correction of the soul."[19] Aristotle's notion of tragic catharsis would seem to owe more than a little to the Pythagorean notion

17. *Eth. Nic.* 1152a27–29.

18. Consider *Pol.* 1336b9–12 together with 20–23.

19. Iamblichus *Life of Pythagoras* 111 Deubner; for the link between "correction" (*epanorthōsis*) and musical catharsis cf. 64. Compare Aristides Quintilianus II.4 (57,11–12), I.12 (30,15–24) Winnington-Ingram.

of a musical-poetic education of the passions. While Aristotle surely goes beyond the Pythagoreans—in the first instance, by replacing what was essentially a private and philosophic education with one that is public and practical—he shares with the Pythagoreans the notion of a catharsis which is universal in its application or which provides "correction," moral improvement or education rather than a cure or therapy properly speaking.

4. Catharsis and Spiritedness

The precise manner in which tragic catharsis must be understood to operate is a subject for speculations that would take us too far afield. I have attempted to show that tragic catharsis as Aristotle understands it most probably involves a partial rather than a total purgation of the passions of pity and fear. Aristotle did not regard the passions as simple "diseases" or as evil in every respect. He considered them a natural and necessary element in the human soul, and a potential support for virtue; and there is reason to believe that he regarded pity and fear as particularly salutary in this respect. Equally important, however, and for the most part neglected by recent interpreters, is the question whether the effect of tragic catharsis is limited to the passions of pity and fear. Aristotle defines tragedy in the *Poetics* as "effecting through pity and fear the catharsis of passions of this sort [*tēn tōn toioutōn pathēmatōn katharsin*]." In Book VIII of the *Politics*, he speaks of a catharsis which affects not only "the pitying and the fearful" but "the generally passionate [*tous holōs pathētikous*], as well as others insofar as each shares in things of this sort [*tōn toioutōn*]" (1342a12–14). Despite much torturing of the phrase *tōn toioutōn pathēmatōn*,[20] these passages taken together strongly suggest that

20. Bernays has argued at some length (*Zwei Abhandlungen*, pp. 24–31) that *toioutōn* means little more than *toutōn* and refers only to pity and fear, and he is followed by a number of scholars; the contrary view is maintained, I think successfully, by J. L. Beare, "Anaphoric *ho toioutos* in Aristotle," *Hermathena* 18 (1914–19), 116–35, and R. Schottlaender, "Eine Fessel der Tragödiendeutung," *Hermes* 81 (1953), 22–29.

while tragic catharsis indeed operates through pity and fear, its effect extends to other passions as well. That it extends to all the passions appears to be ruled out by the necessity of assigning some meaning to the qualifying *toiouton;* on the other hand, the fact that Aristotle speaks in the *Politics* of "the generally passionate" makes it unlikely that he has in mind only those passions immediately connected with pity or fear—for example, the "philanthropic" passion alluded to in the *Poetics*.[21]

There is, perhaps, another alternative. By "passions of this sort" Aristotle could mean that class of passions which is associated with the experience of "pain" rather than of pleasure or desire, passions which have their locus in what Plato had identified as the "spirited" (*thymētikon*) part of the soul.[22] In Plato's *Republic*, "spiritedness" (*thymos*) appears

21. That catharsis extends to all the passions was the view of Corneille (see Kommerell, pp. 32–50, 67–68); that it extends only to passions such as *philanthrōpia* (*Poet.* 1452b38–53a3) was the view of Lessing, and seems to be the position of those modern scholars who do not follow Bernays' interpretation of *tōn toiouton pathēmatōn*. The weaknesses in the current interpretations are briefly but effectively stated by Schottlaender, who returns to something like the view of Corneille.

22. A distinction among "painful," "pleasurable," and "enthusiastic" passions seems to be presupposed in a fragment of Theophrastus (fr. 90 Wimmer), and may underlie the definitions of the passions in the *Rhetoric* (consider, e.g., 1382a21). It is elaborated and brought into connection with the Platonic doctrine of the soul by Aristides Quintilianus, II.5 (58,10–21) Winnington-Ingram. (Cf. Croissant, pp. 15–19.) An important but neglected piece of evidence for a connection between catharsis and spiritedness is provided by a Homeric scholion apparently deriving from Porphyry's *Homeric Questions* and reflecting Aristotelian doctrine: "They ask why he began from the wrath [of Achilles]; . . . in the first place, in order that the part of the soul that is of this sort may be purified of the passion [*ek tou pathous apokatharieusēi to toiouton morion tēs psychēs*]" (Schol. A on *A*.1; A. Trendelenburg, *Grammaticorum Graecorum De Arte Tragica Iudiciorum Reliquiae* [Bonn, 1867], pp. 75–77); cf. Stark, p. 70. Of particular interest here is the apparent use of *toioutos* to refer to the spirited part of the soul. In the *Poetics* itself Aristotle once (1456b1) lists "anger and whatever else is of this sort" (*orgēn kai hosa toiauta*), together with pity and fear, as the passions to be represented in tragedy, and he also speaks of the tragic poet as imitating "harsh" characters such as Achilles (1454b11–15). Cf. Nicev, pp. 36–38, 79–85. According to Quintilian (VI.2.20), tragedy "has to do with anger, hatred, fear, envy, and pity" (*circa iram, odium, metum, invidiam, miserationem versatur*).

together with desire and reason as one of the parts of the soul, and as the principle of soul of the warrior class of Plato's best regime. Though *thymos* frequently carries the simple meaning of "anger," it encompasses a range of passions bearing on men's social and political relationships—moral indignation, friendship, the desire for honor and superiority.

In the Platonic presentation, spiritedness appears to play a generally salutary role in political life. In war, the soldiers' spirited pursuit of victory makes them good fighters, while in peacetime the rewards of honor make them insensitive to the pleasures which dominate the lives of most men. At all times, it appears, the soldiers will be disposed to follow the counsels of prudent or reasonable rulers, just as spiritedness in the soul acts as a powerful ally of ruling reason in controlling the desires. At the same time, however, Plato also indicates that spiritedness is not in itself reasonable, or that it poses definite dangers for politics when emancipated from the guidance of reason or the rule of a class of philosophic guardians.[23] In the *Laws,* he speaks with some emphasis of the dangers of spiritedness. As the Athenian Stranger there says: "There is in the soul either a certain passion or a certain part, spiritedness, an innate possession that is hard to contend with and hard to fight, and it overturns many things with unreasoning force." Spiritedness, he continues, is one form of "ignorance" (*agnoia*), indeed, a particularly dangerous form, for ignorance combined with "strength and might" is the cause of "great and unmusical wrongs" (*megala kai amousa hamartēmata*).[24]

Aristotle's most extended statement on the subject of spiritedness occurs in his discussion of the natural endowment required of the citizens of the best regime in Book VII of the *Politics.* In the *Republic,* Plato had indicated that the spirited warriors would have to be at once harsh toward the city's enemies and gentle toward their friends or fellow citizens. In an obvious allusion to this Platonic discussion, Aristotle remarks:

23. Consider particularly *Republic* 439e–40b and 547b–50b.
24. *Laws* 863b–d.

For what some say ought to be present in the guardians is to be friendly to those known to them and savage toward those who are not known, and it is spiritedness that produces friendliness [to philētikon]; for it is the power of the soul by which we are friendly. A sign of this: spiritedness rises up especially against familiars and friends rather than against those who are unknown when it believes there has been a slight. Therefore Archilochus spoke fittingly to his spiritedness in accusing his friends: "Indeed you were wounded by friends." And what is ruling and free is present in all from this same power; for spiritedness is adept at ruling [archikon] and unbeatable. But one ought not to maintain that they should be harsh toward those who are unknown, for one ought not to be this way toward anyone, nor are magnanimous men [hoi megalopsychoi] savage in their nature, unless toward those who commit injustice. And this they will especially feel toward their familiars, as was said before, if they believe they have been done an injustice. And it is reasonable that this should happen; for among those they suppose to be in their debt for some benefit, in addition to the injury they hold they have been deprived of this too; thus it is said "harsh are the wars of brothers," and "who loves intensely will hate as much." [1327b38–28a16]

By appearing to deny that spiritedness necessarily involves hostility to outsiders and emphasizing instead its connection with friendship or what one may call group solidarity, Aristotle seems to go even further than Plato in regarding spiritedness as a politically salutary quality of soul. In the last analysis, however, Aristotle's reservations against spiritedness are not fundamentally different from those of Plato. The excesses of spiritedness are rooted in its very character as a social passion, and not even "magnanimous men"—according to Aristotle's ethical teaching, those who most perfectly embody the morality of gentlemanship—are exempt from them. In spite of the fact that the magnanimous man is presented by Aristotle as somewhat contemptuous of that honor which acts as the primary support of gentlemanly virtue,[25] he is, as it seems, never wholly free of an inner dependence on the honor or

25. Eth. Nic. 1124a4–19.

dcference of friends and fellow citizens. Indeed, precisely because of the centrality of honor in his way of life, the gentleman would seem to be particularly susceptible to the excesses of spiritedness. It is true that spiritedness in some of its manifestations—for example, righteous indignation—is a noble passion and a mark of goodness of character.[26] At the same time, however, spiritedness is capable of great crimes. Anger, jealousy, and hatred in domestic life can lead civilized men to monstrous acts; and the gentleman's desire for honor and distinction is only a step removed from the desire to demonstrate one's superiority by acts of gratuitous arrogance or hybris, a desire which is transformed in its most extreme form into a longing for tyrannical power. It is not clear whether Aristotle fully shares Plato's view that even the best bred gentlemen nurture in their souls a secret desire to become tyrants.[27] But he does insist that spiritedness in general is of such a character that it "perverts rulers and the best men."[28] More generally, according to Aristotle: "Spiritedness is a passion that is bestial in its disposition, unrelenting in its hold, harsh and violent in its power, a cause of murders, ally of misfortune, companion of injury, instigator of dishonor and waste of substance, and finally of destruction."[29] Because no thematic discussion of spiritedness has survived among Aristotle's writings, and because Aristotle appears to discard the tripartite psychology of Plato's *Republic*, little attention has been given to the possibility that the phenomenon of spiritedness figures importantly in his political thought, and

26. *Rhet.* 1386b11–12; cf. 1389a10–35 and *Eth. Nic.* 1116b23–17a9.
27. *Republic* 619b–e.
28. *Pol.* 1287a31–32; cf. 1286a33–35, 1267a14 and context.
29. Stobaeus III.553,9 Henze. This remark, unjustifiably omitted from the standard collections of Aristotelian fragments (cf. Stark, pp. 89–90), together with similar statements preserved by Stobaeus (III.548,15 and 550,18 Henze = Aristotle frs. 660 and 661 Rose), appears to derive from a lost Aristotelian treatise probably entitled "On the Passion of Anger" (*peri pathous orgēs*, according to the list of Hesychius [no. 40]; but cf. Diogenes Laertius V.21 [no. 37]).

still less in his reflections on poetry.[30] For Aristotle as for Plato, however, the phenomenon of spiritedness appears to be of fundamental importance for understanding of nature of human sociality, and thereby the limits or the nature of political life in particular; and for both the phenomenon of spiritedness is profoundly problematic. Spiritedness is indispensable for the best city just as it is an inescapable fact of political life as such; but it represents at the same time a grave danger, as it constantly threatens the predominance in politics of prudence or reason.

That Aristotle's doctrine of tragic catharsis should be understood in the light of the problem of spiritedness is surely a plausible suggestion. The passions associated with spiritedness—fear, pity, indignation, anger, jealousy, love of honor—are the common fare of tragic poetry; and the very idea of the tragic would seem intimately connected with the ambivalent nature of these passions. If it is granted that Aristotelian catharsis is more plausibly understood as purification than as purgation or evacuation, it makes excellent sense to connect catharsis with a range of passions which are neither simply salutary nor simply harmful for men and societies. On this understanding, catharsis would serve to purify the spirited passions of their dangerous excesses. Cathartic tragedy would thus serve as the education par excellence of spirited gentlemen in political virtue or prudence.[31]

30. See, for example, W. W. Fortenbaugh, *Aristotle on Emotion* (New York, 1975), pp. 23-44.

31. An important consequence of understanding catharsis as affecting not only pity and fear but all the spirited passions is that tragic catharsis can no longer be understood (on the analogy of the catharsis of enthusiasm) as simply homoeopathic: the catharsis of anger will be brought about, not by anger, but by pity and fear. Yet tragic catharsis can be regarded as loosely analogous to a homoeopathic catharsis by the fact that passion is cured by passion. That Aristotle himself so regarded it is strongly argued by the testimony of Olympiodorus, who describes the "Aristotelian mode" of catharsis as "the one that heals evil by evil and through a battle of opposites creates a balanced state" (*ho kakōi to kakon iōmenos kai tēi diamachēi tōn enantiōn eis symmetrian agōn*), or as he also puts it, "this one heals evil by evil, at least in the sense of healing passion by passion" (*ho men gar kakōi to kakon iatai, eige pathos pathei*) (*Commentary On Plato's First Alcibiades* 145 Westerink). The account of Olympiodorus is

5. Tragic Error

It will be asked whether the interpretation of catharsis outlined here finds any support in the account of tragedy in Aristotle's *Poetics*. As was pointed out earlier, it is not clear whether the *Poetics* in its original form contained an elaboration of Aristotle's understanding of catharsis; as the text currently stands, the only explicit reference to catharsis occurs in the celebrated sentence of Chapter 6. This state of affairs has led some scholars to the view that the single reference to catharsis is an inorganic addition to the text of the *Poetics* as originally conceived by Aristotle.[32] On the other hand, Aristotle does speak repeatedly of pity and fear, and his prescriptions for the construction of tragic plots depend directly on his view of the importance of those passions for realizing a genuine tragic effect. Accordingly, it seems legitimate to assume that Aristotle's

---

complicated by the fact that he also refers to the "Aristotelian" or "Peripatetic" mode of catharsis as the "Stoic" mode, and at one point describes the operation of the "Stoic" mode in the following terms: it "healed opposites through opposites, on the one hand applying desire to spiritedness [*tōi men thymōi tēn epithymian epagōn*] and thus softening it, on the other spiritedness to desire, thus making it more robust and leading it toward manliness, like the curved sticks that those who want to straighten bend in the opposite direction, in order that by bringing them around toward the opposite a balanced state will result [*ek tēs eis to enantion periphoras to symmetron anaphanē*]; in this way, then they strove to establish a proper tuning [*harmonian*] in the soul through this sort of mode" (p. 54). Now it is certainly odd that Olympiodorus can identify as "Stoic" a procedure which is criticized by Seneca on good Stoic grounds (consider particularly *On Anger* I.8.7 as well as the passages cited above, chap. III, n. 53; cf. Nicev, pp. 184–85). At the same time, if my analysis is correct, the "Stoic" mode of Olympiodorus cannot simply be collapsed with his "Aristotelian" mode, since nothing in Aristotle's own theory of tragedy suggests a cathartic role for "desire." The "Stoic" mode would seem to reflect in the first place the revival of the Platonic notion of the tripartite soul by Posidonius (Galen *On The Opinions of Hippocrates and Plato* V.450,9 ff. Müller); it may reflect more distantly the allopathic "catharsis" practiced by the early Pythagoreans (consider particularly the reference to a *harmonia* in the soul).

32. See, for example, Howald, pp. 188 and 196, Else, *Aristotle's Poetics*, pp. 225–32, 423 ff.

technical prescriptions for composing tragedies reflect his understanding of catharsis. At the very least, it seems legitimate to work on the assumption that there is a link between catharsis and the fundamental discussion in Chapter 13 of the requirements of the tragic hero, and in particular of the notion of tragic error or the tragic flaw (*hamartia*).

According to the argument of *Poetics* 13, the best or finest form of tragedy is one showing the fall of a man who is neither simply good in a moral sense nor simply evil, but somehow between these two. This is a man, Aristotle says, "of the sort who does not excel in virtue and justice and yet who suffers misfortune not through vice [*kakia*] and wickedness but rather through some error [*di' hamartian tina*]—one of those who is in great repute and good fortune, such as Oedipus or Thyestes and noteworthy men from families of this sort." The best tragic plot, then, will exhibit a change "not from misfortune to good fortune but the opposite, from good fortune to misfortune, not through wickedness but through great error [*di' hamartian megalēn*], either such a man as was mentioned or one rather better than worse."[33] What kind of character is the tragic hero supposed to have, and what is the nature of the "error" to which he appears prone? These questions have been much disputed, both with respect to the meaning of the word *hamartia* in Aristotelian usage and with respect to the application of the notion of tragic error to actual heroes in Greek tragedy. At the present time, there is wide agreement that Aristotelian *hamartia* should be understood as simple intellectual error or mistake rather than as morally culpable fault or flaw.[34] It is usually argued that the error of the tragic hero cannot be moral in nature because Aristotle excludes from the outset that the hero

33. *Poet.* 1452b28–53a17.
34. This is the position adopted in the recent comprehensive account of J. M. Bremer, *Hamartia: Tragic Error in the Poetics of Aristotle* (Amsterdam, 1969). The consensus has, however, been powerfully challenged by T. C. W. Stinton, "Hamartia in Aristotle and Greek Tragedy," *CQ* n.s. 25 (1975), 221–54.

will be morally flawed in any fundamental way, while at the same time requiring his error to be "great."[35] In this connection, the example of Oedipus seems decisive. In Sophocles' *Oedipus Tyrannus,* the play which appears to serve as *the* model for Aristotle's best form of tragedy, the crimes of the hero are committed in total ignorance of the factual situation in which he stands. Oedipus' murder of the unknown man who turns out to be his father would have been regarded, certainly by any Greek of the fifth century, as no crime at all: it was a natural or innocent mistake, a case of justified homicide committed purely in self-defense.[36]

Interpretation of Aristotle's doctrine of *hamartia* has been vitiated in the first place by a consistent failure to give proper consideration to the problem of Aristotle's relationship to Greek tragedy. It is generally admitted that Aristotle's theory of tragedy cannot possibly be understood as a purely descriptive or analytic theory of Greek tragedy; and Aristotle makes quite clear that his doctrine of *hamartia* is to be applied not to tragedy as such but only to the best or finest form of tragedy. At the same time, however, it is assumed that Aristotle's theory of tragedy and of tragic error in particular must be descriptive to some extent; and it is universally held that Sophocles' *Oedipus* provides one, if not the only, example of the best or finest form of tragedy as Aristotle understands it. Yet both assumptions are in fact highly questionable. Aristotle nowhere explicitly identifies the *Oedipus* or any other actual tragedy with his own best form of tragedy. In particular, the view that

35. Typically Kurt von Fritz, *Antike und moderne Tragödie* (Berlin, 1962), p. 4: "The hamartia should therefore be as great as possible, the imperfection small. How then could they be identical with one another?"
36. Thus von Fritz, p. 7. This is also the view of Else, who attempts to argue that catharsis is to be understood as the "purification" which the model tragic hero himself undergoes when it is recognized, by the audience, that his crime is merely accidental (*Aristotle's Poetics,* pp. 436–46). Strangely, Else himself admits that "the pronouncement that a homicide . . . had been accidental apparently established the doer at once as *katharos:* there was no further requirement of religious purification" (p. 432).

Aristotle offers Oedipus as an example of tragic error in Aristotle's sense is based on a misreading of Aristotle's actual statement on the subject: Oedipus is offered as an example not of one who suffers misfortune through error but of "one of those who are in great repute and good fortune."[37]

In any event, the sensible procedure would seem to be to attempt to determine the meaning of Aristotle's tragic error as far as possible without reference to Greek tragic practice. The crucial passages in determining Aristotelian usage occur in the *Nicomachean Ethics*. While a full analysis cannot be attempted here, I shall discuss briefly two passages which seem to point to an understanding of tragic error quite different from that currently dominant.[38]

In the course of the discussion of justice in Book 5 of the *Ethics,* Aristotle undertakes to distinguish several varieties of legally relevant injury:

> . . . when the injury occurs contrary to reasonable expectation [*paralogōs*], it is an accident [*atychēma*]; but when it is not contrary to reasonable expectation, it is an error [*hamartēma*], for one is in error when the source of responsibility is in oneself, but it is only an accident when it is outside; and when one knows but does not deliberate, it is an unjust act [*adikēma*], for example what happens through anger [*thymon*] and other passions that are necessary or natural in human beings; for when they injure and err [*blaptontes kai hamartanontes*] in this way they commit injustice and perform unjust acts [*adikēmata*] but they are not by

37. It is true that Aristotle appears to identify the tragedies dealing not only with Oedipus but with several other standard tragic protagonists with his own best kind of tragedy (compare *Poet.* 1453a19 with 1452b31). Here too, however, Aristotle's point seems more limited than it is often taken to be: the examples are intended as illustrations of heroes who fall into misfortune, not of heroes who fall into misfortune through great error of their own, as the wording of a22—*ē pathein deina ē poiēsai*—confirms.

38. The evidence is intelligently discussed by Stinton, pp. 221–35, who concludes that Aristotelian usage permits understanding tragic hamartia in a range of senses including moral senses; see also A. W. H. Adkins, "Aristotle and the Best Kinds of Tragedy," *CQ* n.s. 16 (1966), 78–102, Gerald K. Gresseth, "The System of Aristotle's *Poetics*," *TAPA* 89 (1958), 312–35, and R. W. Harsh, "Hamartia Again," *TAPA* 76 (1945), 47–58.

this fact unjust or wicked; for the injury is not through wickedness. But when it is from moral choice [*ek proaireseōs*] then it is unjust and wicked.[39]

This passage is usually cited to support the view that acts committed through "error" are unintentional and therefore not morally culpable. It is by no means clear, however, that "error" in the strict sense is not culpable. What would seem to distinguish error from mere accident is the responsibility of the agent: if accident is the result of simple ignorance, error seems to be the result of culpable ignorance—the difference between, for example, accidental homicide and manslaughter.[40] More important, however, is the fact that "error" in Aristotle's usage is not limited to this narrow and technical sense. Even those committing unjust or fully culpable acts can be described as "erring" if their acts are committed under the influence of "anger" (*thymos*) or other "necessary or natural" human passions.

One may agree with those who insist that the distinctions drawn by Aristotle in this passage are not immediately applicable to tragic poetry. Yet it is necessary to pay particular attention to Aristotle's purpose in drawing these distinctions. The key to understanding the various statements of the *Ethics* on the question of legal or moral culpability lies, it would appear, in Aristotle's concern to modify current legal practice and the conceptual understanding embodied in it. Athenian legal practice, at any rate, failed to distinguish in principle between acts committed through culpable negligence and acts committed through passion: both were considered "involuntary."[41] It is this tendency to regard crimes of passion as simply involun-

39. *Eth. Nic.* 1135b11–25. Cf. 1110b24–33, 1111a33–b1 and *Rhet.* 1374b4–9.

40. The culpable is distinguished from the nonculpable in Roman jurisprudence (Gaius *Institutes* III.211, Justinian *Institutes* IV.3.3–8) precisely by the test of "reasonable expectation" (Harsh, p. 52).

41. Of the three Athenian courts with jurisdiction in murder cases, the Areopagus dealt with "deliberate homicide" (*phonos ek pronoias*), the Palladion with "involuntary homicide" (*phonos akousios*), and the Delphinion with "justified" or accidental homicide (*phonos dikaios*). Aristotle agrees with Athe-

tary which Aristotle is concerned above all to correct. Hence his restriction of the term *hamartēma* to acts of culpable negligence alone, and his extension of the term *adikēma* to acts committed through passion. If Aristotle does not emphasize the fact that the performance of unjust acts through passion rather than from moral choice involves a mitigation of culpability, he does so primarily for practical or rhetorical reasons.

A passage in Book VII confirms and extends this interpretation. In the course of the discussion there of "moral weakness" (*akrasia*), Aristotle remarks that moral weakness "is blamed not only as error [*hamartia*] but also as a kind of vice [*kakia tis*], either simply or in part." Yet he makes clear at the same time that this is true only of moral weakness with respect to certain passions. For while "desire" resembles "moral choice" to a very high degree, "anger" (*thymos*) "seems least of all in accordance with moral choice."[42] Or as Aristotle argues in the context just considered: "what comes about from anger is finely judged not to be from forethought, for it is not the one acting in anger who initiates the action but the one who angers"; accordingly, moral weakness with respect to honor, "anger," or the spirited passions generally is not regarded as vicious or blameworthy simply. Aristotle's defense of the nobility of anger or spiritedness (*thymos*) in Book VII is indeed striking:

> spiritedness in some way hears reason but mishears it, as nimble servants who run off before hearing everything that is said to them and then fall into error [*hamartanousi*]. . . . For when reason or imagination indicates the outrage or slight, as it were syllogizing that it ought to fight against such a man it rages straightway. But desire, if reason or perception only say "it is

nian practice that crimes of anger should not be considered to be simply "deliberate" (*Eth. Nic.* 1135b26), but he disagrees with the view that they are simply "involuntary" (*Eth. Nic.* 1111a24-v1). This view is the common view: "many hold that love too is involuntary, and some feelings of anger and natural needs, because they are powerful and beyond nature, and we forgive them as being naturally capable of doing violence to nature" (*Eth. Eud.* 1225a20-23). Cf. J. W. Jones, *The Law and Legal Theory of the Greeks* (Oxford, 1956), pp. 272-73.

42. *Eth. Nic.* 1111b18-19.

pleasant," surges toward enjoyment; so that spiritedness somehow follows reason and desire does not. It is therefore baser, for the one who is morally weak with respect to spiritedness is somehow worsted by reason, but the other by desire and not by reason. Again, forgiveness follows rather the natural impulses, but spiritedness and rage are more natural than the desires for excess and for unnecessary things.[43]

An interpretation of tragic *hamartia* in the light of Aristotle's notion of moral weakness with respect to anger and the spirited passions generally makes excellent sense as an explanation of the apparent disproportion between the moral imperfection of the tragic hero and the seriousness of tragic error. The excesses of the spirited passions are granted forgiveness by most men both because they reflect natural or necessary human impulses, and also because those impulses are in very large measure useful and admirable from a social or political point of view. Yet the errors caused by the spirited passions are, as Plato had put it, "great and unmusical." It is necessary to think only of the hero who served as the model of Greek aristocratic behavior. The same qualities which made Achilles an excellent warrior contributed to his defiance of duly constituted authority, with all its devastating consequences for the Greek host before Troy.[44] The fall of Aristotle's tragic hero would be occasioned, then, by a "great error" which is at once wholly disproportionate to the hero's moral imperfection and a necessary expression of it: tragic error is not simply a mistake of fact or a mischance, but a moral failure which issues ineluctably from the character of the hero.

Whether or to what extent such an understanding of tragic error accords with Greek tragic practice is not a question that can

43. *Eth. Nic.* 1149a25-b8; cf. 1147b20-48a5, 1135b25-27. Compare Theophrastus fr. 77 Wimmer: "In assessing the kinds of error . . . those committed in accordance with desire are worse than those in accordance with spiritedness."

44. Consider in this connection *Poet.* 1454b8-15. Although the text is uncertain, Aristotle appears to approve Homer's presentation of Achilles as at once good or decent (*epieikēs*) and a "model of harshness" (*paradeigma sklērotētos*).

171

be pursued here. But it is necessary at least to consider the possibility that Aristotle's theory is consciously intended to correct what Aristotle regarded as a fundamental deficiency in the moral outlook characteristic of Greek tragedy altogether. If contemporary legal thought had failed to assign a proper degree of culpability to crimes of passion, the same may also be said of the thought of the tragic poets. For the tragedians (and ultimately for Homer, whom the tragedians follow in this as in other respects), responsibility for crimes of passion tends to be shifted wholly or in part to the gods, or to a mental blindness (*atē*) traceable to the intervention of the gods.[45] It is at least a plausible hypothesis that Aristotle objected to the intervention of the gods in tragedy to the same extent and for the same reasons that Plato had objected to it in his critique of tragedy in the *Republic*. Indeed, it could be argued that what separates Sophocles' *Oedipus* from Aristotle's version of the best tragedy is precisely the element of divine intervention: the downfall of Oedipus occurs not through moral error as much as through divinely manipulated chance.[46] Aristotle's own theory, by contrast, would appear to require that the hero's downfall follow unambiguously from his moral error, or that the hero be held unambiguously responsible for yielding to the passion which occasions the tragic deed. This is by no means to say that Aristotle holds any simple theory of poetic justice. The suffer-

45. An excellent account is given by Hugh Lloyd-Jones, *The Justice of Zeus* (Berkeley, 1971). For Aristotle's view of the relation between Homer and the tragedians see Carnes Lord, "Aristotle's History of Poetry," *TAPA* 104 (1974), 195–229; for the notion of *atē* and its relation to Aristotle's view of tragedy see R. D. Dawe, "Some Reflections on Ate and Hamartia," *HSCP* 72 (1968), 89–123.

46. For an analysis of the *Oedipus* and of Sophoclean tragedy generally which emphasizes the importance of divine intervention in the prosecution of family curses, see Lloyd-Jones, pp. 104–28. Consider above all *Poet.* 1454a37–b8, where Aristotle equates divine intervention in tragedy with "irrational" action and argues that it should be excluded entirely, or else—and the alternative seems clearly presented as less desirable—"it ought to be outside the tragedy, as in the *Oedipus* of Sophocles." It is also of interest that this passage contains the only explicit criticism of Homer in the entire *Poetics* (cf. Else, *Aristotle's Poetics*, pp. 470–71).

ing of the hero may be deserved in the sense that it is proportionate to the seriousness of the crime itself; it will not be deserved in the sense that it is proportionate to his moral culpability. Indeed, it would seem to be this disparity between punishment and desert which most clearly defines tragedy for Aristotle as for the tragic poets themselves.

In attempting to understand the mechanism of catharsis or the manner in which it is effected by the tragic plot, one would have to begin, I think, with the question of the relation of punishment to desert in the tragic hero and in the expectations of the audience. If my argument is correct, catharsis will be intimately related to the audience's reaction to a hero whose susceptibility to spirited passion leads him into error and punishment, and its ultimate effect will be to fortify the audience against a similar susceptibility. It is probably safe to assume that not all of the citizens of Aristotle's best regime or even of ordinary societies will be morally weak in the technical sense: moral weakness as such seems to be the exception rather than the rule.[47] But all can be expected to share a certain susceptibility to passion, and in particular to the passions associated with spiritedness. Particularly for gentlemen who are disposed to be susceptible to the spirited passions and to condone and even to admire such susceptibility in others, tragedy provides, as it seems, a salutary demonstration of their dangerous excesses. It is this demonstration or its psychological reflection which constitutes the central lesson of tragedy as Aristotle appears to understand it.

The foregoing remarks are intended to be suggestive rather than definitive, and to mark out a line of future investigation. But I hope they suffice to show that the *Poetics* cannot simply be assumed to contradict the interpretation of Aristotle's view of the political significance of tragedy presented here. It is hardly necessary to point out that the *Poetics* itself is a notoriously elusive work. If progress is to be made in interpreting the argument of the *Poetics,* the relation between Aristotle's literary and

47. *Eth. Nic.* 1152a25–27.

his political theory will have to be given greater attention, I think, than has been customary in the recent past.

6. Comedy

It is usually assumed without argument that Aristotle regarded tragedy as the highest form of poetry. One is compelled to wonder whether this assumption is really sound. If it is indeed true that tragedy as tragedy is inescapably tied to the experience of punishment or suffering,[48] and if the punishment or suffering visited on the heroes of tragedy is necessarily disproportionate to their offense, it would seem that the morality of tragedy altogether must remain fundamentally imperfect. Moreover, if it is true that in tragedy altogether "learning comes through suffering,"[49] there would appear to be a tension or contradiction between the tragic view of the relation between knowledge or wisdom and happiness and what one may call the philosophic view. In tragedy, even at its best, there is a fatal disjunction between learning, knowledge, or wisdom on the one hand and happiness on the other: the happiness of the noble heroes of tragedy depends on a fundamental delusion which is exposed only at the price of misery. It is on the basis of such a view of human life, it would seem, that "the poets" argue that the divine is envious of or inimical to human happiness.[50] Aristotle does not take seriously this argument. For Aristotle as for Plato, the very possibility of the philosophic life—of a life combining learning or knowledge with happiness—shows that the tragic view of the human situation is inadequate.

The obvious candidate as an alternative to tragedy is comedy. Aristotle says little about comedy either in the *Politics* or

48. It is not possible here to discuss the notorious problem of the apparent inconsistency between the argument of *Poetics* 13 and that of the chapter immediately following, where Aristotle commends as the best tragic plot one in which the hero experiences recognition prior to commiting the tragic deed (1453b37–54a9). See I. M. Glanville, "Tragic Error," *CQ* 43 (1949), 47–57; Else, *Aristotle's Poetics*, pp. 450–52.

49. Aeschylus *Agamemnon* 177.

50. Consider *Met.* 982b28–83a5.

the *Poetics*. But there is at least one suggestive link between Aristotle's doctrines concerning tragedy and his statements on comedy: comedy too is imitative of human "error" as distinct from human vice.[51] What are the "errors" represented in comedy? It is tempting to suppose that if tragedy for Aristotle is concerned with the spirited passions and their excesses, comedy for him is concerned with the erotic passions and their excesses. To do so, however, would be to disregard the fact that, according to Aristotle himself, comedy originated in the lampoons (*psogoi*—literally, "blames") of iambic poets, and that much of Greek comedy prior to Aristotle had concerned itself with political rather than erotic subjects. It seems likely that Aristotle considered comedy at least as much a poetry of spiritedness as tragedy.[52]

When Plato reproaches comedy for retaining too much of the element of accusation or blame, he probably means the reader to think above all of the attack on Socrates in Aristophanes' *Clouds*. At the same time, however, he suggests the possibility of a kind of comedy which imitates human error in a spirit of "teaching" rather than blaming, and indicates that such a form of comedy could educate more effectively than law itself precisely because law is necessarily accusatory.[53] One may wonder whether comedy might not be potentially superior in this respect to tragedy as well. Perhaps the right kind of comedy could satisfy Aristotle's requirement for a poetry of spiritedness which can educate men in the dangers of spiritedness, but which is more nearly in harmony with a properly philosophic view of morality, knowledge and happiness.

To what extent such a view of comedy may have been reflected in the promised discussion of comedy in the second book of the *Poetics* it is not possible to say. That Aristotle held a doctrine of comic catharsis has sometimes been argued. I

51. *Poet.* 1449a32–37.
52. *Poet.* 1448b24–49a1, *Eth. Nic.* 1128a4–7, 13–14 ff. Cf. Lord, "Aristotle's History of Poetry," pp. 197–204, 222–23.
53. *Laws* 934e ff. (compare 935c7 with d2). Cf. Lycurgus *Against Leocrates* 102.

believe this to be highly unlikely.[54] Yet this is by no means to say that Aristotle regarded comedy as a form of poetry necessarily lacking in moral seriousness. In any case, there is a substantial body of indirect evidence which could be thought to support the kind of hypothesis here suggested. This is the evidence of linkage between Aristotelian poetic theory and the theater of Menander, the founder of the so-called New Comedy. Menander, who is said to have been a pupil of Aristotle's successor Theophrastus and a friend of the Peripatetic politician Demetrius of Phaleron, purified comedy of its accusatory tendencies, while at the same time giving particular and

54. The late sources which are sometimes cited (see particularly Rostagni, pp. 20-31, 128-41) as indirect evidence for an Aristotelian doctrine of comic catharsis must be used with the greatest caution. This is particularly true in the case of the Byzantine compilation known as the *Tractatus Coislinianus* (G. Kaibel, *Comicorum Graecorum Fragmenta* [Leipzig, 1899] I.50; see Lane Cooper, *An Aristotelian Theory of Comedy* [New York, 1922]), which is generally admitted to be of very doubtful value. I believe it is also true in regard to the doctrine of poetic catharsis—a catharsis extending to comedy as well as to tragedy—which appears to be presupposed by the Neoplatonists Iamblichus (*On the Mysteries* I.11) and Proclus (*Commentary on Plato's Republic* I, 42 and 49-50 Kroll). Although Proclus admits that Plato's expulsion of comedy and tragedy from the best regime of the *Republic* "has provided much ground for criticism both to Aristotle and to the champions of these kinds of poetry" (49,17-19), the context of his discussion provides no other reason for connecting the doctrine he there expounds with Aristotelian catharsis. Not only do Proclus and Iamblichus not use the word *katharsis* (only the verb *apokathairō* appears, the corresponding nouns being *aphosiōsis* and *aperasis*); the doctrine they both present is fairly clearly, it would seem, not a doctrine of catharsis in the Aristotelian sense at all. It appears to rest on the notion that the experience of tragedy and comedy provides the occasion for satisfying or releasing excesses of passion in a harmless manner through vicarious identification with the sufferings and joys of the characters. On this view, tragedy and comedy neither purify the passions of their base or dangerous elements nor purge or eliminate them altogether; they merely moderate the force of the passions so as to make them more amenable to the control of reason. As Proclus puts it: "through these it is possible to satisfy the passions in a moderate manner and, in satisfying them, to make them manageable with a view to education" (*dia toutōn dynaton emmetrōs apopimplanai ta pathē kai apoplēsantas euerga pros tēn paideian echein*) (49,14-16). I would suggest that this doctrine is of specifically Neoplatonic provenance (this seems indicated in particular by the manner in which it is alluded to by both Proclus and Iamblichus), having originally been

thematic attention to the problem of spiritedness.[55] If it is true, as is sometimes said,[56] that Menandrian comedy is the true successor to Attic tragedy, it could be that Aristotle did not look altogether unfavorably on this development.

7. Poetry and Prudence

We have seen that Aristotle appears to envisage a kind of higher education centering on the cultivation not of moral character properly speaking but rather of practical reason or "prudence" (phronēsis). To the extent that tragedy and comedy serve to moderate the passions which constantly threaten to obstruct prudent action, it makes sense to consider them as contributory to such an education. Yet there would also seem to be a more direct sense in which dramatic poetry or poetry generally constitutes an education in prudence. In Chapter 9 of the Poetics, Aristotle tells us that "poetry is more philosophic and more serious than history, for poetry narrates rather the universals, while history narrates the particulars."[57] Poetry does not narrate the universals simply: it presents the universals by way of the particulars or as they manifest themselves in particulars. It differs from history by the fact that it is able to

---

formulated in response to Plato's own suggestions in order to supply that "defense" of poetry which Plato himself had seemed anxious to encourage (Republic 606a–b, 607d–e). It may have been in part the influence of this doctrine which induced the author of the Tractatus Coislinianus to formulate a doctrine of comic catharsis modeled on the Aristotelian definition of tragedy. On the unlikelihood of comic catharsis for Aristotle see particularly L. A. Post, "Aristotle and Menander," TAPA 69 (1938), 24–25.

55. According to Eth. Nic. 1128a22–24, "new comedies" depend on "innuendo" (hyponoia) rather than "scurrility" (aischrologia), the hallmark of older comedy. For the relation between Menander and the literary doctrines of the Peripatos see T. B. L. Webster, Studies in Menander, 2d ed. (Manchester, 1960), pp. 195 ff.; A. Barigazzi, La formazione spirituale di Menandro (Turin, 1965); and C. Lord, "Aristotle, Menander and the Adelphoe of Terence," TAPA 107 (1977), 183–202. Menander's first play was evidently entitled simply Anger (Orgē).

56. Thus, for example, U. von Wilamowitz-Moellendorf, Einleitung in die griechischen Tragödie (Berlin, 1921), p. 56.

57. Poet. 1451b5–7.

present the universals shorn of the unique and contingent particulars which make any historical event inimitable. The universals presented in poetry are the universals of "action" (*praxis*), of human moral and political action in the broadest sense. Poetic "imitation" is not imitation of action in the sense that it merely reflects events of actual life or of history. Rather, it imitates action in a manner designed to bring out the universals of action. In so doing, it renders action imitable by its audience. It provides, in other words, models of moral and political behavior that can stimulate and guide acting men.

There is a striking congruence between what poetry provides and what prudence requires. Prudence is an intellectual habit or a kind of knowing which encompasses both particulars and universals. It requires both an experience of the world and a correct understanding of that experience. It requires an ability to adapt the universals of moral and political action to particulars, to the contingent circumstances of moral and political life.[58] Precisely because of the contingent character of these circumstances, there can be no science or art of action properly speaking: "philosophy" by itself cannot serve as an adequate guide to moral and political behavior. On the other hand, mere experience or familiarity with the unique events of "history" is equally insufficient, though it is useful and even in some degree indispensable for political men.[59] Only poetry, as it seems, provides the proper combination of generality and specificity that is necessary for the development of prudence in the full sense of the term.

In what way precisely Aristotle may have conceived of poetry as the central instrument of an education in prudence must plainly remain a matter for speculation. It is important not to overstate the extent to which Aristotle can be supposed to have defended the study of poetry in the name of prudence.

58. *Eth. Nic.* 1141b8–22. For a recent treatment of the notoriously difficult question of the nature of practical reasoning in Aristotle's ethical writings see Anthony Kenny, *Aristotle's Theory of the Will* (New Haven, 1979), pp. 111–71.
59. Consider *Rhet.* 1360a33–37 (cf. 1359b30–32).

That he thought poetry as such could educate to prudence, or even tragedy or comedy as such, is by no means evident, and I have tried to argue that Aristotle is very likely to have shared the reservations of Plato regarding the moral deficiencies characteristic of contemporary tragedy and comedy. In a number of respects, but particularly in its view of the role of the divine in human life, contemporary tragedy would appear to be incompatible with prudence in the Aristotelian sense; and this would most likely be true of any poetry in which the universals of action are presented under the aspect of religious law. At the same time, Aristotle clearly believed—contrary to the view of early modern thinkers such as Hobbes or Descartes, for example—that the models of human behavior held up by poetry are not necessarily incompatible with prudence, or that there is a kind of poetry which can provide models of imitation that are within the grasp of ordinary men, models that can benefit prudent action instead of threatening it by imposing universal standards which are too exalted to be applicable to the ordinary circumstances of human life. Aristotle's final view of this question will have depended crucially on his final view of prudence itself, a question of notorious complexity which cannot be discussed here. Suffice it to say that Aristotle appears to presuppose what would be denied by the thinkers of early modernity—that prudent action involves and indeed is inseparable from moral virtue.

5

Politics and Culture

---

1. Education and Culture

The preceding discussion has explored the senses in which the musical activities of mature citizens in Aristotle's best regime can be understood as a form of education properly speaking. As is evident from the entire course of Aristotle's argument in *Politics* VII–VIII, however, the leisured "pastime" (*diagōgē*) of the citizens of the best regime can at best be only partially understood as serving the purpose of education. "Education" (*paideia*) as Aristotle uses that term is primarily and fundamentally education to moral and political virtue. From a certain point of view, it is possible to identify the actions deriving from moral and political virtue as the primary content of the leisured pastime of a class of "gentlemen" (*kaloikagathoi*), the class intended by Aristotle to form the citizen body of his best regime. From another and higher point of view, however, moral and political action, like economic action, partakes of the "necessary and useful" as distinct from the "noble" (*to kalon*). From this point of view, the one adopted finally, if unemphatically, in the *Politics* as well as in the *Nicomachean Ethics,* the leisured pastime of political men or of gentlemen is one which is essentially apart from politics and which transcends politics. The primary content of their leisure is "pastime" in the precise sense—the cultivation of the mind in a manner that is at once pleasant and serious or noble, or what may conveniently be called "culture."

180

In conclusion, then, an attempt must be made to elucidate the nature and purpose of the cultured pastime of the citizens of Aristotle's best regime, and the implications of this notion for the proper understanding both of the argument of *Politics* VII-VIII and of Aristotle's political thought generally. It will be necessary to organize my discussion around an analysis of the difficult and widely misunderstood argumentation concerning the best way of life with which Aristotle introduces his entire treatment of the best regime in the *Politics*.

2. *The Best Way of Life* (I)

Aristotle's treatment of the question of the best or most desirable way of life in the first three chapters of *Politics* VII forms a kind of preface to the last two books of the *Politics*. That its importance, and its thematic connection with the later argument (in particular that of Book VIII), have not been sufficiently recognized is due in the first instance to a failure to appreciate the rhetorical difficulties which Aristotle had to confront in attempting to discuss the question of the best way of life within the limits of "political science."[1] Aristotle announces at the outset (1323a21-23) that his discussion will rely on a prior treatment of the question "in our public discourses" (*en tois exōterikois logois*). The provenance of Aristotle's argument is of more than bibliographic interest: the account of Chapter 1 will prove to be "exoteric" not only in name.[2] Chapter 1 addresses the question of the way of life which is best "so to speak for everyone" (1323a19-20) or for men generally. Aristotle begins

1. Commentators have been more concerned with detecting signs of interpolation or revision than with the argument itself. Susemihl-Hicks (pp. 48-49) regard Chapters 2 and 3 as interpolations by a later editor; Theiler (pp. 69-71) thinks they are additions by Aristotle himself. Theiler's approach is rightly criticized by Friedrich Solmsen, "Leisure and Play in Aristotle's Ideal State," *RhM* 107 (1964), 196, n. 18.

2. The chapter has been discussed by J. Bernays, *Die Dialoge des Aristoteles* (Berlin, 1863), who thinks the "exoteric" source was a lost dialogue, and by Jaeger (pp. 276-80), who believes it was the *Protrepticus* (cf. also Ingemar Düring, *Aristotle's Protrepticus* [Göteborg, 1961], pp. 254-55). For reasons which will become apparent, I incline to follow Bernays.

by appealing to the familiar doctrine of the three kinds of "goods." He argues that the best or happiest way of life, for the individual as for the city, is a life devoted to the pursuit of the goods of the soul, "virtue" and "wisdom" (*phronēsis*), in preference to external goods or the goods of the body. Aristotle's brief discussion concludes with the following remark:

> Let this much be said by way of a preface . . ., that the best life both for the individuals and for cities is the life accompanied by virtue and sufficiently equipped so as to be capable of a share in the actions that accord with virtue. As regards possible objections, we must ignore them for the purposes of the present inquiry, but will take them up later, in case anyone is not persuaded by what has been said. [1323b37–1324a4]

Aristotle's apology for the inadequacies of his "exoteric" discussion should induce the reader to wonder just what has been left unsaid. To judge from the argument of Chapter 1, the question of the best way of life is essentially the question of the relative priority of external (and bodily) goods and the goods of the soul. Aristotle seems to argue that there are two ways of life which lay claim to being the best life: the life devoted to the pursuit of external (and bodily) goods, and the life devoted to the pursuit of "virtue and wisdom." Elsewhere, however, Aristotle distinguishes three ways of life—the "life of enjoyment," the "political" life, and the "philosophic" life. According to one formulation: "The philosophic life is concerned with wisdom [*phronēsis*] and the search for truth, the political with noble actions (these are the actions that come from virtue), and the life of enjoyment with the pleasures of the body."[3] The word *phronēsis* in Aristotelian usage can denote, as in the passage here cited, scientific or philosophic wisdom, but it may also refer to various kinds of practical intelligence—mere sanity or soundness of mind (cf. 1323a32–34), "good sense," or that "prudence" which Aristotle regards as a fundamental constituent of moral virtue. In Chapter 1, there is

3. *Eth. Eud.* 1215a35–40; cf. *Eth. Nic.* 1095b14 ff.

no indication that the *phronēsis* of which Aristotle speaks is anything other than wisdom of the latter sort.[4] The argument of Chapter 1 is sufficiently general and ambiguous so as not to rule out the particular claims of the philosophic life (the word *aretē* is general enough to accommodate excellence of mind as well as moral virtue: cf. 1324a25–30); but it pays no special attention to them, and in so doing leaves the impression that for practical purposes the best way of life is the practical or political life, the life devoted to virtue and "noble actions." It would seem that "for the purposes of the present inquiry," which is above all a practical or political inquiry, the claims of the philosophic life may be safely ignored.

3. The Best Way of Life (II)

Aristotle begins Chapter 2 by announcing that he will take up the second of the questions proposed for treatment at the beginning of Chapter 1 (1323a20–21), the question whether happiness is the same or different for individuals and for the city. According to him, the two kinds of happiness are indeed the same, and all would agree they are the same (1324a8–13). At first sight, one would think that the question of the identity of public and private happiness had been resolved in the previous chapter: has Aristotle not already decided that the best or happiest life for the city as for the individual is a life accompanied by virtue? In fact, the question was not resolved. "Virtue," as

4. Consider 1323b22–23 ". . . virtue and wisdom and action in accordance with them" (*aretēs kai phronēseōs kai prattein kata tautas*), as well as the parallel *phronēsis-phronimos* in b34 and 36 (cf. *Eth. Eud.* 1216a40). This creates considerable difficulty for Jaeger's view that the chapter borrows from the *Protrepticus,* as this work is an exhortation to philosophy. Consider the difference between *Pol.* 1323b1–2 and *Protrepticus* fr. B94 Düring (as well as *Eth. Eud.* 1214b30–33, which Jaeger also regards as inspired by the *Protrepticus*), and between *Pol.* 1323b7–12 and *Protrepticus* fr. B42, where the similarity noticed by Jaeger (p. 279) is less important than the difference it presupposes. The use of *phronēsis* in its practical sense is not unexampled in the *Protrepticus* (consider fr. B68 and the remarks of Düring, p. 191), but the theoretical sense predominates. For Aristotle's use of the term generally see C. J. Rowe, "The Meaning of *phronēsis* in the *Eudemian Ethics,*" in *Untersuchungen zur Eudemischen Ethik,* ed. P. Moraux and D. Harlfinger (Berlin, 1971), pp. 73–92.

indicated earlier, is an ambiguous word; the real question raised in Chapter 2 is not whether happiness for the city and for the individual consists in a virtuous life, but whether it consists in the *same sort* of virtuous life.[5]

There are, Aristotle explains, two matters which require consideration: it is necessary to ask whether a life of participation in the concerns of the city is more desirable than the way of life of an alien (*ho xenikos bios*), and secondly, what regime and what disposition or orientation (*diathesis*) is to be considered best for the city. It is the second question which primarily concerns Aristotle. Its investigation is a proper task of "political thought and speculation": by contrast, the first question, which concerns only individuals, is a matter of merely peripheral interest to "the present inquiry" (1324a13-23).

In order to elucidate the second question, however, Aristotle is compelled to explain at length the precise character of the problem regarding the participation of individuals in public life. It seems that those who agree that the most desirable way of life is the life "accompanied by virtue" disagree as to whether a "political and practical" way of life is the most desirable, or rather one "with no ties to any external things, of a speculative sort, which some say is the only philosophic life" (*ho pantōn tōn ektos apolelymenos, hoion theōrētikos tis, hon monon tines phasin einai philosophon*). "For," Aristotle continues,

> these are the two ways of life which are evidently preferred by those who are most ambitious in regard to virtue, both now and formerly—I mean the political and the philosophic. It makes no small difference where the truth lies, for the sensible man will necessarily order things with a view to the better end, both for the individual and for the regime. [1324a25-35]

Evidently, the two questions raised by Aristotle in Chapter 2

5. Newman (on 1324a5) wrongly assumes, I think, that the question whether the happiness of the city resembles the happiness of the individual "in springing from virtue and being proportionate to it" is not settled in Chapter 1; cf. Raymond Weil, *Aristote et l'histoire: Essai sur la Politique* (Paris, 1960), p. 47 n. 176. But the discussion of Chapter 1 does not prove that the happiness of individual and city are alike in every respect.

are not only related but intimately related. Aristotle's second question—"what regime and what orientation" are best for the city—is, it would appear, precisely the question whether the best way of life "for the regime" is the practical and political life or rather a kind of speculative or philosophic life.

In the sequel, Aristotle presents in summary form the views of the advocates of the political and the philosophic life. According to the latter, "despotic" rule over one's neighbors, a kind of rule, that is, which benefits the rulers while disregarding the interests as well as the wishes of the ruled, is inseparable from the greatest injustice, while "political" rule, a kind of rule which benefits the rules and is freely accepted by them, is an inconvenience and an impediment to one's own well being.[6] The views of the advocates of the political life are practically the reverse. According to them, the practical or political life is the only one benefitting a "real man" (*anēr*); and those who take part in politics and public life have no less scope for virtuous action than do private men.[7] And there are some who go so far as to say that the "despotic and tyrannical variety of regime" is alone truly happy (1324a35-b3).

"And in some cases this is the very definition of the laws and the regime—despotic rule over one's neighbors." With this remark Aristotle turns to consider the question which forms the central concern of his inquiry, the question of the orientation of the regime, or the best way of life for the city considered in its relation to other cities. He begins by observing that while the laws of most cities represent little more than a random accumulation, in those cases where the laws aim at a single end that end is invariably the forcible rule or "mastery" (*to kratein*) of other cities. This is true above all of Sparta and Crete, where "education and the bulk of the laws are ordered almost entirely with a view to war" (1324b5-9).

6. For the distinction between political and despotic rule see particularly *Pol.* 1254b2-55a3, 1255b16-20, 1277b7-16, 1278b30-79a21.

7. That this assertion would have been regarded as arguable appears from *Eth. Nic.* 1179a6-8. For the "real man" consider *Eth. Nic.* 1095b19-23 and Xenophon *Hiero* 7.3.

Most men, it seems, identify despotic rule with the political art. They do so unreasonably, for, as Aristotle points out, they would never tolerate from their fellow citizens the injustices they practice toward others. According to Aristotle, one ought not attempt to exercise despotic rule over everything, but only over what is fit for despotic rule, just as one ought to hunt animals rather than men for the table and for sacrifice (1324b32-41). Some men are naturally apt for despotic rule while others are not: those who are fit to be slaves may be acquired in war and ruled despotically, but there can be no justification for treating free men as slaves.[8] The preparations and practices undertaken with a view to war must be regarded, therefore, not as "the supreme end of all things" but rather as existing for the sake of that end. War, conquest, and despotic rule are in no way essential to happiness or the good life (1324b41-25a10).

In Chapter 3, Aristotle returns to the question whether the best way of life for the individual is one of isolation—"the alien's way of life"—or one of active participation in the affairs of the city. Though strictly speaking peripheral to Aristotle's inquiry, this question must be resolved, it seems, for the benefit of those who may not have been fully persuaded by the argument of Chapter 1 (cf. 1324a2-4). It appears that the advocates of the life of isolation refuse political office or rule of any kind on the grounds that the way of life of a "free man" is more desirable than that of a statesman or political man. Their opponents respond that happiness or well-being—"doing well" (*prattein eu*)—is impossible for someone who "does nothing" (*ton mēden prattonta*). According to Aristotle, both are

8. Consider *Pol.* 1256b23-26. That Aristotle suggests without explicitly drawing this conclusion is an indication of the difficulty created for the argument here by his doctrine of natural slavery, which might seem to support a "despotic" orientation. Actually, the fact that Aristotle makes provision for the promise to the slaves of the best regime of their eventual freedom (1330a32-33) would suggest that they are not exclusively natural slaves, and hence that even the best regime rests to a certain extent on the illegitimate exercise of despotic rule.

right in some respects and wrong in others. In particular, the advocates of the political life are correct in holding that happiness consists in "action"; but it is wrong to suppose, as some of them do, that the best kind of action is the exercise of sovereign rule over everyone. For it is both just and noble to share power with equals, or to yield it to one who is superior in virtue (1325a18–b14). "If what we have said is correct," Aristotle goes on, "and happiness is to be identified with wellbeing [*eupragia*], then the best way of life both for every city and for the individual would be the active [*praktikos*] life" (1325b14–16).

This conclusion is somewhat surprising, as it is hardly clear that the reasoning which is meant to dispose of the question of the best life for the individual also settles the question of the best life for the city. Are we to infer, then, that the best life not only for the individual but for the city as well is one of active participation in "political" rule, or that it is indeed essential to the happiness of the city that it involve itself in the affairs of other cities? It is this question that is addressed by Aristotle in the immediate sequel.

> But the active life does not necessarily involve a relation to others, as some suppose, nor are those thoughts alone active which are for the sake of results achieved in action, but much more so those speculations and thoughts which have no end beyond themselves and are for their own sake. . . . And neither is it necessary that cities situated by themselves and preferring to live in this manner be inactive, for their parts may be active; for there are numerous mutual relations between the parts of a city. And this holds as well for human beings individually; otherwise, all would not be well with god and the universe, which have no external actions apart from those that are proper to them. It is evident, then, that the best life is necessarily the same both for each human being and for cities and human beings generally. [1325b16–32]

To speak of an active or practical life which consists in the pursuit of "speculations" which have no end beyond themselves is to speak of a way of life which is no longer "active" in any tolerable sense of the term. Obviously, Aristotle has enlarged its sense in such a way as to include even the activity of philosophy. The question is whether in so doing he does not compromise the entire preceding argument regarding the superiority of the life of active participation in politics. Has Aristotle yielded to his own preoccupations to the extent that he forgets, as one scholar puts it, that his subject is politics?[9]

It seems to me that Aristotle argues as he does precisely because he does not forget for a moment that his subject is politics. To begin with, Aristotle's interpretation of the active or practical life as one which does not exclude the pursuit of philosophy is something very different from an acceptance of the claims of the advocates of "the alien's way of life." The latter is a way of life which, as Aristotle had remarked, "*some say is the only philosophic life*" (1324a28–29); in fact, it is not the only philosophic life.[10] The example of Socrates shows that nothing intrinsic to the activity of the philosopher prevents him from living the life of a citizen and participating in politics. While it is true that the theoretical activity of the philosopher is primarily "for its own sake" or does not necessarily serve the city, there is nothing that prevents a philosopher from benefiting his city by acting as the educator or advisor of political men, or indeed, as the example of Aristotle shows, from elaborating a political science that is meant to benefit political men. In any event, Aristotle would appear to be thinking in the first instance not of philosophers of any sort, but

9. Solmsen, p. 196. He adds: "We have to accept the oscillations of Aristotle's argument and the ambiguity of his conclusion; they are indicative of a deeper conflict between diverging tendencies of his mind." Jaeger speaks in a similar vein (p. 281) of the "inevitable conflict between Aristotle's philosophical and his sociological conscience."

10. Thus also Newman on 1324a27; cf. Susemihl-Hicks and Theiler (pp. 69–70). Aristotle is undoubtedly thinking of the characteristic distinterest of the pre-Socratic philosophers in political matters (consider particularly Aristotle fr. 66 Rose); he may also have in mind Aristippus and the Cyrenaics (consider Xenophon *Memorabilia* II.1.13). See G. Müller, "Probleme der aristotelischen Eudaimonielehre," *MH* 17 (1960), 121–43.

rather of practical men who secede from politics for reasons of safety, convenience, or private enjoyment.[11]

It would be wrong to suppose, however, that a way of life which combines philosophical speculation with political action is for Aristotle in some way intrinsically superior to a life devoted only to philosophy. Aristotle indicates that thoughts and speculations which have no end beyond themselves are "much more" active, and hence productive of greater happiness, than thoughts which are in the service of action (1325b17–21). Indeed, there can be no doubt that Aristotle believed the philosophic life as such to be happier or better than the political life as such.[12] It is only because Aristotle manages to interpret the philosophic life as a life of "activity" that he can conclude, toward the end of Chapter 3, that the "active" life is the best way of life both "for each human being" simply and "for cities and human beings generally."[13] And yet why should Aristotle at once suggest and deny the superiority of the philosophic life?

4. The Problem of Political Rule

Aristotle's argument must be understood in the context of "the present inquiry", which is in the first place and above all a practical or political inquiry. The announced intention of that inquiry is to seek the way of life which is best, not for man simply, but "so to speak for everyone" (1323a20). For all practical or political purposes or for the great majority of men, it would

11. Consider *Eth. Nic.* 1179a6–8. For the political inactivity of much of the hereditary nobility in Athens during the fourth century see, for example, Paul MacKendrick, *The Athenian Aristocracy, 399 to 31 B.C.* (Cambridge, Mass., 1969), pp. 3–27.

12. *Eth. Nic.* 1177a12 ff.

13. The apparent redundancy of *tois anthrōpois* (1325b32) has aroused suspicion, and Susemihl-Hicks regard it as further evidence of the interpolated character of the argument of Chapters 2 and 3. In fact, however, it would appear to provide a precise indication that the best life for the city and for most men—for "so to speak everyone" (1323a20)—is in Aristotle's final view not necessarily the best life for "every single human being" or for man simply.

seem, the best life is the life of "action" in accordance with virtue. But the central concern of Aristitle's inquiry is, as has been seen, the question of the best way of life for the city; and in order to answer this question in a satisfactory manner, it proves necessary to take account of a way of life which is usually associated with individuals rather than with cities. For the purposes of Aristotle's inquiry, the question of the philosophic life is important only in its relation to the question of the best life for the city.

As was indicated earlier, the question to which the latter half of Chapter 3 is implicitly devoted is the question whether an active participation in "political" rule is essential to the happiness of the city. Aristotle's explicit answer is that it is not: a city situated by itself and preferring to live in isolation may achieve happiness through its own internal activity. And yet precisely by suggesting the superiority of an individual way of life devoted to the pursuit of thoughts and speculations which have no end beyond themselves, Aristotle opens his audience to the possibility that a life of self-sufficient activity is the most desirable for a city as well, regardless of where it is situated. This possibility must suggest itself all the more insistently as Aristotle studiously avoids all mention of "political rule" and the easy solution which that notion would provide.

Why is Aristotle reluctant to leave it at saying that the best way of life both for the individual and for the city is a life devoted to the activity of political rule? I believe the reason lies in his certainty that political rule as exercised by the city is an impossible halfway house on the road to despotic rule or "mastery." If political rule, or as Aristotle also calls it, "hegemony" (cf. 1327b4–5), is indeed essential to a city's happiness, no city will voluntarily abandon its pretensions to such rule except in the face of *force majeure*. Political rule as exercised by the city resembles less the rule of citizen over citizen than the rule of husband over wife (cf. 1252a26–27): sovereign states cannot agree to rule and be ruled in turn. But neither can they agree to accept a position of permanent inferiority. Political rule is essentially unstable: if it is not merely a mask for despotic rule, it is always threatening to become despotic rule. Aristotle glances at the experience of Athens as well as of Sparta when he remarks: "Of those who have held the hegemony in Greece some have established democracies in the cities and others oligarchies, in each case with a view to their own regimes, and with an eye to their own interests rather than those of the cities themselves" (1296a32–36). The distinction between "hegemony" and "empire" (*archē*) is in practice often difficult to trace; Aristotle does not hesitate to speak of hegemonial cities which do not serve the interests of the cities they rule.[14]

The problematic character of political rule on the level of the city is most strikingly visible in the fact that the same individuals who support political rule within the city are also inclined to favor a despotic way of life for the city as a whole: they advocate in foreign policy a course of action which they would be ashamed to pursue toward their fellow citizens (1324b32–35). Most men abhor tyranny at home; at the same time, "most men admire despotic rule over many men" (1333b16–17). Political rule as exercised by the city is problematic because it goes against the human grain. There is something in the nature of men and cities that inhibits if it does not render impossible a hegemonial rule which genuinely looks to the interests of the ruled. There is, it would seem, a specific irrationality in political life which causes men to deny to the citizens of other states the same human consideration they accord their own. The division of the human race into a number of independent and potentially hostile communities is, in spite of its manifestly arbitrary character, a permanent and irreducible aspect of human life: the distinction—the necessarily invidious distinction—between "we" and "they," between fellow citizen and foreigner, is the fundamental political fact. At the root of this phenomenon is, as it seems, that permanent

14. Consider Aristotle's treatment of the origins of the Athenian empire in *Ath. Pol.* 23.2 and 24.2; cf. *Pol.* 1333b41–34a2.

feature of human nature which Aristotle, following Plato, calls "spiritedness."

5. *Spiritedness and the Best Regime*

Aristotle's assertion, in the course of his discussion later in Book VII (1327b23–28a 16) of the natural endowment required of the citizens of the best regime, that spiritedness is the source of "friendliness" (*to philētikon*) seems designed to prepare his explicit correction of the Platonic view that harshness or savagery toward strangers is a necessary concomitant of spiritedness. In Aristotle's view, spiritedness is the source of that affection or friendship (*philia*) which, as it seems, constitutes the natural or spontaneous bond of human communities and in particular of the political community.[15] But it is also something more. Spiritedness is productive both of "the element of ruling and the element of freedom" (*to archon kai to eleutheron*); it is a "ruling thing" (*archikon*) (1328a6–7). The same impulse which interests men in the defense of their own or of the city also encourages more aggressive tendencies. The desire to subdue others and to rule over them is no less natural than the desire to remain free of alien rule, and the two desires are inextricably connected. Both are inseparable from a certain harshness, from a kind of anger or self-assertiveness which is by its very nature unreasonable or immoderate.[16] Cities or peoples that are capable of maintaining their independence do not voluntarily abstain from a policy of expansion if circumstances

15. Compare *Pol.* 1253a29–30 and 1278b19–23 with 1262b7–8 ff. and *Eth. Nic.* 1155a22–23. For the significance of "friendship" in classical political thought see Abram Shulsky, "The Infrastructure of Aristotle's Politics" (Ph.D. dissertation, University Chicago, 1972), pp. 117–27, and David Bolotin, *Plato's Dialogue on Friendship* (Ithaca, N.Y., 1979).

16. In the course of his discussion (*Eth. Nic.* 1126a36–b2) of the virtues and vices connected with the passion of "anger" (*orgē*), Aristotle remarks that "we sometimes praise those who have the defect and call them gentle, and we call those who are harsh, manly, as being capable of rule [*tous chalepainontas andrōdeis hōs dynamenous archein*]." It should be noted that the virtue representing the "mean" in regard to anger has no name, and that Aristotle is forced to apply to it the word—"gentleness" (*praiotēs*)—usually associated with the

permit it. Aristotle makes clear that while the barbarian nations of Europe may lack the political capacities required for empire, they do not lack the will to empire. Indeed, being more spirited than other nations, they are dominated to a greater extent by the appetite for war and conquest. Capacity to rule is a function not only of intelligence or political organization but also of the will to rule, and the latter depends on spiritedness. Because they combine both qualities, the Greeks are capable of ruling "all men," the naturally spirited as well as the naturally slavish (1327a23–33). Precisely because the Greeks and similar peoples possess the greatest natural advantages, they are exposed to the greatest temptations. The human stock of the best regime must be spirited by nature if that regime is to survive; but the spiritedness threatens at the same time the very purpose or reason for being of the best regime.

When Aristotle remarks that the Greek nation has the capacity for ruling all men "if it should unite in a single regime" (1327b32–33), it has sometimes been assumed that he recommends thereby a policy of Greek unity, most probably under Macedonian leadership, for the sake of a war of conquest against the Persian Empire.[17] Such a view cannot plausibly be maintained. The argument of Book VII as a whole rests on the assumption that a policy of war and conquest is incompatible with the way of life of the best regime and indeed of any decent political order. Aristotle does not trace the Greeks' present inability to exercise universal rule to defective political organization, for he notes that they are "excellently governed"; the defect in question must be traced to the effect of Greek

---

defect (1125b26–31). It would seem that the human soul provides no real support for moderate spiritedness—for the reasonable assertion of one's rights and interests. This appears to be confirmed by the parallel treatment of ambition (*philotimia*) (1125b1–25); cf. 1149a25–32.

17. Thus, for example, W. Oncken, *Die Staatslehre des Aristoteles* (Leipzig, 1875) II, 287 ff., M. Defourny, *Aristote: Etudes sur la Politique* (Paris, 1932), pp. 494–95, 527–45; see also Hans Kelsen, "The Philosophy of Aristotle and the Hellenic-Macedonian Policy," *Ethics* 48 (1937–38), especially 60–62.

spiritedness in guarding the freedom of the individual cities. There is little reason to suppose that Aristotle did not believe such an arrangement to be the best one possible. Aristotle teaches (1326a8–b24) that the city is the best political community, and that a regime which encompasses many cities can be a regime in name only. The city is the best political community in the last analysis because only a small community can be fully dedicated to the pursuit of virtue and hence to the best way of life.

This is of course not to deny that external developments may make it necessary for the city to enter into alliances with other cities for mutual defence. Nor is it to deny that under certain circumstances it may be advisable for the city to organize an alliance of cities under its own leadership, or even to establish a permanent hegemony. The foreign policy of the best city will necessarily be influenced by the behavior of its enemies (cf. 1331a14–18), and Aristotle does not pretend to resolve questions which must be the responsibility of statesmen deliberating in a particular case. It is for this reason that Aristotle contemplates with apparent equanimity the possible acquisition by the best city of a naval force suited to a "hegemonial and political way of life" (1327a40–b6), or the use of military power in the quest for "hegemony that aims at benefiting the ruled" (1333b41–34a1). But necessity cannot excuse a deliberate policy of conquest and despotic rule, even if it affects only or primarily those who are naturally apt for such rule.[18] Aristotle

18. In the passage just referred to (1333b38–34a2), Aristotle permits or counsels military preparations "not that they may enslave those who are undeserving of it, but in the first place that they themselves may not be enslaved by others, then in order to seek a hegemony that aims at benefitting the ruled—not at despotic rule over all men [*hēgemonian tēs ōpheleias heneka tōn archomenōn alla mē pantōn despoteias*], and third to exercise despotic rule [*despozein*] over those who deserve to be slaves." Commentators persist in interpreting this remark in the light of the advice Aristotle is supposed to have given Alexander (fr. 658 Rose) to deal with Greeks "hegemonically" but with barbarians "despotically": "Among Greeks, a war of conquest is never permitted, but when conducted by a Greek people against a foreign nation it becomes by that fact a just war" (Defourny, p. 488; cf. Weil, p. 411).

may have been favorable to the Macedonian hegemony in Greece as an arrangement that would serve to liberate the cities from the threat (and in some cases from the reality) of Persian dominance. It is more than doubtful that he applauded the Macedonian conquest of the entire Persian Empire.[19]

Aristotle's awareness of the problematic character of spiritedness is, I would suggest, the deepest reason for his reluctance to recommend the practical or political life as the best way of life for the city. To encourage the city to involve itself in the affairs of other cities with a view to the establishment of hegemonial rule is to give free rein to a passion or complex of passions which must eventually negate the very idea of hegemonial rule. Spiritedness is the impulse to protect, preserve, extend, and exalt what is one's own as against what is alien or foreign; it is this impulse which necessarily governs a city's relation to other cities. Political rule, that form of rule

---

Whatever one may want to think of Aristotle's alleged advice to Alexander, it has nothing to do with his argument in the *Politics*. Although Aristotle at first seems to rule out only wars of conquest directed at enslaving those who do not deserve to be enslaved, the qualification added to his recommendation of hegemony ("not at despotic rule over all men"; cf. 1325a35 and context) shows that he means to exclude all wars of conquest properly speaking. What the third item refers to is not wars against external enemies but rather the use of military force to control the slave population (1328b7–10, 1330a25–30; cf. 1269a34–b12): Aristotle speaks of the exercise, not the acquisition of despotic rule. The proof is the immediate sequel, which shows clearly that the pursuits of peace and leisure are to be preferred to any form of external rule (1334a2–10). Whatever lack of clarity may be thought to exist in this passage derives from the difficulty of distinguishing in principle between the possession of slaves and their acquisition in war, of accepting a slave establishment along Spartan lines while rejecting the despotic orientation of the Spartan regime (compare *despozein* in 1334a2 with *despozein* in 1333b17).

19. There seems to me a strong probability that the reference at *Pol.* 1296a36–b2 to the "one man" among those exercising hegemony in Greece who was concerned to encourage moderate regimes is to Philip of Macedon, as Oncken (II, 267), Defourny (pp. 534 ff.) and others have argued; but see P. Andrews, "Aristotle, *Politics* IV.11.1296a38–40," *CR* 66 (1952), 141–44. It is hazardous to draw any conclusions from the biographical tradition surrounding Aristotle, particularly as it relates to Macedonian politics; but there

which is at least as concerned with the good of the ruled as with
that of the ruler, is not a viable policy for the city as a whole
because the city lacks that spontaneous concern for other cities
which its own citizens feel for one another. In spite or rather
precisely because of the fact that spiritedness, in the form of
"friendliness," supports political rule within the city, it
renders difficult if not impossible the exercise of political rule
by the city itself.

6. Politics and Philosophy

The problem is not one that can be solved by exhorting
lawgivers to found cities in remote places. Aristotle's best
regime, while surely a utopia in one sense, does not presuppose
a forgetting of the fundamental conditions of political life:
Aristotle takes it for granted that the best city will have enemies
(cf. 1326b39–41, 1327a21–25, 1327a40–b3). But neither is it
solved by the simple recommendation of a posture of armed
neutrality. The will to freedom and the will to rule are two sides
of the same coin, and a city wholly occupied in providing for its
own defense is not one that is likely to observe nice distinctions
when it comes to judging the actions and intentions of other
cities. The only solution is the solution adumbrated in the
opening chapters of Book VII. What is required is a radical

---

is evidence that Aristotle was closely associated with Philip and took an active
part in Macedonian diplomacy in the decade following his first departure
from Athens (see Anton-Hermann Chroust, *Aristotle: New Light on His Life and
on Some of His Lost Works* [London, 1973], I, 155–76). This connection need
not imply identity of views, but it seems to indicate that Aristotle found the
tendency of Philip's policy acceptable; and if the passage cited above does
refer to Philip, it reflects a favorable view of the principles of the League of
Corinth. Very different, however, is the case of Alexander. The Peripatetic
school was uniformly hostile to Alexander after his death, a fact it is difficult
to explain solely in terms of practical politics or resentment at the execution of
Aristotle's nephew Callisthenes (cf. Philip Merlan, "Isocrates, Aristotle and
Alexander the Great," *Historia* 3 [1954–55], 76–81). As for the traditional pic-
ture of an intimate collaboration between the two men, a good case has been
made (Chroust, I, 125–32) that Aristotle was never in fact Alexander's tutor,
and a number of sources attest to personal enmity between them.

transcendence of politics as it is ordinarily understood, of the entire sphere of existence defined by the fundamental opposition between "we" and "they" and by the primacy of "action." In Aristotle's formulation, the best way of life for the city is not the practical and political life as ordinarily understood, but a kind of "speculative" life.

To assume that the "speculative" activity of the best city will be limited to the mutual interaction of its different communities or classes, as Aristotle appears to suggest in Chapter 3 (1325b25–27), is to miss the full meaning of his paradoxical assertion. If political activity and in particular political rule within the city is regarded as the highest activity to which men can aspire, the attractions of a policy of external rule will necessarily be greater than if this were not the case. If a life of activity and rule is the best life simply, the perfection of that life will appear to be the exercise of "sovereignty over all" (1324a31–41). In fact, however, most men are somehow aware that political activity by itself cannot be the end of the best life. Political activity is indeed productive of happiness, but not intrinsically so: most men engage in politics not for its own sake but because of the rewards that accompany it. Men engage in politics for the reason they engage in other practical activities, in order to secure leisure and the good things that are enjoyed in leisure. Happiness in the truest sense belongs not with activity but with leisure.[20] In Aristotle's view, true happiness consists in the leisured enjoyment of the mind in the pursuit of speculations and thoughts which have no end beyond themselves, in other words, in the activity of philosophy.

20. "Happiness is held to belong to leisure, for we are busy that we may have leisure, and we wage war in order to live in peace. But the activity of the practical virtues belongs to politics and war, and the actions connected with these are held to be lacking in leisure, and warlike actions completely so . . . ; but the activity of the political man is also lacking in leisure, since apart from political action it procures the advantages of power, honor, or at any rate happiness for him and for the citizens—happiness being different from political activity and something we clearly seek apart from it [*par' auto to politeuesthai peripoioumenē dynasteias kai timas ē tēn ge eudaimonian autoi kai tois politais, heteran ousan tēs politikēs, hēn kai zētoumen dēlon hōs heteran ousan*]" (*Eth. Nic.* 1177b4–15).

And yet philosophy cannot be the activity characteristic of the best city, if only because Aristotle goes to such lengths to show that the best way of life for most men is the practical and political life rather than a life of speculative self-sufficiency. What Aristotle calls for, then, is not a transcendence of politics simply but rather a reorientation of the city within the limits of the practical and political life. The best way of life for the city is not the speculative life simply but rather the closest approximation to that life which is possible on the level of politics. What is required is an activity which provides the intrinsic satisfactions of philosophy without imposing the demands of philosophy or while being accessible to men of ordinary capacities. What is required is a leisured activity which can be regarded by most men as the end or reward of political activity and hence as the genuine locus of public happiness. The activity in question—the way of life characteristic of the best regime—is the leisured enjoyment of music and poetry.

In Chapters 14 and 15 of Book VII, Aristotle returns to and elaborates the problem adumbrated in his preface. The citizens of the best regime must be able to sustain occupation (*ascholia*) and to go to war, but much more should they be able to remain at peace and at leisure; they must be able to do necessary and useful things, but ought rather to do what is noble. The legislator of the best regime must follow a course radically different from that of most actual legislators. For "those of the Greeks who at present are thought to be the best governed, and the legislators who have established these regimes, have manifestly failed to order either the regimes themselves with a view to the best end, or their laws and education with a view to all the virtues; rather, they have diverted them in vulgar fashion to serve those which are thought to be useful and more profitable." This is true in particular of the Spartan regime. The Spartans and those who admire their way of life believe that the best kind of regime is a regime oriented to war and conquest, and that the best form of virtue is the manifestly "useful" virtue of courage (1333a30–b14).

In the sequel, Aristotle turns to the question of the virtues that are useful with regard to leisure. It seems that courage and endurance are necessary for leisure in the way that occupation is necessary for leisure; these virtues properly belong to occupation itself. Moderation and justice, on the other hand, are useful in leisure as well as in occupation; indeed, they are particularly useful in times of peace and leisure, for "war compels men to be just and moderate, but the enjoyment of good fortune and leisure together with peace tends to make them arrogant." But moderation and justice are evidently not enough. The citizens of the best regime will also require, with a view to leisure alone, what Aristotle appears to call the "virtue" of "philosophy" (1334a16-28).

"Philosophy" can mean one of two things. Either Aristotle is speaking of philosophy—theoretical speculation—in the precise sense, or he is speaking in a looser sense of what would today be called "culture."[21] That philosophy in the precise sense can have been intended is, to judge from the argument of the opening chapter of Book VII, extremely unlikely; and Aristotle indicates in Chapter 14 itself that a capacity for speculative thought is not part of the equipment required of the citizens of the best regime (1333a25-30). Aristotle did not regard the regime of philosopher-kings as a serious political possibility.[22] When he summarizes and discusses the teaching

21. The issue has too frequently been blurred. Bonitz (*Index* 821a6) gives the meaning "virtus intellectualis," which is approved by Susemihl-Hicks and Newman; Newman also translates "intellectual aptitude" and "habit of intellectual inquiry" (I, 346-47). The wider sense, while not being exclusive of the narrow sense, is less precise than "habit of intellectual inquiry." The "lover of culture" (*philomythos*) is "in some sense a philosopher," but what he shares with the philosopher is a sense of awe or admiration for the noble and beautiful rather than the sense of his own ignorance and the desire to remedy it. The true philosopher possesses the strength of mind to ascend from opinion to truth or knowledge of nature, while the lover of culture remains within the horizon of habit and convention (*Met.* 982a12-21, 994b31-95a6; cf. *Top.* (142a9). For "philosophy" in the wider sense consider, for example, Thucydides II.40.1, Isocrates *Antidosis* 26.13, Plato *Republic* 498a-b.

22. According to Themistius (*Orations* 8.128 Dindorf = Aristotle fr. 647 Rose), Aristotle taught that philosophy is not only not necessary but a positive

of Plato's *Republic* (1260b37 ff.), he does not even mention the rule of philosophers in the fully elaborated version of Plato's best regime. It is all the more revealing, then, that he should criticize Plato for relying on an institutionalized system of communism to ensure the unity and happiness of that regime rather than on "education," that is to say, on "habit, philosophy, and laws" (1263b36–40). Aristotle cannot be supposed to have forgotten that in the last analysis Plato too had relied less on institutions as such than on "philosophy" and an education preparatory to philosophy. What he means to suggest, I think, is precisely that Plato should have relied less on philosophy in the strict sense of the term than on philosophy in the broad sense of the term. Philosophy in the broad sense does not necessarily exclude theoretical speculation, but its core is traditional culture; and traditional culture means above all literary culture. The core of that "philosophy" which is politically relevant is, in the language of Aristotle and his contemporaries, "music."

7. Culture and Gentlemanship

Aristotle's best regime will be ruled not by philosophers but by "gentlemen." The way of life of the gentlemen is a way of life devoted to the practice of virtue. There is, however, a crucial difference for Aristotle between virtue as it is commonly understood and practiced and the virtue of gentlemen properly speaking. In the satirical formulation of the *Eudemian Ethics,* the Spartans, the most conspicuous embodiment of virtue as commonly understood, are "good men" (*agathoi*) but not "noble and good men," that is, "gentlemen" (*kaloikagathoi*).[23] This is because they perform virtuous deeds not because such deeds are "noble" (*kala*) or choiceworthy in themselves, but because they are useful or necessary for the acquisition of the "good

---

impediment to kingly rulers; it is necessary only that they show themselves ready to listen to and be persuaded by those who "genuinely philosophize."
23. *Eth. Eud.* 1248b8–49a17.

things'' (*agatha*) of life, wealth and honors (cf. 1334a40–b3). As Aristotle says of the Spartans at an earlier point in the *Politics:* "they believe that the good things that men contend for are won by virtue rather than vice, which is correct, but they suppose these to be greater than virtue, which is not correct" (1271b7–10). The gentleman properly speaking is one who performs virtuous deeds for their own sake or because he takes pleasure in doing so; or if there is some reward external to the deeds themselves that he is concerned to win, it is the honor accorded him in recognition of his virtue by those whose opinions he values. At the peak of gentlemanship stands the "magnanimous man" (*ho megalopsychos*).[24] The magnanimous man is more than a little contemptuous of the good things for which men ordinarily contend in the political arena, including even honor. Accordingly, he is not one who is eager to take part in politics, but does so rather as a matter of duty.

The dominant class, the "guardians," of Aristotle's best regime are to be not merely gentlemen but "magnanimous men" (1328a9–10; cf. 1338b2–4). Because or to the extent that magnanimity stands at the peak of gentlemanship or of moral and political virtue altogether, magnanimity points unmistakably toward that which transcends moral and political virtue. The magnanimous man, like the best regime itself, is the reflection of the philosophic life within the practical or political sphere.[25] The rulers of the best regime resemble philosophers above all by the fact that they prefer leisure to occupation and in particular to the occupation of ruling. Plato, it would seem, had attempted to understand leisure as a

24. *Eth. Nic.* 1123b26–24a4.

25. Cf. Harry V. Jaffa, *Thomism and Aristotelianism* (Chicago, 1952), pp. 116–41. The ambiguity of magnanimity has led some scholars, notably R. A. Gauthier (*Magnanimité: L'idéal de la grandeur dans la philosophie paienne et dans la théologie chrétienne* [Paris, 1951], pp. 56–117; cf. Gauthier-Jolif, *L'Ethique à Nicomaque*, II, 272 ff.), to consider it a virtue proper to the philosopher. For the debate on this question see D. A. Rees, "Magnanimity in the *Eudemian* and *Nicomachean Ethics*," in *Untersuchungen zur Eudemischen Ethik*, ed. P. Moraux and D. Harlfinger (Berlin, 1971), pp. 231–43, who rightly decides against Gauthier's view.

characteristic feature of the philosophic life.[26] While Aristotle denies that leisure is coextensive with the pursuit of philosophy strictly understood, he preserves the Platonic connection between leisure and philosophy. He does so precisely by broadening the meaning of "philosophy" itself.[27] The magnanimous rulers of the best regime will spend their leisure not in the pursuit of scientific truth, or not primarily in such pursuit, but rather in the enjoyment of what is noble or beautiful as well as—at least from the perspective of the magnanimous man himself—"useless" in works of music and poetry.[28] Precisely by understanding the pursuit of "philosophy" in this sense as the end of politics or of life altogether, the gentleman is enabled to orient himself toward a way of life which is least exposed to the distempers—the excesses of spiritedness in its various forms—characteristic of the practical or political life.

26. Consider Plato *Theaetetus* 172d–76a, *Phaedo* 66b–d.

27. One may agree with the remarks of Solmsen concerning Aristotle's original use of the word *scholē* without agreeing that his conception of leisure differs fundamentally from that discoverable in Plato's *Laws* (see particularly Koller, *Musse,* pp. 35 ff.). Solmsen (and, though for somewhat different reasons, Kelsen, pp. 62–64) regards Aristotle's teaching as reflecting a specifically "hellenistic" desire for "withdrawal and privacy." But the fact that the leisured activities of the best regime are non- or trans-political in character does not mean they are essentially private: Aristotle states very emphatically not only that education must be public and uniform but that "each citizen should believe not that he exists for his own sake but that all exist for the sake of the city" (1337a26–29); and the culture of the mature citizens of the best regime will take the form primarily of public performances of "theatrical music.".

28. Compare *Eth. Nic.* 1125a11–12 with *Pol.* 1338a37–b4.

APPENDIX

Aristotle, Damon, and Music Education

It has become usual to interpret the history of the idea of music education in antiquity in the light of the notion of "musical ethos." Although this term was conceived and continues to be used as a convenient way of referring to Greek conceptions of the "psychic" power of music in the broadest sense,[1] the tendency has been to speak of musical ethos as a doctrine that is concerned primarily or exclusively with the uses of music in the formation of the moral character of the young. It is just such an "ethical-pedagogic" doctrine—a doctrine which is variously held to derive from Damon and his school, Damon and the Pythagoreans, or Damon and Plato—that is generally ascribed to Aristotle.[2] I have tried to show that Aristotle's argument in behalf of the ethical or educative value of music cannot be construed as a doctrine of musical ethos in the narrow sense, and that Aristotle's more apparent interest in the education of the young presupposes and is indeed incomprehensible apart from his more fundamental interest in the education or culture of adults. If the problem is formulated in the manner suggested here—that is, by distinguishing as sharply as possible between the capacity of music to form character in the young and its capacity to affect the passions and shape the "character of the soul" in mature persons—the way can be opened, I think, to a

1. Consider in particular Abert, pp. 1–4, Anderson, *Ethos and Education,* pp. 1–2, 179–80. That this is in fact what later antiquity understood by *ēthos* in music appears most clearly from Sextus Empiricus *Against the Learned* VI.48–50.

2. Anderson, *Ethos and Education,* p. 129 (Damon), Koller, *Musse,* pp. 1–3, 47–48, 59 (Damon and Plato), Koller, *Mimesis,* pp. 68–69 ff. (Damon and the Pythagoreans). The distinction between "Musikethiker" and "Musikästhetiker" seems to have originated with Abert.

Appendix

more adequate view of the development of the idea of music education than that presently available.

Very little is reliably known of the musical doctrines of that enigmatic figure, the teacher of Pericles and Socrates, Damon of Athens, and of the school which appears to have descended from him.[3] In the virtual absence of direct testimony, it has been customary to rely on what are thought to be the wholesale borrowings from Damon embodied in the discussion of music education in the third book of Plato's *Republic*. Not long ago we were exposed to the opinion that everything of interest in that discussion, and in particular the Platonic doctrine of poetic imitation, is borrowed from or inspired by Damon—or Damon in company with "the Pythagoreans."[4] It is safer to begin by assuming that Plato never simply "borrowed" anything, and to wonder whether the authentic teaching of Damon on the subject of music education was not rather different than the argument of the *Republic* might seem to suggest. That a fresh approach in this matter is necessary has indeed been felt;[5] that one is possible I hope to show. My investigation will concentrate on two pieces of evidence—one neglected and inadequately exploited, the other entirely overlooked: the brief account of Damon and his school in the second book of Aristides Quintilianus, and the (as I shall argue) interpolated section at the end of the eighth book of the *Politics*.

The most important—indeed, the only—extended account of the teaching of the Damonian school occurs in the musical treatise of Aristides Quintilianus (second century A.D.?).

3. For Damon's life and political activities see A. E. Raubitschek, "Damon," *C & M* 16 (1955), 78-83; F. Schachermeyr, "Damon," in *Beiträge zur alten Geschichte und deren Nachleben: Festschrift für Franz Altheim* (Berlin, 1969), I, 192-204.

4. Koller, *Mimesis*. Koller's thesis continues to find favor—see, for example, H. John, "Das musikerzieherische Wirken Pythagoras' und Damons," *Das Altertum*, 8 (1962), 69—despite an effective refutation by Else, "Imitation in the Fifth Century," pp. 73 ff.

5. Warren Anderson, "The Importance of Damonian Theory in Plato's Thought," *TAPA* 86 (1955), 88-102, *Ethos and Education*, pp. 74-81.

Whether or to what extent Aristides has incorporated authentic Damonian material in his own teaching is not a question that can be settled here, though it is fair to say that scholars have not always shown the proper caution in this respect.[6] But Aristides' one explicit reference to Damon is of unusual interest, and it has not, I believe, been properly understood—largely because (as so frequently happens in cases of this kind) the Damonian "fragment" has been isolated from the context which determines its meaning.

The argument of the relevant section of *De musica* II is as follows. Just as individual notes have a definite character (*ēthos*)—some are "male," others "female," and others neutral or mixed (II. 12 [77,19–20 Winnington-Ingram])—so too do intervals and entire harmonies. Accordingly, one may use the harmonies "by applying them to different kinds of souls by way of similarity or by way of opposition; thus you will uncover a weak character that is hidden and heal it and make it better, and you will effect persuasion: if the character is mean or harsh, you lead it through a middle state to its opposite, and if fine and good, you augment it by similarity to a settled and balanced condition" (14 [80,11–16]). Aristides' argument presupposes his distinction between two sorts of "character education" (*ēthikē paideusis*) effected by music: a "therapeutic" education operating "by way of opposition" (*kat' enantiotēta*) on those who suffer from an excess of passion, and an "opheletic" education operating "by way of similarity" (*kath' homoiotēta*) on those who are sufficiently free from passion to lend themselves to the "persuasion" which music is able to effect, or whose character is susceptible of being "assimilated" to the ethos a

6. See H. Deiters, *De Aristeidis Quintiliani Fontibus* (Düren, 1870), K. von Jan, "Damon," *RE* IV, 2073, R. Schäfke, *Aristeides Quintilianus: Von der Musik* (Berlin, 1937), pp. 100–12, Koller, *Musse*, pp. 79–81, Anderson, "Damonian Theory," pp. 98 ff. (cf. Else, "Imitation in the Fifth Century," p. 85 and nn. 53 and 54). Not much progress will be made in resolving this question until Aristides' own teaching—which is not only obscure, but voluntarily obscure (consider especially II.7 [65, 10–21] Winnington-Ingram, where the reading of the manuscripts should certainly be retained)—is better understood.

particular kind of music imitates or embodies.[7] After a brief remark concerning the diagnostic testing of character by different harmonies, Aristides proceeds as follows:

> For the harmonies resemble, as I said, their dominant intervals and limiting notes, and these resemble the movements and passions of the soul. That the notes even of a continuous melody form by similarity a character that did not exist previously both in the young and in those already advanced in years and develop one that is latent was made clear by Damon and his school as well. In the harmonies handed down by him, at any rate, one will find that of the notes employed the female and the male at one time or another either dominate or are used more sparingly or not at all—clearly because a harmony too is beneficial according to the character of each kind of soul. It is for this reason that of the elements of musical composition "note-selection" is regarded as in each case the most useful in the choice of the most necessary notes. (14 [80,23–81,6] = Damon fr. B7 Diels-Kranz])

This passage is of interest in the first place not so much for what Aristides says as for what he fails to say about the doctrines of the Damonian school. If Aristides' remark is read in its context, it becomes clear that the agreement between the Damonian teaching and Aristides' own views is at best a partial one. According to Aristides, music can affect character either "by way of similarity" or "by way of opposition"; according to Damon (and there is no reason to suppose Aristides is not fully reporting the Damonian position), music affects character "by way of similarity" only.[8] For Aristides, music can both form the character and heal the passions. For Damon, as it seems, the ethical or educational effect of music is limited to the formation of character. What is more, music education as

7. II.9 (68,22–69,1); for the distinction "passion"/"persuasion" consider particularly II.6 (59,27–28) and context. In the passage just cited, Winnington-Ingram wrongly marks a period after *enthēseis* (80,14): *kath' homoiotēta/kath' enantiotēta* stands in chiastic relation with *to te phaulon . . . enthēseis/kai peithō poiēseis*, while *ei men . . . symmetron* (80,14–16) only further elaborates the same distinction.

8. Consider Athenaeus 628c = Damon fr. B6 Diels-Kranz, Plato *Republic* 401d1. Cf. Else. "Imitation in the Fifth Century," pp. 83–85.

understood by the Damonian school is operative only in certain periods of life. For Aristides attributes to the school of Damon a concern for the music education not of the young and "those more advanced in years"—as is often assumed—but rather of the young and "those *already* advanced in years" (*tois ēdē pro-bebēkosi*):[9] for Damon, music education is the education on the one hand of children, and on the other of the old. While Aristides regards as an integral and important part of music education the healing of excessive passion in mature men, Damon had limited music education to the formation of character in the young and the very old.

The only obstacle in the way of understanding the Damonian teaching in the manner indicated by Aristides is a story appearing in several late writers, to the effect that several young men indulging in drunken behavior to an accompaniment of Phrygian music were brought to order when Damon instructed the flute girl to play a Dorian tune.[10] But since the same or a similar incident is connected more frequently and on better authority with the name of Pythagoras,[11] and since the Pythagoreans were indeed concerned with the healing or "purification" (*katharsis*) of the passions by means of music, there is no good reason to credit the attribution of this story to Damon.[12]

9. Cf. II.4 (58,3-5). This mistake is made by Anderson, *Ethos and Education*, p. 39, von Jan, pp. 2072-73, and F. Lasserre, *Plutarque: De la Musique* (Olten/Lausanne, 1954), p. 58; Schäfke correctly translates (p. 289) "Menschen vorgerückten Alters."

10. Galen *On the Opinions of Hippocrates and Plato* V, 453 Müller, Martianus Capella IX.926 = Damon fr. A8 Diels-Kranz. Cf. Lasserre, pp. 62-64, Schachermeyr, p. 199.

11. Philodemus *On Music*, Pap. Herc. 1576 fr. 1,16-19 (58) Kemke, Cicero fr. 2 Orelli, Quintilian I.10.32, Sextus Empiricus *Against the Learned* VI.8, Iamblichus *Life of Pythagoras* 112 Deubner, Boethius *On Music* I.1.

12. Aristoxenus fr. 26 Wehrli, Iamblichus *Life of Pythagoras* 64 Deubner, Aristides Quintilianus II.19 (91, 27-31). It is frequently asserted that Damon was himself a Pythagorean, but the only evidence is a questionable scholion to Plato *Alcibiades* 188c (= Damon fr. A2 Diels-Kranz). That Damon was influenced in some degree by Pythagorean musical thought is possible and even likely; yet the fact is that when Aristoxenus testifies (fr. 35 Wehrli) to a

What must be noticed next in Aristides' account of the Damonian teaching is its intention. Aristides appeals to the authority of Damon not so much in order to support his view of the ethical effect of music "by way of similarity" as to support his view of the ethical effect of a harmony (or a harmony as realized in a "continuous melody") as distinguished from its notes or intervals. Aristides' appeal to Damon reflects the musical situation of his own time: it reflects the attenuation of genuine modal ethos which had begun as early as the fifth century B.C., and which eventually permitted the amalgamation of the ancient harmonies in the uniform scale (the so-called Greater Perfect System) of classical music theory. The "harmonies" presupposed in Aristides' analysis are not true *harmoniai*—distinctive scales or "tunings" and the musical idioms associated with them—but "octave-species" (*eidē*) distinguished from one another only by their relative position on a single scale. Since, at least in theory, many harmonies share many of the same notes, it is not evident that the character of a given

---

Pythagorean concern for public education, he conspicuously fails to connect it with the Pythagorean concern for music. It is probably necessary to distinguish between original Pythagoreanism and later Pythagoreanism, which may well have absorbed Damonian ideas (consider Strabo I.2.3, which seems to reflect fourth-century controversies). Even so, the evidence for a Pythagorean theory of musical ethos in the narrow sense is remarkably slight. I do not believe that Hermann Koller (*Mimesis,* pp. 79–104) has succeeded in extracting it from Aristides Quintilianus, nor Rostagni (pp. 55–63) from Iamblichus' account of Pythagoras. According to Iamblichus (*Life of Pythagoras* 64), Pythagoras "established the first education through music by means of both tunes and rhythms, from which result cures of human conditions and passions [*aph' hōn tropon te kai pathōn anthrōpinōn iaseis egignonto*]." This passage hardly suffices to establish a distinction between "ethical" and "cathartic" uses of music, as Rostagni has attempted to argue. And, in fact, it seems clear from the sequel that Iamblichus is speaking only of passions or of pathological or diseased conditions, including bodily conditions; and *tropoi* may well be used to refer to states of the body (cf. 110). To say that the healing of the passions is a "corrective" (*epanorthōsis*) designed "with a view to virtue" (64; cf. 224) is not to say that it is "ethical" in the sense that it is appropriate for the moral education of the young. An account of Pythagorean musical thought may be found in W. Burkert, *Weisheit und Wissenschaft* (Nuremberg, 1962), pp. 348–78.

melody will be decisively affected by the harmony in which it is composed.

Aristides' solution to this difficulty is twofold. In the first place, he argues that a harmony derives its distinctive ethos from the notes which belong to it—from the "limiting notes" which define its range[13] and from the notes determining the intervals between them. Secondly, he stresses the importance of "note selection" (*petteia*) in musical composition (cf. I.12 [29,18-21]). The ethical effect of a given harmony depends, as it seems, on a selective use of the notes belonging to that harmony: only the notes which are "most necessary" in creating that effect are to be employed—for every harmony will necessarily contain notes which conflict with its dominant ethos.

It is sometimes assumed on the basis of this passage that the notion that individual notes have a distinct ethos (and the related emphasis on the importance of "note selection") is Damonian in origin.[14] Aristides' argument seems to me to suggest quite the opposite. The "harmonies" of the time of Damon were true modes rather than segments of a uniform scale; as Aristides himself points out, in very ancient times (the context is a discussion of the modes mentioned in Plato's *Republic*) "they did not always use all the notes" which might seem properly to belong to a particular harmony (I.9 [18,5 ff.]). "Note selection" cannot have been a principle of Damonian theory, for it was guaranteed by the very nature of modal composition. As regards the distinction between "male" and "female" notes, it appears to represent Aristides' interpretation of the "harmonies" of Damon rather than a genuine Damonian doctrine (consider 80,29 *goun*, 81,1 *estin heurein*): it is more than likely that modal ethos was regarded by Damon and his school (and by any musically educated person of the fifth

13. This seems to be the meaning of *tois periechousi phthongois* at 81,24 (cf. Schäfke, p. 289 n. 4, von Jan, p. 2072).

14. von Jan, p. 2072, Anderson, "Damonian Theory," pp. 98-101, Lasserre, pp. 58-59.

century) as determined less by individual notes abstractly considered than by certain types of intervals and the musical idioms or styles which had developed around them.[15]

When Aristides speaks of "the harmonies handed down" by Damon, he is evidently speaking not of musical modes proper (or of a written composition) but of melodic exercises of a certain kind—"Vokaletüden."[16] When he goes on to conclude that the male or the female notes are dominant in these exercises "because a harmony too is beneficial according to the character of each kind of soul," *harmonia* has its normal meaning[17]—since the whole point of Aristides' argument is to establish the ethical distinctiveness of a mode or harmony in its normal sense. The suppressed premise of Aristides' rather elliptical remark is that the Damonian "exercises" are, as their name suggests, compositions designed to embody the characteristic ethical effects of different harmonies. Accordingly, it is wrong to assume that Aristides imputes to Damon or his school the practice of composing individualized melodies for the benefit of "each individual soul" (*psychē hekastē*).[18] Whatever may have been Aristides' own view in this matter, his account of Damonian education mentions human groups or types (the young and the old) rather than individuals; and his interpretation of the Damonian "harmonies" suggests two distinct types (those dominated by male notes and those dominated by female notes) rather than a continuum which could accommodate slight variations in musical ethos to accord with the individual needs of a variety of human characters. What may be inferred from Aristides' account, I think, is that

15. Cf. Aristoxenus *Harmonics* 23, 39. In Aristides' version of the scales mentioned in the *Republic* (I.9 [18–20]), the initial "limiting note" is in many cases the same. Cf. Anderson, *Ethos and Education*, pp. 11–19, I. Henderson, "Ancient Greek Music," *The New Oxford History of Music* I (London, 1957), 345–49.

16. Cf. Schäfke, p. 289, n. 7 (following Meibom).

17. Contrary to what Anderson seems to suggest ("Damonian Theory," p. 99, n. 33).

18. Thus Anderson, *Ethos and Education*, p. 41 (but cf. "Damonian Theory," p. 99).

the harmonic exercises associated with the name of Damon—exercises, it would seem, which had originally been designed for use in education (and primarily, one would suppose, in the education of the young)—were composed in two distinct and even radically different modes or types of modes. Which modes these were, and what was their intended effect, we will now try to determine.

That Damon had recommended for the purpose of education two modes differing widely in ethos will be granted by those who regard Plato's treatment of music education as decisive for the Damonian view. It appears to have been a special claim of the Damonian school that music is capable of fostering all the virtues—"not only courage and moderation, but justice as well";[19] and when Plato emphasizes the need for two harmonies of an opposing character to foster the opposing virtues of courage and moderation (*Rep.* 399a–c), it is likely that he is reflecting something of Damon's own teaching in this matter. Similarly, he distinguishes in the *Laws* (802e)—a passage which may well be the source of Aristides' theory—between a "male" music which is "magnificent and disposes to courage" and a "female" music which "inclines rather to the orderly and moderate". Now the solution that Plato appears to adopt in the *Republic*—the Dorian mode is required in order to promote courage, the Phrygian in order to promote moderation—is generally assumed to represent the view of Damon.[20] But, in the first place, such a view is in itself highly problematic: the Phrygian mode was normally understood to produce feelings of "enthusiasm" or religious exaltation, or the very opposite of "moderation" (*sōphrosynē*) in one of its senses.[21] In the second place, it is not even certain that this was in fact the Platonic position. The argument of the *Republic* is decidedly ambiguous, and already in antiquity there was some

19. Philodemus *On Music* I.13 (7) Kemke = Damon fr. B4 Diels-Kranz.
20. Thus Abert, pp. 84–86, Lasserre, p. 62, John, p. 70, Anderson, *Ethos and Education*, pp. 72–73, 107–09.
21. Consider Euripides *Bacchae* 159 and context, *Pol.* 1340b4–5, 1342a32–b6.

disagreement as to which mode Plato had meant to connect with which virtue.[22] Several ancient commentators seem to have thought that, despite appearances, Plato recognized only the Dorian mode as being suited to the education of the young.[23]

In the treatise *On Music* formerly attributed to Plutarch, we are told that "the relaxed [*epaneimenē*] Lydian mode—the one that is opposite to Mixed Lydian and resembles Ionian—is said to have been invented by Damon of Athens."[24] Not much has been made of this remark, partly because the authority of the Pseudo-Plutarch is worth little in itself, partly because an interest in Lydian music on the part of Damon appears to be ruled

22. Proclus *Commentary on Plato's Republic* I, 61,24–28 Kroll. Though the question cannot be fully discussed here, I am inclined to agree with the ancient Platonists who identified Phrygian as the warlike and Dorian as the pacific mode. The problem of the Homeric hero as it is adumbrated in *Republic* II–III is that his reasoned beliefs regarding the gods render him afraid of death and hence deficient in courage; Phrygian music, by its very irrationalism, overcomes these hesitations and thereby promotes courage. It is too often forgotten (consider the argument of Lasserre, p. 62) that the Phrygian "songs of Olympus" are described by Plato in much the same terms as they are by Aristotle (compare *Symposium* 215b7–d6 and *Minos* 318b with *Pol.* 1340a8–12, 1342a7–11; cf. Proclus I, 62,5–9).

23. This is the argument of Proclus (*Commentary on Plato's Republic* I, 61,28–62,28 Kroll), who appeals to the implicit characterization of Phrygian music in the *Minos* (n. 22 above) and, less cogently, to *Laches* 188d; and it is evidently assumed in [Plutarch] *On Music* 1136e, a passage which is clearly influenced by Aristoxenus. It is sometimes argued (as for example by Anderson, *Ethos and Education*, pp. 105, 126), primarily on the strength of *Laws* 669d–e, that Plato refused to recognize an ethical effect in purely instrumental music. But this is clearly not the view taken in *Republic* 398d ff. The discrepancy may perhaps be explained by the fact that the Athenian Stranger is speaking with men who have not themselves been educated in music, while Socrates' interlocutors in the *Republic* clearly have. At any rate, it is not denied in the *Laws* that different tunes and rhythms have different effects (consider 791a, 802e), only that it is easy to determine precisely what those effects are. That Plato recognized the possibility of a musical "therapy" of the passions is evident from *Laws* 790d–91a. In a more general sense, the way of life of the citizens of the *Laws* is an "education and play" in which music has a central role (cf. particularly 803c–e). For a discussion of the *Laws* in connection with the treatment of music in Aristotle's *Politics* see Koller, *Musse,* pp. 9–28.

24. [Plutarch] *On Music* 1136d = Damon fr. B5 Diels-Kranz.

out by Plato's explicit rejection of the Lydian modes for the purposes of education (*Rep.* 398c). In its context, however, the remark is a suggestive one. It is preceded by a brief discussion of the Mixed Lydian mode, and immediately followed by this statement: "Of these harmonies, then, one is mournful and the other relaxed [*eklelymenēs*], and it was with reason that Plato rejected them and chose Dorian as being suited to warlike and moderate men—though not, by Zeus, as Aristoxenus says in the second book of his *Musicians,* because he was unaware that in these too there is something useful for a regime of guardians."[25] Evidently, Aristoxenus had criticized Plato's treatment of the ethos of the various harmonies on the grounds that the Lydian modes which Plato had summarily rejected also possess a certain educative value. Now it is possible that this understanding of Lydian music was original with Aristoxenus. But the very fact—if it is a fact—that one of the Lydian harmonies was invented by the leading theorist of music education would suggest that an educative value had been recognized in Lydian music before the time of Aristoxenus—by Damon. Even if the story preserved by the Pseudo-Plutarch is not true, it may well reflect a special position accorded the relaxed Lydian mode (or Lydian music as a whole) in the theories of the Damonian school.

In the final chapter of Book VIII of the *Politics,* Aristotle makes use of a distinction between harmonies or types of tunes according to which there are tunes which represent or affect character (*ta ēthika*), tunes which represent or affect action (*ta praktika*), and tunes which repesent or induce religious exaltation (*ta enthousiastika*). A similar distinction seems to be implied in a passage in the *Problems* (XIX.48) dealing with the harmonies employed in the music of tragedy. If one supplements Aristotle's brief remarks concerning the character of the various harmonies with the evidence of the *Problems,* the result is as follows. To the category of "enthusiastic" tunes corresponds the Phrygian harmony; to that of "practical" tunes,

25. [Plutarch] *On Music* 1136e = Aristoxenus fr. 82 Wehrli.

the Hypophrygian (Ionian) and Hypodorian (Aeolian) harmonies; and to that of "ethical" tunes, the Dorian harmony as well as the various harmonies of the Lydian group.[26]

Aristotle attributes the classification employed in the *Politics* to "certain men engaged in philosophy" who are "familiar with the education concerning music." That Aristoxenus in particular is meant has often been assumed. The identification is correct, I think, for it is confirmed by the report of Aristoxenus' views provided by the Pseudo-Plutarch: Aristoxenus had attacked the treatment of music education in the *Republic* precisely on the grounds that Plato had been unaware of the (moral or civic) utility of certain of the Lydian harmonies. Evidently, Aristoxenus considered the Lydian harmonies as in some measure "ethical" or educative—though perhaps not as much or as generally so as the "most ethical" Dorian (cf. 1342a2–3, 28–30). And Aristotle only makes explicit what is implicit in Aristoxenus' distinction between "ethical" and "enthusiastic" harmonies when he criticizes Plato or his Socrates for admitting the Phrygian as well as the Dorian harmony in the education of the young (1342a32–b6).[27]

If it is granted that the classification of harmonies appearing in Aristotle's *Politics* and in the *Problems* bears the stamp of

26. For the text and interpretation of *Problems* XIX.48 see Lord, "A Peripatetic Account of Tragic Music," and chap. III, sec. 3 above.

27. Aristotle's third category is also of interest in this connection. When the Pseudo-Plutarch undertakes to defend Plato against the strictures of Aristoxenus, he defends Plato's understanding of the ethical effect not only of the Lydian modes but of Aeolian and Ionian as well. Of Ionian he says: "he knew that tragedy used this sort of tune-composition as well" (*On Music* 1136e). Plato had treated Ionian as a relaxed or "sympotic" mode (*Republic* 398e6–10); Aristoxenus seems to have disputed this characterization on the grounds that Ionian was used in tragedy. Aristoxenus' view reappears in *Problems* XIX.48, where the "practical" Hypodorian (Aeolian) and Hypophrygian (Ionian) are said to be the modes appropriate to the heroes of tragedy; and it is evidently presupposed by Heraclides Ponticus (Athenaeus XIV.624c, 625b = fr. 163 Wehrli), who describes the Ionian mode as being, among other things, "a favorite of tragedy" (*tēi tragōidiai prosphilēs*). The most extended discussion of the ethos of both modes is that of Heraclides; it is perhaps less idiosyncratic than is usually assumed.

Aristoxenus, it is surely a plausible assumption that Aristoxenus' views in these matters were influenced in some degree by the school of Damon. That this was in fact the case is shown, I think, by what I suggest is an unrecognized document of the Damonian school—the interpolated paragraph which concludes Book VIII of the *Politics*.

The last paragraph of the *Politics* reads as follows:

> There are two things to be kept in view, the possible and the fitting; individuals ought rather to undertake what is possible and fitting for them. But these things too are defined according to the period of life. For example, those who are enfeebled by age have difficulty singing the high-strung harmonies, and nature directs them to use the relaxed ones. For this reason some of those connected with music have rightly blamed Socrates in this matter too, because he rejected the use of the relaxed harmonies in education on the grounds that they have an effect similar to that produced by drink—an effect not of actual drunkenness (for drunkenness is properly a state of excited frenzy) but rather one of stupor. So one ought to become familiar with harmonies and tunes of this sort with a view to a period of life that is to come—that is to say, old age; and also in the event that one of these harmonies is such that it promotes orderliness while affording amusement—as appears to be the case with the Lydian harmony above all. It is clear that three standards are to be observed in education: the mean, the possible, and the fitting. [1342b17–34]

That this passage is not the work of Aristotle has been strongly suspected for some time.[28] The main difficulties are these. To begin with, it is here assumed that "singing" is an appropriate musical activity for older men. But Aristotle had explicitly stated that "singing and the playing of instruments" is appropriate only for the young: "what is fitting" (*to prepon*) for older men is precisely the enjoyment of the performances of others (cf. 1342b17–23 with 40b20–21, 31–39 and 42a1–4). Nor had Aristotle given any indication that special provisions may have to be made for those who are "enfeebled with age."

28. Susemihl-Hicks bracket the passage, and argue the case for spuriousness at length; Newman agrees.

In the second place, it is claimed that the young ought to learn the relaxed modes not only because of their utility in later life but because one of them—the "Lydian," that is, the "relaxed" Lydian—"promotes orderliness while affording amusement,"[29] or because it contributes directly to the (moral) education of the young. It is reasonably certain that Aristotle did not share this view. Aristotle had made it abundantly clear that the Dorian mode is the mode best suited to the education of the young; and while it is true that he seems prepared to accept others as well, the very fact that he leaves the door open to such harmonies "as may be approved by those who are expert in philosophy and the education concerning music" (1342a30-32) shows that the use of other harmonies was not "approved," or at any rate not contemplated, by Aristotle himself. Moreover, it seems quite unlikely that he would have approved the use of the relaxed Lydian harmony under any circumstances. According to Aristotle, the effect of the "relaxed" harmonies is to dispose its listeners *malakoterōs tēn dianoian* (1340b2-3): what they promote is not "orderliness" but a cowardly softness or effeminacy of spirit. It seems probable that relaxed Lydian belongs with those "deviant" harmonies (1342a23-24; cf. 1290a19-29) which Aristotle appears to reserve for the entertainment—the "relaxation" (*anesis* 1341b41)—of the noncitizen class of his best regime. In short, Aristotle seems to share precisely that view of the relaxed harmonies which is the Platonic view. When the author of the final paragraph of the *Politics* criticizes "Socrates" for rejecting the use of the relaxed modes in education on the grounds that they are "associated with drinking" (*methystikai*), he is in effect criticizing Aristotle himself.[30]

29. Here (b31-32) the manuscripts have *dia to dynasthai kosmon t' echein hama kai paideian.* I think *paidian* must be read. The idea of "education" is, as will be suggested shortly, already implicit in *kosmon;* and Aristotle had made it clear that the music education of the young must combine an education to virtue with pleasure, play or amusement (1339b11-25, 1340b14-17, 25-31).

30. Cf. *Pol.* 1340b2 *malakoterōs* with *Republic* 398e6-7 *methē . . . kai malakia kai argia,* e9 *malakai te kai sympotikai.*

What appears to have happened is that a reader of the *Politics* felt himself authorized to contribute a supplementary note concerning a matter which Aristotle had seemed to leave to the judgment of "those who are expert in philosophy and the education concerning music." Of the identity of the interpolator little can be said, except that his evident misunderstanding of Aristotle's real position would appear to mark him as a Peripatetic of a later time. But the authorities he invokes—"some of those concerned with music" (*tōn peri tēn mousikēn tines*)—can be identified, I think, with reasonable certainty. If the information preserved by the Pseudo-Plutarch is correct, the criticism of Plato's handling of the relaxed modes points directly to Aristoxenus. But there is much more in this passage which points beyond Aristoxenus, directly—and unmistakably—to the school of Damon. While Aristotle had spoken only in passing of what is "fitting" for different ages (1340b33, 42b17), the interpolator makes *to prepon* a principle of his analysis (1342b18, 33–34); but *to prepon* appears to have been a fundamental category of Damonian theory.[31] The emphasis on the actual performance of music by the old is at least compatible with what is known of the teaching of Damon, and is perhaps reflected in Plato's prescriptions for a chorus of old men dedicated to Dionysus (*Laws* 665a ff.). At all events, a Damonian concern for the music education of the old is directly attested, as has been seen, by Aristides Quintilianus.

As regards the education of the young, it is clear that the interpolator recommends the use of the relaxed Lydian mode not by itself but in addition to the Dorian (which had just been recommended for this purpose by Aristotle).[32] When he ex-

---

31. Aristides tells us that *mousikē* was defined by "some" as "an art of what is fitting in sounds and movements" (I.4 [4,21]); the inclusion of dance strongly suggests Damon (cf. Athenaeus XIV.628c = Damon fr. B6 Diels-Kranz). Cf. Plato *Republic* 399a7, 400b1–4.

32. This seems to be the point of *meson* in b34—a rather clumsy attempt to harmonize the interpolated passage with the discussion of the Dorian mode which immediately precedes it (cf. b14); and Dorian seems to be the intended reference of the *kai* in b28.

plains that the relaxed Lydian is suitable for the young because it "promotes orderliness while affording amusement," what is implied, I think, is a distinction between the "orderly" (*kosmion*) ethos of relaxed Lydian and the "manly" (*andreion*) ethos of Dorian: while Dorian music teaches the manly virtues, and in particular the virtue of courage (*andreia*), Lydian music teaches the softer virtues—order, moderation, and (perhaps) justice. That this distinction is Damonian in origin is strongly suggested by Aristides' analysis of the harmonic exercises ascribed to Damon in terms of "male" and "female" notes, and by its appearance in close proximity to the name of Damon in Plato's discussion of music education.[33] Further confirmation may perhaps be found in Proclus' interpretation of the brief and very obscure discussion of the Damonian view of metrical ethos which is given in Plato's *Republic*.[34] According to Proclus, Damon regarded the enoplion as having a "manly character" (*andrikon ēthos*), and the dactyl as being "productive of orderliness and equanimity" (*kosmiotētos poiētikon kai homalotētos*); while "both, when mixed together in the right fashion, provide education in the true sense."[35] For Damon, it would seem, music education as a whole is an attempt to instill and to harmonize qualities which, while equally necessary from a social or political point of view, are necessarily and naturally opposed.[36]

There appears to have been an important disagreement between Damon and Aristoxenus on the one hand and Plato and

33. *Republic* 399e10–11 *biou . . . kosmiou te kai andreiou;* cf. Laws 802e.
34. *Republic* 400b–c = Damon fr. B9 Diels-Kranz.
35. *Commentary on Plato's Republic* I, 61,5–14 Kroll. A similar distinction appears in Aristides Quintilianus' discussions of harmony and meter (II.14 [82,1–2], 15 [82,24–25, 83,27]). Also of interest is Aristides' definition of the Damonian *prepon* as a "harmony" (*symphōnia*) of noble or praiseworthy qualities (I.4 [5,12–13]).
36. The reconstruction of Damon's "Areopagitica" by H. Ryffel, "Eukosmia," *MH* 4 (1947), 23–38, fails to recognize, I think, the precise meaning of *kosmos* and related terms in Damonian theory, though rightly stressing the aristocratic or conservative tendency of Damon's thought as a whole.

Aristotle on the other regarding the nature of the relaxed harmonies, in particular the relaxed Lydian. This mode—invented, according to one account, by Damon himself—seems to have formed an integral part of music education as understood by the Damonian school. Its educational utility was recognized, though perhaps less fully, by Aristoxenus; it was denied by Plato and Aristotle. Plato seems (and it is necessary to stress the qualification) to have accepted the Damonian principle that different modes are required to promote the opposing virtues of courage and moderation, or that the Dorian mode by itself is not sufficient for the purposes of education. With Aristotle this principle is abandoned, and the Dorian mode is recognized—possibly in connection with the musical revolution of the fourth century, which made of the old Dorian mode the central of seven species of the octave—as a "mean" which promotes a "mean and settled" character,[37] a character at once moderate and manly. As regards the notion of music education itself, I have tried to show that Damon restricted it to the young and the very old. Only with Plato is musical *paideia* understood to encompass mature men as well as the young, the healing of the passions as well as the formation of character; and if some trace of the Damonian concern for the old or superannuated remains in the Platonic presentation, it disappears in the sober restatement (which in other respects is similarly comprehensive) of Plato's position by Aristotle.

37. *Pol.* 1342b14–16, 1340b3–4.

Selected Bibliography

I. Aristotle's Politics: *Editions, Translations, Commentaries*

Barker, Ernest. *The Politics of Aristotle*, translated with an introduction, notes, and appendixes. Oxford, 1946.

Dreizehnter, Alois. *Aristoteles' Politik*, critically edited with an introduction and indexes. Munich, 1970.

Gigon, Olof. *Aristoteles: Politik*, translated and edited. Zurich, 1955.

Immisch, Otto. *Aristotelis Politica*. Bibliotheca Teubneriana. Leipzig, 1929.

Newman, W. L. *The Politics of Aristotle*, with an introduction, two prefatory essays, and notes critical and explanatory, 4 vols. Oxford, 1887-1902.

Ross, W. D. *Aristotelis Politica*. Scriptorum Classicorum Bibliotheca Oxoniensis. Oxford, 1957.

Susemihl, Franz, and R. D. Hicks. *The Politics of Aristotle*, a revised text with introduction, analysis, and commentary. London, 1894; rpt. New York, 1976.

II. Other Classical Texts Frequently Cited

Aristides Quintilianus. *De Musica*, ed. R. P. Winnington-Ingram. Bibliotheca Teubneriana. Leipzig, 1963.

Aristotle. *Ethica Nicomachea*, ed. Ingraham Bywater. Scriptorum Classicorum Bibliotheca Oxoniensis. Oxford, 1894.

Aristotle. *Fragmenta*, ed. Valentin Rose. Bibliotheca Teubneriana. Leipzig, 1886.

Diels, Hermann, and Walther Kranz, eds. *Die Fragmente der Vorsokratiker*, 6th ed., 2 vols. Dublin/Zurich, 1972.

Plato. *Opera*, ed. John Burnet, 5 vols. Scriptorum Classicorum Bibliotheca Oxoniensis. Oxford, 1900-7.

Wehrli, Fritz. *Die Schule des Aristoteles*, 10 vols. Basel, 1944-59.

Selected Bibliography

III. Other Works

Abert, Hermann. *Die Lehre vom Ethos in der griechischen Musik*. Leipzig, 1899.

Anderson, Warren. "The Importance of Damonian Theory in Plato's Thought," *TAPA* 86 (1955), 88–102.

——.*Ethos and Education in Greek Music*. Cambridge, Mass., 1966.

Bernays, Jacob. *Grundzüge der verlorenen Abhandlung des Aristoteles über Wirkung der Tragödie*. Breslau, 1857. Reprinted in *Zwei Abhandlungen über die aristotelische Theorie des Drama*. Berlin, 1880.

Boyancé, Pierre. *Le culte des Muses chez les philosophes grecs*. Paris, 1936.

Bremer, J. M. *Hamartia: Tragic Error in the Poetics of Aristotle*. Amsterdam, 1969.

Busse, A. "Zur Musikästhetik des Aristoteles," *RhM* 77 (1928), 34–50.

Croissant, Jeanne. *Aristote et les mystères*. Paris/Liège, 1932.

Dalfen, Joachim. *Polis und Poiesis: Die Auseinandersetzung mit der Dichtung bei Platon und seinen Zeitgenossen*. Munich, 1974.

Defourny, Maurice. *Aristote: Etudes sur la Politique*. Paris, 1932.

Dirlmeier, Franz. "Katharsis pathēmatōn," *Hermes* 68 (1940), 82–87.

Dodds, E. R. *The Greeks and the Irrational*. Berkeley, 1966.

Döring, August. *Die Kunstlehre des Aristoteles*. Jena, 1876.

Else, Gerald F. "Imitation in the Fifth Century," *CP* (1958), 73–90.

——.*Aristotle's Poetics: The Argument*. Cambridge, Mass., 1963.

Fink, Eugen. *Metaphysik der Erziehung im Weltverständnis von Plato und Aristoteles*. Frankfurt am Main, 1970.

Flashar, Helmut. "Die medizinischen Grundlagen der Lehre von der Wirkung der Dichtung in der griechischen Poetik," *Hermes* 84 (1956), 12–48.

Grube, G. M. A. *The Greek and Roman Critics*. Toronto, 1968.

Howald, Ernst. "Eine vorplatonische Kunsttheorie," *Hermes* 59 (1919), 187–207.

Jaeger, Werner. *Aristotle: Fundamentals of the History of His Development*. 2d ed. Trans. R. Robinson. Oxford, 1948.

Kahl, Alexis. *Die Philosophie der Musik nach Aristoteles*. Leipzig, 1902.

Koller, Ernst. *Musse und musische Paideia: Die Musikaporetik in der aristotelischen Politik*. Basel, 1956.

Koller, Hermann. *Die Mimesis in der Antike*. Berne, 1954.

Selected Bibliography

Kommerell, Max. *Lessing und Aristoteles.* Frankfurt, 1940.

Lord, Carnes. "Aristotle's History of Poetry," *TAPA* 104 (1974), 195-229.

――――."A Peripatetic Account of Tragic Music," *Hermes* 105 (1977), 175-79.

――――."Aristotle, Menander, and the *Adelphoe* of Terence," *TAPA* 107 (1977), 183-202.

Neubecker, A. J. *Die Bewertung der Musik bei Stoikern und Epikureern.* Berlin, 1956.

Nicev, Alexandre. *L'énigme de la catharsis tragique dans Aristote.* Sofia, 1970.

Oncken, Wilhelm. *Die Staatslehre des Aristoteles.* 2 vols. Leipzig, 1875.

Rostagni, Augusto. "Aristotele e Aristotelismo nella storia della estetica antica," *Studi italiani di filologia classica* n.s. 2 (1922), 1-147.

Schadewaldt, Wolfgang. "Furcht und Mitleid? Zur Deutung des aristotelischen Tragödiensatzes," *Hermes* 83 (1955), 129-71.

Schottlaender, Rudolf. "Eine Fessel der Tragödiendeutung," *Hermes* 81 (1953), 22-29.

Solmsen, Friedrich. "Leisure and Play in Aristotle's Ideal State," *RhM* 107 (1964), 193-220.

Stark, Rudolf. *Aristotelesstudien.* Munich, 1954.

Stinton, T. C. W. "Hamartia in Aristotle and Greek Tragedy," *CQ* n.s. 25 (1975), 221-54.

Theiler, Willy. "Bau und Zeit der aristotelischen Politik," *MH* 9 (1952), 65-78.

Index

Achilles, 171
Aeolian (harmonies), 118, 214
Agathon, 143
Aristides Quintilianus, 24, 85, 157, 204–210, 217
Aristophanes, 175
Aristoxenus, 24, 115–116, 141, 143, 213–215, 217–219
Athens, 27, 61, 191

Bernays, Jacob, 151

Catharsis, 33–34, 105, 109–13, 119–127, 129, 131–140, 142, 148–150, 152, 158–160, 164–166, 173, 175
Chiron, 76
Citizen(s), 36–38, 40–43, 48, 50, 56, 138–143, 145, 147, 157, 161, 163, 173, 180, 186, 188, 190–192, 196, 198–199
City, 36, 41, 44, 48–50, 53, 136, 182–192, 194–198
Comedy, 44, 46, 148–149, 151, 174–177, 179
Courage, 54, 59, 66, 93–94, 198–199, 211, 218–219
Crete, 185

Damon, 25, 203–213, 215, 217–219
Demetrius (of Phaleron), 176
Descartes, René, 21–22, 179
Dionysius, 124, 217
Dorian (mode), 99, 114–118, 143–146, 207, 211–214, 216–219
Drawing, 54, 58, 63

Euripides, 70

Gentlemen(ship), 32–33, 35, 65, 153–154, 162–164, 173, 180, 200–201
Gymnastic, 53–54, 56, 58–61, 62, 65–66, 70, 101, 102

Habit, habituation, 32, 36–39, 42–43, 46, 58, 65–66, 70, 74, 93, 95, 97–99, 102–103, 153–158, 200
Happiness, 41, 50, 55–56, 78–81, 138, 174–175, 183–184, 186–187, 189–190, 197–198
Heidegger, Martin, 25
Hesiod, 158
Hobbes, Thomas, 20–21, 179
Homer, 75–77, 81, 89, 158, 172
Horace, 85
Hypodorian (mode), 114–116, 118, 143–144, 214
Hypophrygian (mode), 114–116, 118, 143–144, 214

Imitation, imitate, 18–19, 23, 83, 88–92, 103–104, 114, 117, 148, 175, 178–179, 204
Ionian (harmonies) 118, 212, 214

Jaeger, Werner, 25–28
Justice, 135, 156, 199, 211, 218

Legislator(s), 30, 32, 36, 38, 48, 154–155, 198

225

Index

Leisure, leisured activity, 32–33, 35,
40–41, 54–57, 62, 67, 71, 77, 79,
81, 93, 138, 147, 180, 197–199,
201–202
Lessing, 151
Letters, 53–54, 58, 60–62
Lydian, Mixed Lydian (mode),
113–118, 140, 143–146, 212–219

Macedonia, 193, 195
Medes, 72
Melanippides, 146
Menander, 176
Moderation, 93–94, 199, 211,
218–219
Music, *mousikē*, 85–89

Odysseus, 81
Oedipus, 166–168, 172
Olympus (tunes of), 83, 88, 95,
112–113, 127–128, 132, 139–140,
143

Pastime (*diagōgē*), 55–58, 61, 67,
70–74, 76–85, 93, 103–104, 111,
139–140, 147, 180–181
Pericles, 204
Peripatetics, 24, 26, 85, 97, 120,
129, 157, 176, 217
Persia, Persians, 72, 193, 195
Philosophy, 21, 25, 30–31, 35,
39–40, 50, 64, 66, 69, 109–110,
150, 158, 174, 178, 182–185,
188–190, 197–202, 216–217
Philoxenus, 146
Phrygian (mode), 114–118, 120,
127–129, 133, 140, 143–144, 146,
207, 211, 213–214
Plato, 19–20, 22–23, 25–26, 28, 35,
51, 174–175, 179, 192, 200–204,
209, 211–214, 216–219
Play, 43, 54–55, 57, 61, 70–74,
76–82, 84, 152

Pleasure, 54–55, 57, 69–74, 76,
78–85, 87, 90–93, 106, 111, 119,
131–134, 138, 152, 154, 160–161,
182
Plutarch, 212–214, 217
Political philosophy, 19, 22, 26, 30
Political science, 26–27, 30–32, 181,
188
Problems, 24, 47, 97, 114, 116, 118,
120, 133, 140, 143, 145, 213–214
Proclus, 218
Prudence, 32, 35, 39, 66–67, 70, 72,
104, 154–157, 164, 177–179, 182
Pythagoras, Pythagoreans, 25,
122–124, 158–159, 203–204, 207

Reason, 35–36, 38–40, 42, 46–47,
58, 65–66, 103, 153–156, 161,
164, 170–171, 177
Relaxation, 54–55, 57, 70, 72,
76–82, 111, 138–139, 145, 147,
152, 216
Rousseau, Jean-Jacques, 20, 22

Sappho, 115
Socrates, 35, 90, 188, 204, 214–216
Sophocles, 116, 167, 172
Sparta, Spartans, 44, 49–50, 53, 59,
74–75, 77, 101, 185, 191, 198,
200–201
Spiritedness, 160–164, 170–171,
173, 175–176, 192–196, 202
Statesmen, 30, 32, 40, 186

Theophrastus, 176
Thyestes, 166
Timotheus, 146
Tragedy, 23, 33–34, 89–90, 92,
119–120, 131, 133–135, 137–141,
143, 147, 151–152, 159, 164–169,
171–177, 179, 213

Zeus, 77, 213

226

EDUCATION AND
CULTURE IN THE
POLITICAL THOUGHT
OF ARISTOTLE

Designated by G. T. Whipple, Jr.
Composed by Strehle's Computerized Typesetting
in 11 point Compugraphic Baskerville, 2 points leaded,
with display lines in Baskerville.
Printed offset by Thomson-Shore, Inc.
on Warren's Number 66 text, 50 pound basis.
Bound by John H. Dekker & Sons, Inc.
in Holliston book cloth
and stamped in Kurz-Hastings foil.

Library of Congress Cataloging in Publication Data

Lord, Carnes.
    Education and culture in the political thought of
Aristotle.

    Bibliography: p.
    Includes index.
    1. Aristotle.   Politics.   2. Education—Philosophy.
I. Title.
LB85.A7L67   370'.1   81–15272
ISBN 0-8014-1412-1   AACR2